THE
TRIBAL LIVING
BOOK

THE
TRIBAL LIVING
BOOK

BY DAVID LEVINSON AND DAVID SHERWOOD
ILLUSTRATIONS BY MARYLOU FINCH

JOHNSON BOOKS: BOULDER

© 1984, 1993 by David Levinson and David Sherwood
All rights reserved.

Library of Congress Cataloging-in-Publication Data
    Levinson, David 1947–
      The tribal living book: 150 things to do and make from traditional
cultures / by David Levinson and David Sherwood.—2nd ed.
        p.   cm.
    Includes index.
    ISBN 1-55566-104-1
      1. Handicraft.   2. Industries, Primitive.   I. Sherwood, David.
II. Title.
TT157.L44   1993   93-10533
600—dc20   CIP

Revised Edition
  2 3 4 5 6 7 8 9

Cover Design: Bob Schram/Bookends

Printed in the United States of America by
Johnson Printing Company
1880 South 57th Court
Boulder, Colorado 80301

To Deborah and Amelia

Contents

Acknowledgments

We have many people to thank for helping us with this book: Mrs. Elana Sherwood for contributing the chapters on the Shaker basket and fingerweaving, Marlene Martin for her help and advice and for sharing her embroidery expertise, Ethan Hugo for helping build the wigwam and the earth lodge frame and for testing the board games, Timothy J. O'Leary for his help in locating many obscure sources and for sharing his vast knowledge of the lifeways of the peoples of the world, John Beierle for his advice on using the Human Relations Area Files data archive, and Abraham Maramba for supplying information about the lifeways and folklore of the Philippines.

We especially acknowledge the contribution of Marylou Finch and thank her for illustrating the book. Many of the instructions would be difficult to follow without her clear illustrations. We also want to acknowledge that the illustrations in Chapter 4 were taken directly from Frank Lebar's *The Material Culture of Truk*, and those in Chapter 37 from Caroline F. Jayne's *String Figures and How to Make Them: A Study of Cat's-Cradle in Many Lands*. We thank the Smithsonian Institution and the American Museum of Natural History for granting permission to use the photographs in Chapters 39 and 45.

Finally, we wish to thank our families—Deborah, Ethan, and Diane and Amelia, David, and Lola—for their patience, advice, and encouragement.

Introduction

Have you ever wanted to build an outrigger canoe, shoot a dart with a blowgun, or cook tortillas from scratch? How about communicate with your friends in sign language? Or scamper up a 100-foot tree trunk?

If you have ever wanted to do such things or even wondered or fantasized about them, *The Tribal Living Book* is for you. With the instructions in this book you can build an outrigger canoe just like the Samoan Islanders of the South Pacific, shoot a blowgun like the Jivaro Indians of Ecuador, or sign with your friends in Plains Indian sign language. We provide detailed information about and instructions for more than 150 projects and activities of over 100 tribal peoples from six continents and the seven seas, including dwelling construction, working with natural materials, crafts, musical instruments, board games, sports, food gathering, hunting weapons, recipes, food preservation, and social relationships, among others. The projects and activities we have chosen are varied enough so that anyone—young or old, novice or craftsperson, homebody or outdoorsperson—will find plenty to keep busy with.

For the most part we have emphasized objects you can make or activities you can carry out with natural materials found in North America. This has made it possible for us to make and field-test many of the projects ourselves or to get the advice of contemporary craftspersons who use natural materials and tribal techniques. We have tried to be as authentic as possible, describing the objects and activities just as the tribal people do them. Of course, you are free to make any changes you want—in fact, tribal designs often make such changes easy.

Why did we write this book? Like many people, when we enter a bookstore or library we head for the back-to-nature, alternative life-style section. Our bookshelves have filled over the years with these types of books and magazines. As professional anthropologists who make our living studying different cultures around the world, we have often been disappointed in these publications. What is missing is the kind of how-to information we provide here. Our purpose in writing this book, then, is to add something new and different to what is already available about natural living, alternative life-styles, and appropriate technologies.

What do we mean by tribal? We mean a non-Western, non-industrialized society whose members live primarily off the land, speak their own language (different from the language spoken in other cultures), and share a common set of customs and beliefs about the world. In the past few hundred years, some 5,000 different tribal cultures have been identified around the world. Today, there are still several thousand left, with populations ranging from a few dozen to several million, although most no longer live a purely tribal life. Instead, they have combined their tribal ways with some of the conveniences of modern living. The tribal cultures you are probably most familiar with are the Native American tribes which occupied North America prior to the arrival of Europeans. The well-known and highly priced Native American arts and crafts are a good example of the work produced by tribal peoples around the world.

As we said, the projects and activities we have included come from over 100 different tribal cultures from all over the world. Since you may be interested in knowing something about these cultures, we have marked their locations on the map at the end of Appendix A and have written brief profiles of some of them in Appendix A.

The Tribal Living Book is for people interested in the lifeways of people in other cultures, and especially for those who want to enrich their own lives by learning about and experiencing the customs of faraway places. It is based on the seemingly contradictory belief about human nature that all people are the same yet different. We are all the same because we all have families, we all eat food, we all relax and play, we all live in some type of dwelling, and we all must learn certain basic skills in order to survive. But we are different in how we go about doing these things—the type of house we live in, how we get and eat our food, how we raise our children, how we spend our free time, and so on. In this book we emphasize tribal ways of life that are worth knowing about and some that are even worth incorporating into our own daily lives.

PART I
Dwellings

1
Igloo

An igloo is made from snow and ice. To build an igloo you'll need packed powdery snow at least 30 inches deep covered by at least another 6 inches of soft powder. And you'll need to be in a climate cold enough so that the temperature rarely rises above the freezing point in the winter months. With these two conditions, you should have no trouble building a sturdy, roomy igloo. The plans given here are for the type of igloo used by the Netsilik Eskimo of northern Canada with some modifications introduced from the type of igloo used by the Copper Eskimo, also of northern Canada. It takes a Netsilik husband-and-wife team little more than an hour to build an igloo. You should figure that it will take you two to three hours.

The insulating qualities of snow are such that even in sub-zero weather the temperature inside the igloo will remain about 10 to 20 degrees above freezing. The temperature will vary, of course, depending on the size of the igloo, the number of occupants, and the heat source. For heat and light the Netsilik use a small stone oil lamp set about three feet off the floor.

The major problem with igloo living is overheating. If it becomes too warm inside the igloo, the ceiling snow will soften and entire snow blocks might melt and fall into the interior. Overheating can be controlled somewhat by cutting one or more small ventilation holes in the roof.

Nomadic peoples most often live in circular dwellings such as tents, huts, tipis, and igloos. Sedentary peoples more often live in rectangular or square dwellings.

Dimensions

An igloo is a round, domed structure with a base diameter of 9 to 16 feet and a height of 6 to 9 feet from floor to ceiling. Since the igloo is built partly with snow removed from the interior, the floor will be 2 to 3 feet below the outside snow level.

Materials

You will need two types of snow: (1) hard, packed powder at least 30 inches deep, and (2) soft powder at least 6 inches deep. If you want to add a window you'll also need freshwater ice. Ice should not be used for the walls or roof as it lacks the insulating qualities of snow. The only tools needed are a straight-edged knife, a long stick or pole, and a snow shovel.

Figure 1.1 *Cross-section of an igloo*

Construction

• Select as a site a flat, circular area 9 to 15 feet in diameter covered by at least 30 inches of packed powder and 6 inches of soft powder. Clear the soft powder to one side with the snow shovel or by hand.

- On the cleared site outline the igloo dimensions by cutting a circle in the snow with the knife. The longer the knife blade, the better. Determine the size of the igloo by the number of occupants, how long you plan to stay, and the amount of usable snow.

- Begin building the igloo with blocks of the packed powder. Start building with snow taken from inside the circle marking the outside of the igloo. In that way, as the walls go up, you'll be digging out the floor. Using the knife, cut blocks of snow about 24 inches square and 8 to 12 inches thick. The blocks for the base of the walls can be somewhat larger and those for the top sections somewhat smaller. Cut only a few blocks at a time and place them around the circle, working up and around in a spiral fashion. Angle each ascending row of blocks so that it extends a bit further inward than the row beneath it. In that way you'll give the igloo its domed shape.

    Fit the blocks together by gently pressing them into place and by trimming and cutting the edges. The blocks for the roof must be fit carefully and tightly. The roof must be domed for two reasons: first, so that the igloo stays up, and second, so that water from the melting snow will run down the interior walls rather than drip into the center of the igloo.

- If you are working with another person, one should be working outside plastering the blocks with soft powder while the other sets the blocks in place from the inside. When completed, the seams of the blocks should be covered by soft powder so that the igloo looks like a heap of snow.

- Once the walls and roof are in place and plastered, cut an entrance way at snow level in the side facing away from the prevailing wind. The opening should be small, about 2 feet wide by 3 feet high. Finally, cut a 3-inch round ventilation hole in the roof. The basic igloo is now finished.

Optional Features

- If you're planning to spend more than one night in the igloo, you'll want to add an entrance passage to the entrance way. This passage will help keep the snow and wind out and, if large enough, can be used as a storage area. An entrance passage is nothing more than a domed or rectangular tunnel of snow blocks anywhere from 4 to 15 feet long and 3 to 4 feet high. The opening from the passage to the outside should be higher and wider than the opening from the passage to the igloo. As shown in Figure 1.2, the passage can be either straight, curved or T-shaped. If T-shaped, either end of the T can be blocked to keep out the wind.

- You can add some light to the igloo by setting a window in the south side. If freshwater ice is available, cut a small, rectangular piece 2 to 6 inches thick. Cut a square hole in the south wall of the igloo, making sure that the hole is smaller than the ice slab. Place the slab over the hole and press the trim until it fits tightly. Pack the seams with snow. Do not use seawater ice, as it is often green and does not let much light pass through.

- A table and sleeping ledge(s) can be fashioned from snow. To build a sleeping ledge, set a wall of snow blocks about 3 feet high 3 feet out from a wall. Fill the space between the ledge wall and the igloo wall with snow. Pack and smooth the snow until the ledge is a suitable height and length. A snow table can be built in the same way. Remember that you should not sleep directly on the snow. Make sure to place some insulation—cloth, canvas, branches, moss, etc.—between yourself and the snow.

Figure 1.2 *Igloo entrance passage designs*

3

2
Wigwam

The wigwam was the most widely used of the various types of dwellings built by the native peoples of North America. It was used by dozens of Native American groups who lived as far north as Ontario, Canada, as far south as North Carolina, as far east as Massachusetts, and as far west as the Mississippi River.

The name wigwam is an English corruption of the Chippewa word *wagiwam*, meaning dwelling. In the Chippewa language, a wigwam is actually called a *waginogan*, meaning a bent dwelling.

The Chippewa wigwam described here is made with saplings, birchbark shingles, reed mats, and basswood fiber ties, as shown in Figure 2.1. Other types of wigwams may be covered entirely with birchbark or reed mats or have siding made from black ash, chestnut, cedar, or elm bark. A wigwam can be erected in less than an hour, but it may take days or weeks to sew the bark shingles and reed mats and to prepare the fiber ties. Once these materials are made, however, they can be stored and used for several years. If you're in a rush or looking only for quick, temporary shelter, twine can be substituted for the fiber ties and canvas or pine boughs used in place of the bark and reed coverings.

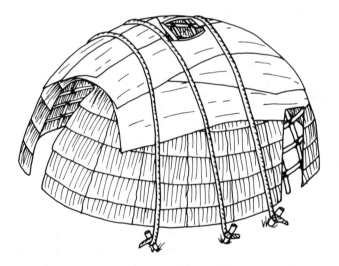

Figure 2.1 *Chippewa wigwam*

Although a wigwam is easy to build and can provide sleeping space for up to eight people, wigwam living is not especially comfortable. It is dark inside, ventilation is poor, head space is limited, and if a fire is burning the top fills with smoke. The Chippewa used the wigwam mostly for sleeping and preferred to cook outdoors whenever the weather permitted. The main advantages of a wigwam are that it is sturdy, portable, and easy to build.

Dimensions

The size of the wigwam you choose to build depends on the number of occupants. The typical Chippewa wigwam, which was 12 feet long, 10 feet wide and 5½ feet high at the center slept 6 to 12 people.

Material Manufacture

● Basswood fiber ties (also called basswood bark or basswood fiber) are made from the fiber found between the bark and the wood of the basswood (*Tilia americana*) tree. Begin by cutting a slab of bark about 6 feet long and 3 feet wide from the trunk of a standing basswood. Free the slab by making a long, vertical cut and peeling the bark around the trunk, prying and cutting as necessary. Cut the bark slab into 4-inch widths and soak the strips in water until the soft, yellow inner fibers can be peeled easily. This soaking process may take a few hours to a few days. Remove the inner fibers, cut them into long, narrow strips, coil the strips and set aside to dry. When dry, the strips are ready for use. The fiber can usually be separated from the bark more easily if the peeling is done in the summer months. If basswood is not available, the fibers can be made in the same way from the inner bark of the swamp ash or the slippery elm.

● For support and frame poles use freshly cut, straight supple saplings less than 1 inch in diameter at their broadest point. The Chippewa preferred ironwood (*Ostrya virginiana*) because of its strength and flexibility, but oak, birch, willow, or hickory saplings will do just as well. Avoid pine saplings as they are too weak and rigid. You'll be using the saplings to make two kinds of poles. First, frame poles, which should be debarked and sharpened at the butt end, are set in the ground, bent inward, and tied to opposing frame poles. Second, support poles, which should also be debarked but need not be sharpened at one end, are attached horizontally to the frame poles. The number and length of the poles you'll need depends on the size of the wigwam.

● Birchbark for the roofing shingles is best peeled from the paper birch (*Betula papyrifera*) in the spring as soon as the snow starts to melt or in the late fall well after the first frost. Bark gathered in the summer months is likely to separate into layers and shred, and bark gathered in the winter is difficult to peel. The trunk of the birch should be at least 6 inches around (the broader the better) and relatively free of the black splotches called eyes. Cut the bark from the trunk below the first branches but above the snow line. For the amount of bark needed to make shingles, it is best to fell the tree first.

To remove the bark, make one, long vertical cut. A quick, slashing cut with the knife is best; if you hold the blade square to the tree the knife will jump, leaving a ragged edge. As shown in Figure 2.2, carefully pry the bark off the trunk with the knife blade or a beveled stick. Pry slowly, making sure not to split the bark. When removed, roll the bark strip against the grain and tie with twine or basswood fiber. Try to use the sheets immediately. If that is not possible, you can restore flexibility by soaking the bark in water or by steaming it.

Each shingle is made from two or more bark strips sewn together, as shown in Figure 2.3. To make the shingles, lay the strips out end to end and overlapped by 2 to 3 inches. Sew the strips together at the overlap with heavy thread (carpet thread works well), thin strands of basswood fiber, or debarked, split roots of either the tamarack or spruce tree. Finish

Materials
(1) 22 frame poles of debarked ironwood, hickory, birch, oak, or willow saplings, each 10-12' long and 1'' diameter

(2) 14 support poles of debarked saplings, 8 12' long and 6 8-10' long

(3) basswood fiber ties, 40 ties each 6-12'' long, 6 lengths each about 20' long

(4) 10 siding mats from cattail or bulrush reeds, each mat about 5' wide and 4-5' long

(5) roofing shingles from birchbark, each shingle 2-4' wide and 6-10' long

(6) a small axe, a long-blade knife, a large sewing needle.

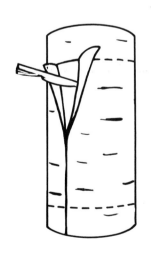

Figure 2.2 *Peeling birchbark*

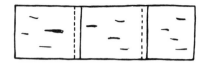

Figure 2.3 *Birchbark roof shingle*

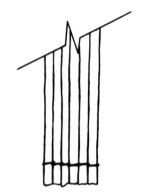

Figure 2.4 *Reed wall mat*

Figure 2.5 *Roof framework*

Figure 2.6 *Wigwam framework*

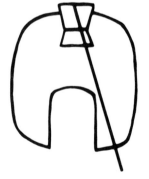

Figure 2.7 *Top view of wigwam showing smoke hole flap*

the shingles by sewing a stick at each end, much like that found at the bottom of a pull shade. Depending on the size of the peeled strips, each shingle should be 2 to 4 feet wide and 6 to 12 feet long.

• The wall mats are made from either cattail or bulrush reeds. The reeds should be dried in the sun (make sure to turn them periodically) and then boiled in a large pot before sewing. Using reeds about 5 feet tall, lay them out on the ground side by side to form a mat about 4 feet long. Sew the reeds together with heavy thread, basswood fiber, or split roots. Sew by passing the needle through and around each reed and then through and around the next reed and so forth. Sew a number of parallel rows about 8 to 10 inches apart. Leave one end of the mat unbound for flexibility while binding the other, as shown in Figure 2.4.

Construction

• Before starting to build, study Figures 2.1, 2.5, and 2.6. The key to a sturdy wigwam is a sturdy frame. First, select an appropriate site. The best site is a flat area at the top of a slight rise free of stones, tree stumps, and large surface tree roots. Mark the wigwam dimensions with sticks or stones. Gather the construction materials together and place them to one side. Keep the ties handy (looped through your belt is a good place), as you'll be grabbing for them at all stages of construction.

• Set the 22 frame poles in opposing rows around the circumference. Place 5 poles along each long side, 24 inches in from the corners and 24 inches apart. Place 6 poles on each short side, 14 inches in from the corners and 14 inches apart. Make sure to leave a larger opening at one end between the two central poles as an entrance way. When setting the poles, the sharpened end should be planted about 10 inches into the ground and the poles slanted slightly outward.

• Starting with the 5 pairs of poles on the long sides, bend each opposing pair into the center so they overlap by 8 to 12 inches and lash them together with basswood fiber ties, as shown in Figure 2.5. Follow the same procedure for the opposing pairs on the short sides. Make sure to lash all poles to one another at each point where they cross. Lash the horizontal support poles to the frame poles as shown in Figure 2.6. Again, make sure to lash all poles together at all points where they cross one another and make sure to leave an opening for an entrance way at one end. The frame is now complete.

• Lean the reed mats against the sides with the unfinished edge of the mats up, then lash the mats to the framework with fiber ties. Lay the birchbark shingles over the roof framework, leaving a smoke hole about 2 feet square in the center of the roof. Make sure that the shingles overlap one another and hang down over the siding mats. Secure the shingles by passing long lengths of basswood fiber over the structure from front to rear and side to side. Secure the fibers with stakes or heavy stones. If necessary, the shingles can be further secured by lashing them directly to the frame.

• Inside the wigwam build a log or stone hearth directly beneath the smoke hole. You can control the draft by adding a bark or reed mat smoke screen to the roof as shown in Figure 2.7. Tie the screen to the framework at one end and tie to a long pole at the other. You can use the pole to turn the screen away from the wind.

3
Earth Lodge

The earth lodge is an underground dwelling traditionally used by many Native Americans in the mid- and northwest. The plans given here are for the type used as a winter home by Klamath of northern California and southern Oregon. A Klamath earth lodge is a circular, semisubterranean structure with a flat-topped, earth covered, hip roof (see Figures 3.1 and 3.2). The lodge is erected over a circular pit dug from 2 to 4 feet deep. Depending on the number of occupants, the lodge can range in size from 12 to 35 feet in diameter with a ceiling height of 10 to 12 feet. The living area is entered through a hatchway in the roof. An earth lodge is one of the most energy efficient dwellings ever designed. It is cool in summer and, with a small fire, warm in winter.

Unlike constructing a wigwam or igloo, building an earth lodge is a big job. Figure that it will take four adults, working full-time, at least three months to build a good-sized earth lodge. But, once built, your lodge will last for years, although you will need to repair or replace the roof periodically.

The plans here are for the typical Klamath lodge with some modifications taken from the lodge used by the Modoc, the Klamath's neighbors to the south. As with other vernacular dwellings, manufactured materials can be substituted for natural ones.

The Lapp Earth Lodge
The Lapp people of Northern Scandinavia used an earth-covered dwelling, called the turf cot, as a spring and autumn home. Unlike North American earth lodges, which are semisubterranean, the turf cot is built above ground on the slope of a hill. The framework rests on two curved central arches formed by four curved poles joined together at the top. A square chimney sits on the arch. Poles running from the ground to the arch are covered first with bark sheets and then with turf. The turf cot is usually circular or oblong and may have an extra room that is rectangular in shape.

Dimensions

As vernacular dwellings go, an earth lodge is large. Klamath lodges varied in size from 12 to 34 feet in diameter and from 10 to 12 feet in height. Spacious lodges housed as many as 10 to 12 people at one time. The plans given here are for a lodge with a 30-foot diameter, a 10-foot ceiling, and a 2-foot pit.

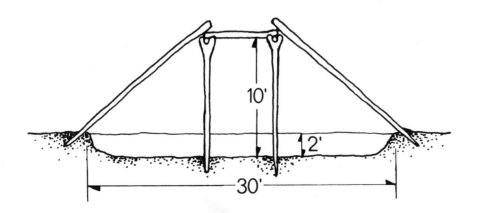

Figure 3.1 *Cross-section of the earth lodge*

Materials

An earth lodge has three main parts: (1) the central frame, (2) the roof, and (3) the hatchway. The frame, roof rafters, and hatchway are made from whole tree trunks, poles or split logs. The roof is shingled with swamp grass mats and then covered with loose grass and earth. All wooden parts are lashed together with cord made from rolled swamp grass, although you may find it easier to use rope or twine or even nails. In addition, you might find it easier, although less pleasing aesthetically, to shingle the roof with plastic sheets or tarpaper rather than grass mats. The mats, however, will provide better ventilation and reduce humidity inside the lodge.

Central Frame. The frame consists of four central posts, two long plates, two short plates, and four corner braces (Figure 3.2). For a lodge 30 feet in diameter you will need:

4 center posts—12 feet long, 7-12 inches in diameter, forked or notched at one end;

2 long plates—15 feet long, 5-10 inches in diameter;

2 short plates—5 feet long, 5-10 inches in diameter;

4 corner braces—18 feet long, 5-10 inches wide, split and sharpened at one end.

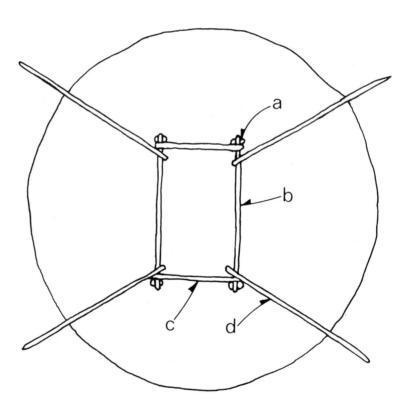

Figure 3.2 *Top view of the earth lodge: (a) forked central posts, (b) long plates, (c) short plates, (d) corner braces*

Roof. The roof consists of four layers: first, about 75 rafters of straight poles or rough, split planks, each about 18 feet long and 3 to 6 inches wide placed 1 to 3 inches apart, as shown in Figure 3.3; second, shingles made from swamp grass mats, each about 5 feet wide and 12 feet long; third, a thick layer of loose, dry grass; and fourth, a 6- to 12-inch layer of earth.

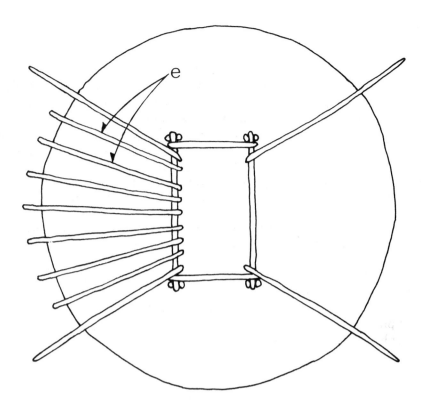

Figure 3.3 *Top view showing the rafters: (e) rafters*

Hatchway. A rectangular hatchway 10 by 15 feet placed directly in the center of the roof serves as both an entrance way and smoke hole. The wood frame for the hatchway consists of four 10-foot poles or planks, two 5-foot tie rods, and five 5-foot poles or planks (see Figure 3.4). These poles or planks should be debarked. The hatchway opening can be covered at night with a mat which can be rolled and stored at one end during the day.

The hatchway is reached from the outside by a stairway laid along the roof and from the inside by a ladder. To make the stairway and ladder you will need four tree trunks with short limbs left on and 10 2-foot long sticks to serve as rungs.

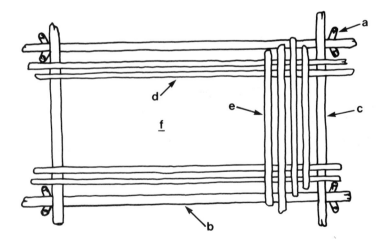

Figure 3.4 *Top view of hatchway framework: (a) central posts, (b) long plate, (c) short plate, (d) hatchway joists, (e) hatchway sheathing, (f) hatchway opening*

Lashings. All logs, poles, and planks are lashed to one another with cord made from rolled swamp grass (*Scirpus lacustris*). Store-bought rope or twine or even nails work equally well.

Equipment. You will need an axe, chainsaw, bucksaw, knife, spade, pitchfork, sewing needle, splitting maul, wedges, and buckets. If time is a consideration, a back-hoe or bulldozer to dig the pit will be a big help.

Material Manufacture

• First, cut, split, and debark the logs, poles, and planks you'll need. The best place to find long, straight poles is a thick stand of pine or cedar trees. Remember, when removing branches, to chop up with the grain. Sharpen each of the four center posts and the four corner braces at one end. Ideally, the four center posts should also be forked at one end. If there is no natural fork, notch them so they will hold the plates. Logs for the corner braces and rafters should be split in half, although poles will do. Only the poles for the hatchway frame need to be debarked. Removing bark is easier if you use a sawbuck and a long-bladed knife.

• Second, make swamp grass cord by taking two strands of dried swamp grass, laying them side-by-side on your bare thigh, and then rolling them together, first down your thigh and then rapidly up your thigh.

• Third, the shingles are made from bundles of dry swamp grass twined together at 6-inch intervals with swamp grass, as shown in Figure 3.5. Make sure the bundles butt together tightly. Each shingle mat should be about 5 feet wide and 12 feet long.

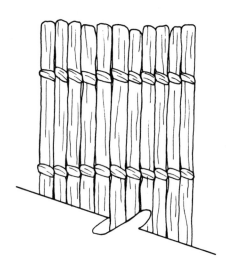

Figure 3.5 *Swamp grass mat*

Construction

Figures 3.1–3.4 provide construction details. Review them before starting to build the earth lodge.

Excavation. Dig out a pit about 30 feet in diameter and 2 feet deep. The sides of the pit should either be vertical to the ground or slope slightly outward. The pit floor should be flat and free of rocks and tree roots. Pile the excavated earth around the outside of the pit; you will use it later to cover the roof.

Frame. Set the four central posts to form a 5- by 10-foot rectangle in the center of the pit. Make sure to sink each post at least 2 feet into the ground. The openings of the forks or notches should be in the long direction. Place the two long plates in the center post forks and secure. Place the two short plates on the long plates, inside the posts, and secure. Attach the corner braces as shown in Figure 3.2. Each brace should extend about 2 feet beyond the pit perimeter and be sunk into the ground.

Rafters. Place the rafters at a 45-60° angle, as shown in Figure 3.3. The rafters should be placed 1 to 3 inches apart from one another. Lash each rafter to a plate and extend it about 1 foot beyond the pit perimeter. There is no need to sink the ends in the ground, as the weight of the roof will hold them in place.

Hatchway. Construct the hatchway over the rectangular opening formed by the long and short plates, as shown in Figure 3.4. You will need to make some adjustments to the rafters so that both they and the hatchway joists and sheathing fit neatly. Attach the mat to one end of the hatchway opening.

Roofing. Working from the hatchway down, attach the shingle mats to the rafters. Overlap the mats by about 8 inches. From the ground to about halfway up all around, cover the mats with a 4 to 6 inch layer of dry grass. Then, working from the top down, cover the entire roof with 6 to 12 inches of earth.

Ladder and Stairway. Construct both the stairway and interior ladder from small tree trunks with short branches left on to hold the rungs. The cross-sticks used as rungs should be lashed to the vertical trunks. Lash the interior ladder to the end of the hatchway opposite the mat and stand it on the lodge floor. Lay the exterior stairway on the roof and partially bury it in the earth covering. The earth alone should hold it firmly in place.

Interior Design

If you so desire, cover the floors and/or walls with grass mats. A sub-flooring of loose, packed grass can also be used. Underneath the hatchway and closer to the non-ladder end build a stone fire pit. Use the space behind the ladder and the pit edges under the rafters for storage.

4
South Pacific Tinimei

Tinimei *is a general term used for various buildings on Romonum Island. More specific terms are* iim, *sleeping house;* wuut, *meeting house;* fanarg, *cook house;* imwen ira, *women's hut. A small* tinimei *is called a* woowen.

The *tinimei* (tinny-may) is the general name given to buildings constructed by the people living on Romonum Island in the eastern Carolines. As shown in Figure 4.1, a *tinimei* is a rectangular, gabled structure with extensions on all four sides. Both the central and extension roofs are covered with palm leaf thatch. This open-sided, steeply gabled building is ideally suited to the warm, humid climate in the tropical Pacific.

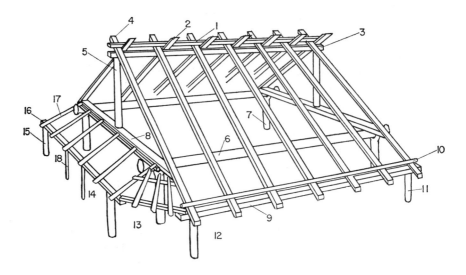

Figure 4.1 *Major structural features of the tinimei: (1) secondary ridgepole, (2) rafter, (3) ridgepole, (4) end rafter, (5) king post, (6) wall plate, (7) corner post, (8) end plate, (9) side extension wall plate, (10) eave purlin, (11) side extension corner post, (12) side extension, (13) corner extension, (14) end extension, (15) end extension corner post, (16) end extension wall plate, (17) end extension rafter, (18) door post*

As with most products of tribal technology, much of the work in building a *tinimei* goes into preparing the natural materials—cutting, shaping, and fitting the timbers; rolling the coconut husk fibers; and wrapping the thatch. The actual assembly of the building should take a team of four people no more than a day or two.

Of the four vernacular dwellings in this book the *tinimei* is the one best suited to the use of commercial construction materials. The Romonum Islanders use timbers from the breadfruit tree for the posts, plates, poles and rafters; lashing twine made from the sennit coconut; and thatch made from leaves of the ivory nut palm. Since the timbers are cut and trimmed to square, rectangular or circular dimensions, you can readily substitute commercial lumber purchased in standard sizes from any lumberyard. Likewise, you can use nylon or other rot- and slip-resistant rope in place of the coconut fiber twine. In place of the palm leaf thatch you can use bark sheets, roofing paper, or even heavy sheets of plastic.

Tinimei vary in size depending on their use. The plans given here are for one 25 feet long by 15 feet wide by 15 feet high in the center. The four extensions add about 2 feet to each side beyond the above dimensions.

The *tinimei* has six major structural sections: (1) central frame, (2) roof frame, (3) two side extensions; (4) two end extensions; (5) four corner extensions; and (6) the roof thatching. You will probably find it easiest to build the *tinimei* by making the parts for each section first and then assembling them following this sectional sequence.

Materials

Central Frame
4 corner posts—4 inches by 4 inches by 9 feet long
2 wall plates—2 inches by 4 inches by 27 feet long
2 end plates—2 inches by 4 inches by 16 feet long

Roof Frame
2 king posts—4 inches by 4 inches by 10 feet long
1 ridge pole—2 inches by 4 inches by 27 feet long
1 secondary ridge pole—2 inches by 3 inches by 27 feet long
14 rafters—2 inches by 2 inches by 27 feet long
2 eave purlins—1 inch by two inches by 27 feet long
4 diagonal roof stringers—10 feet long, 2 inches in diameter
2 long roof stringers—25 feet long, 2 inches in diameter
12 gable stringers—four 8 feet long, four 6 feet long, four 4 feet long, all 1 inch in diameter

Side Extensions
4 side extension corner posts—4 inches by 4 inches by 7 feet long
2 side extension wall plates—2 inches by 4 inches by 27 feet long

End Extensions
4 end extension corner posts—4 inches by 4 inches by 7 feet long
2 end extension wall plates—2 inches by 4 inches by 15 feet long
2 secondary end extension plates—1 inch by 2 inches by 15 feet long
12 end extension rafters—1 inch by 2 inches by 3 feet long

Corner Extensions
4 corner extension outer stringers—1 inch by 2 inches by 4 feet long
4 corner extension inner stringers—1 inch by 2 inches by 2 feet long
12 corner extension rafters—1 inch by 2 inches by 3 feet long

Roof Thatch
225 bindings rods—5 feet long by ½ inch in diameter
2,000 or more palm leaves—the Romonum use leaves from the ivory nut palm (*Coelococcus amicarum*), which are about 2 feet wide and 4–5 feet long. Other palms with leaves suitable for thatch are the Jamaica thatchpalm (*Thrinax parviflora*) and the brittle thatchpalm (*Thrinax microcarpa*). When figuring the number of leaves you'll need, remember that they are used folded and overlapped.

Lashing
1,000 feet of coir twine. Coir twine is made from the husk fibers of the sennit coconut (described in Chapter 5). If you want to use a different natural cord, instructions for making a variety of types are provided in Chapter 5. You also need 500 feet of tie line to secure the thatch to the binding rods. Any sturdy rot- and slip-resistant line will do.

13

Figure 4.2 *Notched corner post head*

Figure 4.3 *Wall plate in corner post notch*

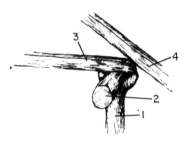

Figure 4.4 *Alignment at corner post: (1) corner post, (2) wall plate, (3) end plate, (4) rafter*

Tools
Assuming that you will use prepared lumber, the tools required will be a knife, shovel, posthole digger, chisel, mallet, hammer, and two forked, 15-foot poles.

Material Preparation

Whether you cut the lumber yourself or purchase it at a lumberyard, a few pieces need special attention before you can start building. First, cut a notch in each of the four central frame corner posts, as shown in Figure 4.2. Second, trim the two central frame wall plates so they fit tightly in the corner post notches, as shown in Figure 4.3. Finally, bevel the upper edges of the central frame end plates at both ends so that the rafters will rest on them securely, **as** shown in Figure 4.4.

Roof Thatch

• Gather the palm leaves and use while still green. If possible gather leaves of about equal length. Next, gather the binding rods together. You can use either half-inch dowls, small saplings, or rush reeds. For tie lines to secure the leaves to the rods the Romonum use mid-ribs of fronds taken from coconut palms. Any rot- and slip-resistant line will work as well. Ideally, the line should be stiff enough so that you can push it through the leaf without using a needle or awl.

• Sit on the ground with your legs crossed or outstretched and lay two binding rods across your thighs. Prepare a pile of leaves for binding by folding them over by one-third and working the fold back and forth until it sets.

• Take two leaves and wrap them around one end of the binding rods, as show in Figure 4.5. Wrap a few more leaves around the rods as shown in Figure 4.5.

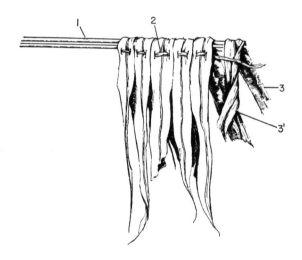

Figure 4.5 *Thatch sheet: (1) binding rods, (2) tie line, (3,3') ends of wrapped leaves*

• Tie them on as shown in Figures 4.5 and 4.6. The tie line should run parallel to and about one inch off the lower binding rod. Continue wrapping and tying leaves until there is room for only two more at the end of the binding rods. Wrap and tie the last two leaves as you did the first two. Secure the tie line by bringing it back three leaves from the end, looping it through the lines which secure each of the last three leaves.

Follow this same sequence for as many thatch sheets as you will need for the main roof, extension roofs, and end gables.

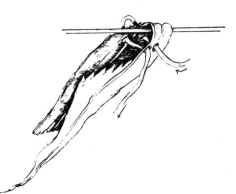

Figure 4.6 *Tying leaf to binding rod*

Construction

Building the *tinimei* is easiest if you follow the steps below in order. Figure 4.1 and the figures in this section provide the construction details.

Central Frame. Gather together the four corner posts, two wall plates, and two end plates. Measure off an area on flat ground 25 feet long by 15 feet wide. Dig one 4-foot posthole at each corner of the rectangle. Place a large, flat stone in the bottom of each hole and set the corner posts in the holes with the notches opening in the long direction. Fill the holes with dirt, sand, or gravel and pack.

• Set the two wall plates in the post notches as shown in Figure 4.3. The plates should extend beyond the posts one foot at each end, with the plane of the top surface of the plates higher than the tops of the posts. If the two posts don't provide sufficient support for the wall plates, add additional posts as needed.

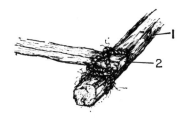

• Set the end plates in place atop the wall plates and running across the ends. Lash in place using the diagonal lashing shown in Figure 4.7.

Figure 4.7 *Lashing end plate (2) to wall plate (1)*

Roof Frame and Side Extensions. Raise the ridgepole with the two long, forked poles. Center the king posts on the two end plates and rest the ridgepole on the king posts. The ridgepole should extend one foot beyond the king posts at each end. Until the rafters are in place, you will need to support the ridgepole with the forked poles. To check their fit, set one pair of alternating rafters at each end of the central frame. Rest the rafters so that they extend one foot beyond the ridgepole and two feet beyond the wall plates. Make sure that the rafters sit firmly on the beveled ends of the end plates. Remove the rafters and set them aside.

• Measure out two feet from each corner post. Dig a 4-foot post hole at each of these spots and set the side extension posts in place as you did with the central frame corner posts. The posts shoud rise about 3 feet above the ground. Place the side extension plates on the posts, adding extra posts as needed.

• Beginning with one pair of end rafters, set the seven pairs of rafters in place as shown in Figure 4.1. Lash the rafters to the ridgepole, using the lashing shown in Figure 4.8. Set the secondary ridgepole in the cradle formed by the rafters extending above the ridgepole. Lash it to the rafters, and then lash the rafters to the wall plates.

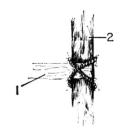

Figure 4.8 *Lashing rafter (1) to ridgepole (2)*

• Lash the four diagonal and two long roof stringers to the underside of the rafters as shown in Figure 4.9, then lash the two eave purlins to the lower end of the rafters, and, finally, close the gables with the vertical end gable stringers as shown in Figure 4.10.

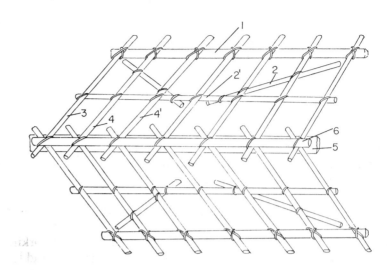

Figure 4.9 *Roof framework (shown from above): (1) wall plate, (2,2') stringers, (3) end rafter, (4,4') principal rafters, (5) ridgepole, (6) secondary ridgepole*

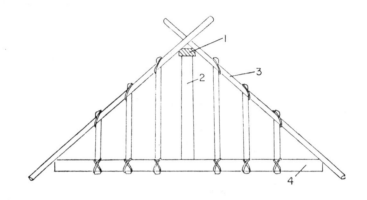

Figure 4.10 *Gable end framework: (1) ridgepole, (2) king post, (3), rafter, (4) end plate*

One unique structural feature of the tinimei is that there are no tie beams or ceiling joists to prevent the sides from spreading outward under the weight of the roof. Joists are unnecessary for two reasons. First, the roof exerts relatively little downward pressure, as it is steeply pitched and covered with palm thatch, which is much lighter than conventional roofing materials. Second, the rafters are partially supported by the side extension plates, further reducing the pressure on the central posts and wall plates.

End Extensions. Place one secondary end plate at each end of the structure so that it rests on the extending portions of the main wall plates and butts against the main end plate. The ends of the secondary plates should extend one foot beyond the main wall plates at each end.

● Measure 3 feet out from each central frame post and dig four 4-foot postholes. Set the posts in the holes, then fill and pack. The posts should extend about 3 feet above the ground and should be the same height as the side extension posts.

● Place the end extension plates on the posts so they extend 1 foot beyond the posts at each end. Set six end extension rafters in place at each end. Run the rafters from the secondary end plates to the end extension plates so they extend 1 foot beyond the plates. Lash the rafters to the plates.

Corner Extensions. Run the outer stringers from the side extension wall plates to the end extension plates, as shown in Figure 4.11. Lash the stringers to the plates. Run the inner stringers from the end extension rafters to the main structure end rafters and lash in place as shown in Figure 4.11. Lash the corner extension rafters to the inner and outer stringers.

16

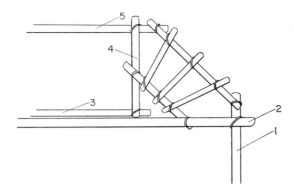

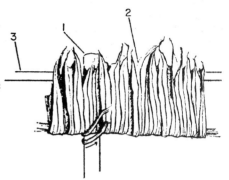

Figure 4.11 *Corner extension framework: (1) side extension wall plate, (2) central frame end rafter, (3) secondary end plate, (4) end rafter extension, (5) end extension wall plate*

Thatching the Roof. The thatch sheets are attached to the rafters with cord lashing. You can use either a separate length of cord for each thatch sheet or one length of cord for each rafter.

• Starting from a bottom, right-hand corner on one side of the roof, place one thatch sheet so that it covers the eave purlin and extends a few inches beyond the side extension wall plate, as shown in Figure 4.12. Working across the bottom row, place thatch sheets next to one another and lash each in place, as shown in Figure 4.13. The adjacent thatch binding poles should overlap one another and be lashed together, as shown in Figure 4.14.

Figure 4.12 *Tying thatch sheet to rafter: (1) rafter, (2) thatch sheet, (3) eave purlin*

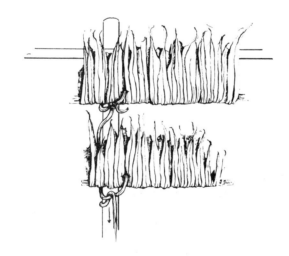

Figure 4.13 *Tying thatch sheets to rafter*

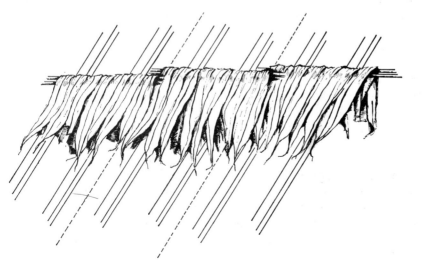

Figure 4.14 *Row of thatch sheets tied to rafters*

• Following the same procedure, thatch one side of the roof up to the ridgepole and then thatch the other side. Each row of thatch should overlap the row below it by one-third of its length. When you reach the top on each side, any extra line should be wrapped around the ridgepole and tied off with a square knot. Make sure that each thatch sheet is tied securely to two rafters. Thatch the gable ends by lashing thatch sheets to the vertical poles as shown in Figure 4.15.

Figure 4.15 *Thatch sheets on gable end*

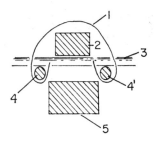

Figure 4.16 *Roof capping: (1) capping sheet, (2) secondary ridgepole, (3) transverse rod, (4,4') thatch sheet binding rods, (5) ridgepole*

• Cap the area over the ridgepole as shown in Figure 4.16. Lay the thatch sheets along the secondary ridgepole two layers thick, with the binding poles on opposite sides. Force the binding poles around the secondary ridgepole so that they rest between it and the main ridgepole. Then, to secure them in place, force short dowels, reeds, or sticks through the thatch between the two ridgepoles.

PART II
Basic Skills and Materials

5
Cordage

Cord *is several threads twisted or woven together.* Line *is a thin, strong cord.* String *is a small cord, smaller than a rope but larger than a thread.* Twine *is a strong cord of two or three threads twisted together.* Rope *is cord one-inch or more in diameter.*

As the list below suggests, you can use almost anything to make rope, cord, twine, line, and string. This is not surprising, as cord is used all over the world in the manufacture and assembly of so many different items—mats, rugs, dwellings, containers, clothing, snares, fish nets, hammocks, bows, and musical instruments, to name just a few.

Cord is made in a variety of ways. The raw material can be used in its natural state and twined, braided, twisted, rolled, plaited, or woven. How the cord is made depends on the nature of the raw material and the use to which the cord will be put. For example, it would be a waste of time to braid basswood fibers for use as lashings in a wigwam. On the other hand, horsehair line can be used only after it is rolled and twisted.

The secrets to making cord by hand from animal and plant materials are nimble fingers and lots of practice. It is also important to make sure that the raw materials are correctly prepared. You can save yourself time and frustration by making short pieces of cord before attempting to make longer lines.

Animal Materials

Hair

horse	Asia, Russia, Europe, North America
human	South America, North America
cow	Europe
yak	Asia, India
goat	Asia, Middle East, North America
camel	Middle East
buffalo	North America
sheep	North America, Europe
rabbit	North America

Skin

deer	North America, Russia
sea mammals	North America, South America
buffalo	North America
ox	North America
fish	North America
rabbit	North America

Sinew (back and leg)

deer	Russia, North America
guanaco	South America

moose	North America
elk	North America
buffalo	North America

Plant Materials

Tree Root

pine (*Pinus*)	Europe
black spruce (*Picea mariana*)	Europe, North America
European white birch (*Betual pendula*)	Europe
bog-fir (*Abres*)	Europe
red cedar (*Thuja plicata*)	North America

Tree and Shrub Bark (outer or inner)

sea hibiscus (*Hibiscus tiliaceus*)	South America, India, Africa, Asia
scouler willow (*Salix scouleriana*)	Europe, North America
fig (*Ficus lacifera, Ficus gymnorygma*)	India, South Pacific
linden (*Tilia cordata*)	Africa, South Pacific
baobab (*Adansonia digitata*)	Africa
acacia (*Acacia sp*)	Africa
red cedar (*Thuja plicata*)	North America
basswood (*Tilia americana*)	North America
slippery elm (*Ulmus rubra*)	North America
moosewood (*Dirca palustris*)	North America
ijomo (*Helicia odorata*)	South Pacific
wegodo (*Urena lobata*)	South Pacific

Tree and Shrub Leaf Fiber

palm (numerous species)	South America, Asia, Africa
yucca (*Yucca baccata, Yucca decipiens, Nolina matapensis*)	North America, Central America
agave (*Agave hetercantha*)	North America, Central America, Africa

Grasses and Sedges

grasses—long, flat, prairie, marram (*Carex*, numerous species)	Asia, Europe, North America, India, South America
hay	Europe
straw-oat, rye, wheat	Europe

Other Plants

Kelp stem (*Macrocystis pyrifera*)	North America
hemp (*Cannabis sativa*)	North America, Asia
Indian hemp (*Apocynum cannabinum*)	North America, Asia, Middle East
nettle fibers (*Urtica dioica*)	North America
milkweed fibers (*Asclepias syriaca*)	North America
iris (*Iris ensata*)	India
elm shoots (*Ulmus wallichiana*)	India
sagebrush (*Artemisia tridentata*)	North America
antelope brush (*Purshia tridentata*)	North America
sennit coconut husk (*Cocus nucifera*)	South Pacific
rattan fiber (*Calamus*, numerous species)	Africa, South Pacific, Asia
bamboo fiber (*Bambusa*, numerous species)	India, China

21

rushes (*Juncus*, *Scirpus*, numerous species)	North America, Europe, India
palm shoots (*Arecaceae*, numerous genera and species)	North America, South America, Africa, South Pacific
heather (*Calluna valgaris*)	Europe
reeds (*Phargamites*, *Arundo*, numerous species)	Africa, Middle East
mescal (*Lophophora williamsii*)	North America

Fish-Skin Line

The Ingalik people of Alaska make lines for fishing, snares, and wrapping from the skin of the dog-salmon (*Oncorhynchus keta*). The skin must be dry and free of all flesh. It need not be scaled, unless you plan to make very thin line.

• Clean the skin by scraping with a knife or stone. Remove and discard the tail and head sections. Cut the skin in half lengthwise with a sharp knife and fold each skin half over and over in one-inch widths. Cut the line in the desired width from each folded half. Unfold the lines and then work them through your teeth, stretching, twisting, and pulling them until round.

Babiche (Rawhide) Line

Like many other people around the world, the Ingalik also make line from untanned rawhide. Skin of the caribou, sea mammals, mountain sheep, or moose is used. Sea mammal skin is preferred, but caribou skin is more widely available.

For grass cord, basswood fiber, spruce root cord, and milkweed fiber instructions, see Chapters 2, 3, 14, and 18.

• Soak a large piece of untreated skin in water for seven to ten days until the hair pulls off easily. Remove the hair by scraping the skin with a knife or sharp stone, then air-dry the skin.

• Cut the line from the dried skin. This is a two-person operation, with one person cutting and the other pulling. Lay the skin flat and, starting from an outer edge, cut from underneath, pulling toward yourself, round and round toward the center of the skin. At the same time, the other person should pull the skin tight and free the line from the surrounding skin.

• Stretch the line on a stretching frame constructed from four hardwood poles. Take two 4-foot poles and lash or nail them together to form an X. Lash one 3-foot pole to the top and another to the bottom of the X to form a frame about three feet square. Stretch the line by tying one end to a cross piece and then tightly winding the line around the outside frame.

Coconut-Husk Twine

People in the South Pacific make coir twine from the husk fibers of the sennit coconut (*Cocus nucifera*). Being strong and durable, coir twine is used to lash the poles of log huts together. A hut 20 feet long by 18 feet wide by 15 feet high might require as much as 18,000 feet of coir twine— six months' to a year's work for one person.

Coir twine can be made only from the husk fibers of the sennit coconut, the longest variety of coconut, with mature fruit reaching 22 inches in length. Other coconuts are too short and their fibers too brittle to be of use in twine making.

• Collect half-ripe sennit coconuts and split each husk into five long segments. Boil the segments in salt or fresh water for several hours. Remove from the water and peel the husks from the flesh. Beat the husks with a mallet to remove dirt, flesh, and short fibers. Peel the long, red fibers from the husk, dry them in the sun for three hours, and then separate them into thinner strips.

• Roll two or more strands of fiber together to form single strands. Roll by placing the fibers on your bare thigh and rolling them together with your palm, first down the thigh and then quickly, without removing your palm, up the thigh. Rolling on a bare thigh is important, as the body oils on the skin will help bind the fibers together.

• Braid three of the strands together to form the twine. Braid two strands together over a single, center strand. Feed in strands as needed for length, leaving the unbraided ends hanging down.

Indian Hemp Cord

Indian hemp is an important source of both handmade and manufactured cord the world over. The instructions here assume the use of the wild hemp (*Apocynum cannabinum*) that grows in North America.

• Cut hemp plants (the taller the better) in the fall. Remove the leaves and dry the stalks in the sun for two weeks. Bundle the stalks and store to be used as needed. Split each stalk down the center with your thumbnail or a sharp knife, then flatten the stalk halves and fold each in half. Peel the inner fiber from each half, working from the middle toward each end. Smooth the rough fibers with a knife or sharp stone.

• Roll two or more fibers together to form a cord, using the same rolling technique as in making coir twine.

Agave Leaf Twine

The Tarahumara people in northern Mexico rely on the agave (*Agave heteracantha*) for fiber for cordage. The agave is a type of cactus with a broad stump and long, broad, green leaves about 16 inches long.

• Gather agave leaves, being careful of the sharp spines and edges. Scrape off the sharp spines and boil the leaves. Cool and scrape with a knife to remove the leaf pulp. (Dry leaves should be beaten with a mallet rather than scraped.) Wash the remaining fibers in running water. Using two or more fibers, twist into twine using the down-the-thigh, up-the-thigh technique.

Pine Root Twine

The Lapp people of northern Scandinavia make twine from the slender roots of the pine tree. Any type of pine tree can be used, as long as the roots are no more than one inch thick.

• Select and dig up pine tree roots, debark them, and split them into halves or quarters. Coil the split roots, then soak for one week in the mud at a lake bottom or under wet ground moss. If such soaking is not feasible, boil for a half-day in a solution of two or three large spoonfuls of wood ash in water. Wind the wet cord around a stick or pole and set aside for one day. If the roots are stiff after drying, soak in cold water for a few hours before proceeding.

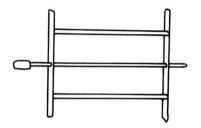

Figure 5.1 *Lapp reel*

• Attach two fibers to a reel like that shown in Figure 5.1. Make the reel from four sticks and one rounded pole. Lash, nail, or screw the four frame sticks together. Cut a round hole in each side stick. Insert the pole through the hole, making sure that it turns easily. Attach the fibers to the reel by tying one end around the pole and winding the reel.

• Wind the fibers (two at a time) off the reel onto round poles, each about 12 inches long. Leave the fibers tied at one end to the reel pole. Working away from the reel, twine the fibers together by twisting the sticks, one to the right, the other to the left. Finish the ends of the twine with thin strips of pine root fiber.

Rush Twine

Rushes are an important source of cordage in North America and Europe. Various rushes, including the common bulrush (*Scirpus lacustris*) and cattail (*Typha latifolia*), can be used. The instructions given here are for rush twine as made in rural Ireland.

• Cut rushes in the late summer. Beat with a mallet and twist to remove the pitch, then dry the rushes in the sun. Tie into bundles and store inside until winter. To make twine, take each rush and twist it, and then twist two twisted rushes together to form a two-ply rope. To lengthen, tie a loop at the end of a rope and hook the next length through.

Horsehair Line

Animal hair is used to make the fine lines needed for fish nets and fishing lines. The rural Irish are particularly adept at this craft.

• Gather a handful or more of long horsetail hair. Obtain two or three goose or swan feather quills and cut each to form a hollow tube three inches long. Using two quills, thread 10 to 20 hairs through each quill tube. Join the two bundles of hairs (one protruding from each tube) by knotting them together at the end.

• With the two bunches of hair knotted together, and the rest of the hair in each tube, rotate the tubes against each other between the forefingers on one hand. If you rotate correctly and rapidly enough, the hairs will feed through the tubes and twist together, forming a single line. You can feed more hair through the tubes with your free hand.

6
Glues

People in technologically simple societies make less use of glues and adhesives than we do. There is a limited number of natural materials that yield useful glues, and glue is more difficult to store and transport than plant fibers used for cordage. When glues are used it is most often to seal objects such as bowls or canoes, to attach delicate materials such as feathers to an arrow shaft, or to repair cracks in wood or stone containers.

There are at least two dozen animal and plant materials that can be used to make glue. For most glues the preparation sequence is the same: collect the material, heat it, cool it, and reheat to use.

Animal Materials

deer hide, horn, hoofs, joints	North America, Europe
buffalo hide, horn, hoofs	North America
buffalo milk curd	North America
human blood	North America, South Pacific
turtle head	North America
fish skin	North America, Europe
fish oil, organs	North America
beeswax	North America, South America

Plant Materials

Tree and Plant Gum or Sap

rakoko root (*Cooperia drummondi*)	Central America
pinyon (*Pinus cembroides*)	North America
pine (*Pinus sp.*)	North America
black spruce (*Picea mariana*)	North America
chokecherry (*Prunus virginiana*)	North America
pawpaw tree (*Asimina triloba*)	Africa
breadfruit tree (*Artocarpus communus*)	South Pacific
milkweed (*Ascelpias syriaca*)	North America
porcupine grass (*Stipa spartea*)	South Pacific

Tree and Plant Parts

guru root (*Nolina matepensis*)	Central America
gotoko root (Phaseolus metcalfei)	Central America
baobab fruit (*Adansonia digitata*)	Africa
coconut husk (*Cocus nucifera*)	South Pacific
touberry (*Cordia subcordata*)	South Pacific
wild ebony fruit (*Diosyros embryopteris*)	Asia
akar fruit seed (*Abrus precatorius*)	Asia

Breadfruit Sap Glue

The breadfruit tree (*Artocarpus communus*) is an important source of food for people living in the South Pacific. It also serves as a source of glue for the Woleai people of the central Carolines. Although not native to North America, breadfruit trees do grow in southern Florida.

• Slash a breadfruit tree in several places to let the sap run. Collect the sap by scraping it off the trunk into a container. Wash the sap in salt water to remove dirt and bark, and then soak in fresh water for three days. Remove from the water and store in a covered container.

• To use, pull the glue from the container with a stick. The glue will come out as a long, white rope. Wind it around the end of a stick, heat, and rub on. When properly heated, it will peel off the stick in a thin sheet.

Beeswax

Beeswax is a natural, sticky, adhesive substance used in both North and South America as a glue. It is prepared in the following way by the Siriono people of Bolivia, who use it to attach feathers to arrow shafts.

• Gather the beeswax from a beehive and boil in fresh water. As the water boils, skim the dirt off the top. Cool the liquid and roll into balls about the size of baseballs. To use, reheat the glue and smear on all parts to be glued.

Evergreen Pitch

The pitch from all varieties of evergreen trees can be used as a glue. Native Americans used pitch to seal bark containers and canoes.

• In the summer, scrape the bark off sections of evergreen trees standing near fresh water. When the gum has oozed out of the trunk, gather it and the bark pieces it is stuck to. Place the gum and bark in a fine-mesh strainer or cheesecloth bag and boil in water. As the gum boils it will liquify and seep through the wire or cloth mesh. Skim the gum off the surface of the boiling water and discard the bark residue. Store the gum, which will harden when cooled, in a covered container.

• To use, boil the gum in water until soft. When nearly soft, add a handful of ground cedar charcoal to the boiling water to help firm the glue. Apply with a flat stick or knife.

Sturgeon Glue Stick

Skin, oil and internal organs of fish are sources of glue in sub-Arctic areas of North America.

• To make the glue, pull the cord from the spinal column of a sturgeon (or, since sturgeon is hard to come by these days, you may want to try the spinal cord of another fish instead). Chop the cord into small pieces and fry the pieces in a heavy pan until they melt. While it is still in the pan and warm, wind the melted cord around the end of a stick, making a mass.

Sandpaper
Sandpaper can be made from sturgeon glue, animal hide, and sand. Cut a small, square piece of moose or other hide. Cover one side of the hide with glue and let it nearly dry. Pour fine sand over the glue and dry it in the sun for six hours.

- To use, heat the mass and rub off some glue. Since you heat only the glue on the outside of the mass, you leave the inside glue hard and ready for future use. You may want to sharpen the butt end of the stick so it can be set in the ground while you are working.

Root Glue

The Tarahumara people of Northern Mexico make an adhesive by combining the boiled roots of the guru (*Nolina matepensis*) and gotoko (*Phaseolus metacalfei*) plants and the root sap of the rakoko (*Cooperia drummondi*).

- Collect the ingredients and combine in water. Boil the mixture until the liquid has nearly disappeared. Let the mixture cool and use without reheating.

7
Vegetable Dyes and Dyeing

In 1856 the English chemist Sir William Perkin accidentally discovered that dyes could be made from extracts of coal tars. This discovery of aniline dyes marked the beginning of a rapid decline in the economic importance of dyes made from vegetable, animal, and mineral materials. Although natural dyes have a long history—they were used in Egypt, Peru, and China for at least 3,000 years before Perkin's discovery—dyeing with natural coloring agents has become something of a lost craft. With the rapid growth of the aniline dye industry in England, Germany, and the United States, aniline dyes almost entirely replaced natural ones. Even Native American groups such as the Iroquois in New York State, who had used vegetable dyes for hundreds of years, quickly switched to aniline dyes.

In the past ten years has there been a revival of interest in natural dyes; many Native American craft items sold today in craft stores are again dyed with natural vegetable and mineral dyes. Although aniline dyes are easier to use and longer lasting and produce surer colors, natural dyes have a number of advantages: they often produce softer, more delicate colors; they pose little threat to one's health; and gathering the plants and making the dyes are fun and educational.

Natural dyes are made from naturally occurring plant, animal, and mineral substances. The vegetable dyes listed here were commonly used by Native Americans, European peasants, and English villagers during the seventeenth and eighteenth centuries.

These dyes can be used today to dye a wide variety of natural fibers, including rushes, wool, vegetable fibers, and cotton, as well as wood, animal hair and fur, rawhide, leather, feathers, and porcupine quills. Synthetic fibers cannot be dyed with vegetable dyes. Vegetable dyes can be made from the roots, bark, branches, leaves, flowers, fruit, and pollen of a variety of trees, bushes, flowers, herbs, and mosses. Usually the vegetable coloring agent must be combined with a mineral setting agent—the mordant—such as alum, grindstone dust, lime, salt, or wood ash. A few plants, such as bloodroot, yield dyes that set without a mordant. Vegetable dyes produce a wide range of reds and yellows, but they do less well with blue, green, and black. Many tribal people prefer mineral or soil coloring agents for blue and black. Wood products such as bowls, baskets, and spoons are often colored green by rubbing them with pond scum, called "frog spit."

The simplest method of dyeing is to place the vegetable coloring agent in cold water and let it sit for a few days. When the solution reaches the desired color the material to be dyed is placed in it and allowed to sit until the color takes. Unfortunately, this method works with only a few dyes and produces inconsistent results. A second method is to prepare the dye by boiling the coloring agent in water. The material to be dyed is then dipped (perhaps more than once) in the dye solution, removed, and dipped in a second solution containing the mordant. The third, and most common, method is to use one solution containing both the coloring and the fixing agents. The material to be dyed is placed in the solution, allowed to stand until the desired color is reached, and removed to dry. The shade of the dye can be controlled by adjusting the ratio of the amount of coloring agent to the amount of water or by dipping the material more than once.

In the following two sections we list some plants useful as dyes and some dye recipes. All of the plants listed can be found in North America. Unless otherwise noted, when the part of the plant used is listed as "bark," we mean the inner bark.

Dye Plants

Common name	Botanical name	Part of plant used
Red		
ground lichen	*Parmelia conspera*	entire plant
yellow figwort	*Orthocarpus luteus*	entire plant
galium	*Galium tinctorium*	root
red elder	*Sambucus pubens*	berries
pokeberry	*Phytolacca americana*	berries
red willow	*Salix laevigata*	bark
sitagapi	*Haematoxylon brasiletto*	bark and branches
alder	*Alnus incana*	bark (outer and inner)
red-osier dogwood	*Cornus stolonifera*	bark
puccoon	*Lithospemum carolinese*	dried root
smooth sumac	*Rhus glabra*	seeds, stalk, pericarp, bark
bloodroot	*Sanguinaria canadensis*	underground stem
eastern hemlock	*Tsuga canadensis*	bark
narrow-leafed yucca	*Yucca glauca*	juice
urto	*Krameria parvifolia*	root
prickly pear	*Opuntia fragilis*	fruit juice
mountain mahogany	*Cercocarpus breviflorus*	root and bark
paper birch	*Betula papyrifera*	bark
nettle	*Urtica lyallii*	entire plant
Rust		
colorin	*Erythrina flabellifomis*	bark
blackbead	*Pithecellobium dulce*	bark
alder	*Alnus incana*	bark
English walnut	*Juglans regia*	green walnuts
Yellow		
common agrimony	*Agrimonia gryosepala*	flowers
betony (woundwort)	*Stachys palustris*	entire plant
blackberry	*Rubus alleghenienses*	berries
curly dock	*Rumex crispus*	root
sweetbrier	*Rosa eglanteria*	entire plant
tumeric	*Hydrastis canadensis*	root
Oregon grape	*Berberis vulgasis*	root

black willow	*Salix nigra*	bark
yellow lichen	*Evernia vulpina*	entire plant
sweet acacia	*Acacia farnesiana*	flowers
pin clover	*Erodium cicutarium*	flowers
goldthread	*Coptis trifolia*	root
American plum	*Prunus americana*	bark
smooth sumac	*Rhus glabra*	stalk and bark
bloodroot	*Sanguinaria canadensis*	bark
wild sunflower	*Ratibida columnaris*	flower
sweet gale	*Myrica gale*	seeds
rabbit brush	*Chyrysothamnus nauseosus*	flowers and buds
wild rhubarb	*Rumex hymenosepalus*	root
fourwing saltbrush	*Atriplex canescens*	leaves and twigs
giant reed	*Arundo donax*	pollen
lichen	*Usnea barbata*	entire plant
	Parmelia borreri	
larkspur	*Delphinium zalil*	flowers

Orange

gray herb	*Thelesperma gracile*	root
bloodroot	*Sanguinaria canadensis*	root
lichen	*Ramalina scopulorum*	entire plant
dodder (love vine)	*Cuscuta paradoxa*	vine

Purple

elderberry	*Sambucus canadensis*	berries
huckleberry	*Gaylussacia frondosa*	berries
maple	*Acer* sp.	rotted wood

Blue

elderberry	*Sambucus canadensis*	berries
water lily	*Nympaea odorata*	roots

Green

lily of the valley	*Convallaria majalis*	leaves
elderberry	*Sambucus canadensis*	leaves

Brown

butternut	*Juglans cinerea*	husk and shuck
pine	*Pinus* sp.	cones
black willow	*Salix nigra*	bark
black walnut	*Juglans nigra*	hulls of nuts

Black

ash	*Fraxinus americana*	bark
silver maple	*Acer saccharinum*	branches, leaves, bark
pinyon	*Pinus edulis*	resin
aromatic sumac	*Rhus aromatica*	leaves and branches
black walnut	*Juglans nigra*	hull of nuts, bark
huckleberry	*Gaylussacia frondosa*	berries
elderberry	*Sambucus canaensis*	bark
American hazel	*Gorylus americana*	bark
butternut	*Juglans cinerea*	bark and root
bur oak	*Quercus macrocarpa*	bark
Kentucky coffeetree	*Gymnocladus dioicus*	root
hickory	*Carya* sp.	nuts

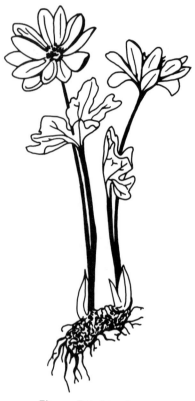

Figure 7.1 *Bloodroot*

Recipes

The recipes below were used by the Iroquois in New York and the Chippewa in Minnesota, Wisconsin, and Ontario. Remember that the shade of color produced by the dye will be affected by the amount of dye material used, its purity, and the time of year you collect it. Do not expect the same amount of dye material from the same variety of plant to produce exactly the same color each time.

Red Dye I
Ingredients (for two gallons):
    paper birch—inner bark
    red-osier dogwood—outer and inner bark
    cedar bark—two cups of ashes
    water—two gallons
Directions: Boil the barks in the water. Sift the cedar ashes through cheesecloth and add to the dye solution. Bring the solution to a boil then add the material to be dyed.

Red Dye II
Ingredients (for one quart of scarlet dye):
    bloodroot—two handfuls of underground stem
    wild plum—one handful of inner bark
    red-osier dogwood—one handful of inner bark
    alder—one handful of inner bark
    water—one quart
Directions: Bring the water to a boil. Add all dye agents. Add the material to be dyed.

Red Dye III
Ingredients (for scarlet dye):
    sumac—seeds, pericarp, stalks
    galium—pulverized roots
    water
    soap
Directions: Wash and clean the sumac seeds, pericarp, and stalks and boil them in water until the solution reaches a deep reddish-brown. Strain the solution through flannel. Add the pulverized galium root. Add the material to be dyed. Slowly bring the solution to a boil and let it boil for a few minutes. Remove the material to be dyed and rinse in cold water, then soak in a solution of soap and water. Rinse in warm water and dry.

Black Dye I
Ingredients (for dyeing rushes):
    butternut—inner bark
    green hazel—inner bark
    water
Directions: Boil the barks in water. Add the material to be dyed and boil for a short time. Remove the material and dry. Repeat the process until a black color is reached.

Black Dye II
Ingredients:
    alder—inner bark
    red-osier dogwood—inner bark
    oak—inner bark
    grindstone dust
    water
Directions: Boil the barks in water. Add the grindstone dust and bring to a boil. Add the material to be dyed. Remove and dry.

Yellow Dye I

Ingredients (for light yellow):

    alder—inner bark, green or dried
    hot water

Directions: Pound bark until it shreds, then steep it in hot water. When the solution takes on a yellow color, add the material to be dyed and bring to a boil. Remove the material and dry.

Yellow Dye II

Ingredients (for deep yellow):

    bloodroot—underground stem, green or dried
    hot water

Directions: Pound stem and steep in hot water. Add material to be dyed and bring to a boil. Boil for a few minutes. Remove and dry. (Note—use considerably less bloodroot than you would for red or orange dye.)

Yellow Dye III

Ingredients (for pale yellow):

    sweet gale—seeds
    water

Directions: Pound the seeds, add to the water, and boil for 15 minutes. Add the material to be dyed and boil for another 15 minutes. Remove the material and wash it in soap and water. Rinse, wrap in flannel, and dry.

Purple Dye

Ingredients:

    maple—two handfuls of rotted wood from an old tree
    grindstone dust—two handfuls
    water

Directions: Combine the rotted wood, dust, and water. Bring to a boil. Add the material to be dyed and bring to a boil again. Boil for a few minutes. Remove the material and dry.

8
Firemaking

Firemaking is one of the key abilities which separates human beings from other animals. People in virtually every society have mastered this basic skill. Strangely enough, however, only a handful of different firemaking techniques have developed over the centuries, with all based either on friction, percussion, or the compression of gases. Instructions for five firemaking techniques are given here. The first four require no special equipment beyond a penknife and a few pieces of wood. Matches and cigarette lighters are handier, of course, but these simple firemaking techniques may prove useful if you find yourself lost in the woods without a lighter or matches.

Tinder

Tinder, the highly flammable bits or shreds of stuff which will catch a spark and start to smolder, is the most important material used in firemaking. Thousands of different materials are used throughout the world as tinder. The Aleut people, for example, twist sea grass into bunches and then pound seal blubber into it. Other materials useful as tinder are fungus, leaves, cotton, wood dust, coconut fibers, sea grass, charred cloth, animal hair, bird down, moss, and straw. Remember that whatever you use, it must be bone dry.

Fire Saw

The Kapauku people of New Guinea make their fires with a device known as a fire saw, consisting of a stick and a bamboo-like vine (Gramineae, *Bambosa*). To make a fire saw, split a stick in half lengthwise

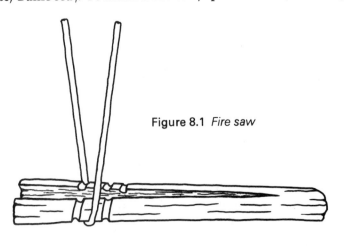

Figure 8.1 *Fire saw*

Hardwoods
white ash
black ash
cherry
rock elm
Douglas fir
locust
white oak
red oak
southern yellow pine
black walnut

Softwoods
white cedar
cypress
white pine
white spruce

from one end almost to the other and wedge a little tinder between the two halves as shown in Figure 8.1. Place the vine underneath the stick directly below the tinder. Step on the stick with one foot, take one end of the vine in each hand and pull it quickly back and forth against the bottom of the stick. The resulting friction will ignite the tinder. The Kapauka can start a fire this way in thirty seconds.

Fire Plow

The Malekula people of the New Hebrides make their fires with a fire plow, consisting of a flat softwood board and a hardwood stick about twelve inches long. (See Figure 8.2.) A piece of broom handle will work well as the stick. Place one end of the board on a small rock and the other end on the ground, kneeling on it to keep it in place. Hold the hardwood stick with both hands and rub it back and forth across the board so that a groove starts to form. It is crucial that the two pieces of wood are aligned so that their grains cross when rubbed together. Work slowly at first, until dust, formed by the two pieces rubbing together, gathers in the groove. Then move the stick faster and faster to produce a spark that will ignite the dust. Place some tinder under the dust as it falls to the ground. When the dust starts to smolder over the tinder blow on it gently to keep it alive. Under favorable conditions, you can make a fire this way in less than sixty seconds.

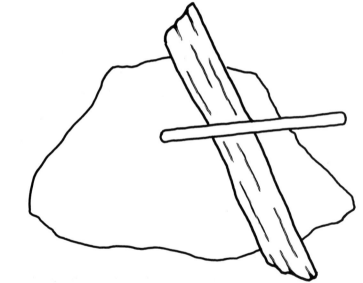

Figure 8.2 *Fire plow*

Fire Drill

The fire drill is one of the most widely used firemaking tools in the world. The Yao people of Mozambique, along with many other tribal peoples, are experts at this technique. The fire drill is simple enough to make and requires no special tools. First, cut a flat surface along one side of a half-rotted log and cut a small depression in the center, as shown in Figure 8.3. Then, on one side of the log, carve a narrow, vertical groove running from the flat surface to the ground. Find a hardwood stick to use as the drill and whittle one end to a blunt point. Kneel on the log to hold it in place and put a little tinder on the ground at the base of the groove. Place a few grains of sand in the depression, insert the pointed end of the drill in the groove, and roll the drill rapidly between your hands while exerting heavy downward pressure. The heat generated by the friction of the drill rubbing against the sides of the depression will cause the resulting sawdust to start smoldering. The sawdust will fall down the groove on to the tinder. By gently blowing on it when it reaches the tinder you can make the tinder ignite. As you twirl the drill between your hands, you'll notice that they gradually slide downward. In order to keep the drill twirling fast enough to maintain sufficient friction you'll either have to quickly shift your hands from the bottom of the drill to the top or have a helper start twirling from the top when you reach the bottom.

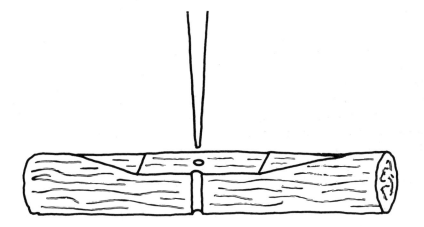

Figure 8.3 *Fire drill*

Strike-a-Light

In their frigid Arctic climate, the survival of the Alaskan Aleut people depends on their ability to make fire. Their method is easy but requires a small amount of sulfur, a chemical occurring in many parts of North America. Locate a quartzite rock and sprinkle a little dried moss or bird down on top of it. Sprinkle a little powdered sulfur on the down or moss. Then, take a second quartzite rock and strike down with it with all your might on the small pile of tinder. The clash of the two rocks will produce a spark, causing the sulfur to blaze and to light the tinder. Native people of Tierra del Fuego in South America use a similar method, but they leave out the tinder and strike flint on pyrites.

Fire Piston

The fire piston is a unique firemaking tool used widely throughout India and the Orient. If made and used correctly, it will be nearly as handy as a cigarette lighter. A fire piston consists of a piston and a cylinder, both of which are usually carved from some hard, tight-grained materials such as horn, ivory, or hardwood. Tinder is attached to the bottom of the piston, which is then rapidly jammed into the cylinder. The heat generated by the rapid compression of gases in the cylinder causes the tinder to ignite.

If you are an experienced woodworker, you might try making a fire piston. While the design is deceptively simple, the actual construction is an exacting process. The piston must fit just right in the bore of the cylinder. If the alignment is not perfect, the fire piston will not work.

The only materials you'll need are wood glue and two pieces of dowel, one ⅜ inch around, and the other ¾ inch around. As for equipment, you'll need a drill and a ⅜-inch bit, a vise, and a selection of wood files, fine-grained sandpaper, thread, nails, and a hammer. Figure 8.4 shows two views of a fire piston made in India.

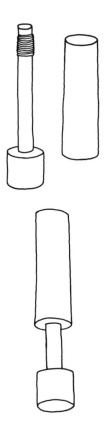

Figure 8.4 *Fire piston*

• To make the cylinder, cut a 3-inch piece from the larger dowel and drill a ⅜-inch hole in the dowel to a depth of 2¾ inches. For the piston, cut a 4-inch piece from the smaller dowel. Insert the piston dowel into the bore to check the fit. The piston should enter the cylinder smoothly without binding, yet just graze the sides. The piston can be made smaller by lightly sanding around the circumference with a piece of fine-grained sandpaper.

• To attach a handle to the piston, cut a 1-inch piece off the larger dowel, bore a ⅜-inch hole in one end, and glue it to the end of the piston (see Figure 8.4). Drive a small nail or screw through the handle into the piston shaft for added strength.

• Carve a small, cup-shaped hollow ⅛ inch deep in the lower end of the piston shaft. Use a round-ended file or small penknife for this job. The hollow will hold the tinder.

• Lightly sand around the outside of the piston shaft about ½ inch up from the lower end. This depression forms the base for the packing, a wrapping of thread which serves as a seal to insure that the air trapped in the cylinder does not escape as the piston is pushed into the cylinder. Tie the thread to the shaft as shown in Figure 8.5, wrapping it around evenly and waxing as you go (ear wax is the traditional material for this, although any wax will do). When the thread is wound several layers thick, tie it off. Wet the thread with a little saliva and insert it in the cylinder to check the fit. It should make a slight "pop" when pulled quickly from the cylinder. You may have to add or remove some thread to achieve this effect.

• To use the fire piston, secure a small piece of dry fungus or other tinder in the hollow at the end of the piston with a little wax. Then, while holding the cylinder with one hand, take the piston in the other hand, place it in the mouth of the bore, rapidly plunge it down to the bottom of the bore and, just as quickly, pull it out. The tinder should be burning when you pull the piston from the cylinder. Don't be frustrated if you don't get it to work the first time—it takes some practice and plenty of patience.

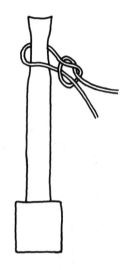

Figure 8.5 *Tying thread to piston*

9
Stone Flaking

Stone was the first material used by human beings to make tools. From as far back as one million years ago up to modern times, men, somewhere in the world, have made their knives, arrow heads, scraper blades, and drill bits from stone. Stone flaking, the oldest stone working technique, involves chipping a narrow, rectangular, sharp-edged piece of stone, called a flake, from a larger stone, called a core, as shown in Figure 9.1.

When chipped correctly from a suitable core, the flake will have an extremely sharp cutting edge, sharper even than the blade of a razor or surgical scalpel. The flake can be used in its rough form for cutting or scraping or reworked to form an arrow head, drill bit, or spear point.

Although stone flaking is arduous, frustrating, and likely to produce crushed or bloody fingers, it does have the romantic appeal of being the one human skill that we can share with our ancestors who walked the plains of Africa one million years ago. Today, with the possible exception of some isolated tribes of Australian aborigines, no group of people relies solely on stone as a source of tools.

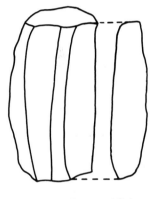

Figure 9.1 *Core and flake*

Materials

The best type of stones for flaking are siliceous rocks such as flint, chert, obsidian, and chalcedony. These rocks, all members of the quartz family, are very hard yet flake easily, often producing a flake with a long, straight, sharp cutting edge like that shown in Figure 9.1. Siliceous rocks can be found lying on the ground or in large deposits in many areas of North America. For the rock to serve as the core, try to find one six inches or more in diameter and roughly rectangular in shape. Depending on the flaking technique used, you may also need a hammerstone, a wood or bone point tool, and a wood or bone flaking tool. A hammerstone is nothing more than a large stone that is as hard as or harder than the core. The point and flaking tools are made from wood or bone as shown in the following figures.

Percussion Flaking

In percussion flaking you strike the core with another rock or with a rock and point tool to chip off the flake. The three major forms of percussion flaking are shown in Figure 9.2. You'll find that anvil and direct percussion flaking are something of a hit or miss proposition, with misses more frequent than hits. Indirect percussion, because you have more control over the point of impact, is a more reliable technique. The key in all three forms of percussion flaking is to hit the core near its edge with a blow strong enough to cause a fracture which runs the length of the core. A common mistake is to strike the core too gently, producing a useless flake, called a dub flake.

Figure 9.2 *Percussion flaking: (a) anvil flaking, (b) direct percussion flaking, (c) indirect percussion flaking*

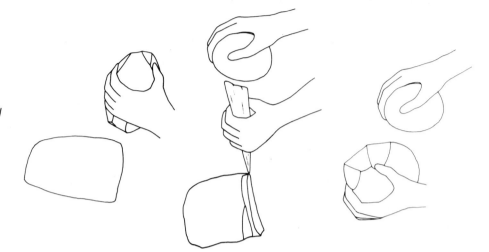

Pressure Flaking

Pressure flaking takes a bit more skill than percussion flaking, as you have to locate a natural fracture point near the edge of the core and apply steady downward pressure at that point with a point tool, as shown in Figure 9.3. Pressure flaking can also be used to fine-trim a flake or core as shown in Figure 9.4. For this kind of flaking you'll need to use a flat flaking tool made from hardwood or bone. By applying pressure at an angle at natural fracture points, you can chip off small pieces to produce a smoother cutting edge or to shape the flake into an arrowhead or point.

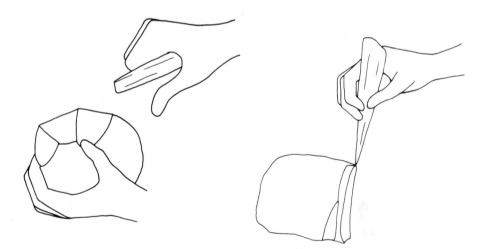

Figure 9.3 *Pressure flaking*

Figure 9.4 *Pressure flaking for trimming*

10
Burden Carrying

Carrying wood, water containers, or any heavy, bulky objects in, out of, or around in the woods is one of those tasks that always seems to fall on human shoulders and backs. As burden carriers, animals and wheeled vehicles often don't work as well as we do in dense forests. Over the centuries, tribal peoples have developed a variety of techniques and tools that make burden carrying easier. The tumpline, burden frame, and carrying on the head are three such inventions still worth using today.

The Tumpline

A tumpline (also called a burden strap, pack strap, or carrying strap) is a flat, woven belt 15 to 20 feet long. As shown in Figure 10.1, the center pad of the line is wider than the lines at each end. The pad is about 2 inches wide and 2 feet long. The end lines are about 1 inch wide and of variable length. The tumpline is used world-wide to haul water containers, wood, produce, baskets, and infants on a person's back. The line is used by tying the end lines to the burden, placing the burden on your back, and then passing the pad over your head and securing it across your forehead or chest. For especially heavy burdens, two lines can be used; one secured across the forehead, the other secured across the chest.

In North America, Native Americans in eastern woodland areas wove tumplines from leather, moose hair, deer hair, or the inner bark of the slippery elm (*Ulmus rubra*) or basswood (*Tilia americana*). Slippery elm bark is the material of choice as it is soft, pliable, and durable. There is no need to give detailed instructions for weaving a tumpline here, as it is finger-woven in the same way as the belt described in Chapter 18, with only two differences in technique. First, use longer center strands and shorter outer strands for the tumpline, as opposed to the belt. Second, make sure to tie off the outer strands in the tumpline when the center pad is completed.

A strong, durable tumpline will support the weight of anything you can hoist on your back and it will last for many years. The tumpline can also be used in tree climbing, trapping, emergency shelter construction, and first aid. A sturdy tumpline should be part of the equipment inventory of every serious outdoors person.

The Burden Frame

The Iroquois Indians who occupied much of what is now New York State prior to the arrival of European settlers were continually faced with the problem of hauling wood, game, bark, and their possessions through

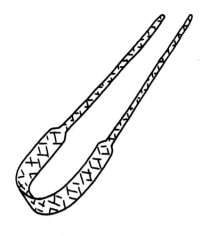

Figure 10.1 *Tumpline*

the woods. Their solution to this problem was the burden frame, supported on the back by a tumpline. Burden frames, like back packs, can be elaborate, but they can also be quickly and easily assembled in the woods when needed. To make a frame like the one shown in Figure 10.2 you'll need two freshly cut hickory (*Carya* sp.) or ash (*Fraxinus americana*) saplings, basswood fiber ties (see Chapter 2) and a tumpline. The saplings should be about 3 feet long and equal in diameter. The piece for the vertical support should be a little longer than that for the horizontal support.

• Assembling the frame is a relatively simple operation. First, cut the saplings and prepare the lengths of basswood fiber. (Sturdy hemp or nylon rope can be used instead.) Drill one hole through each end of the horizontal support. Whittle in about an inch on each end of the vertical

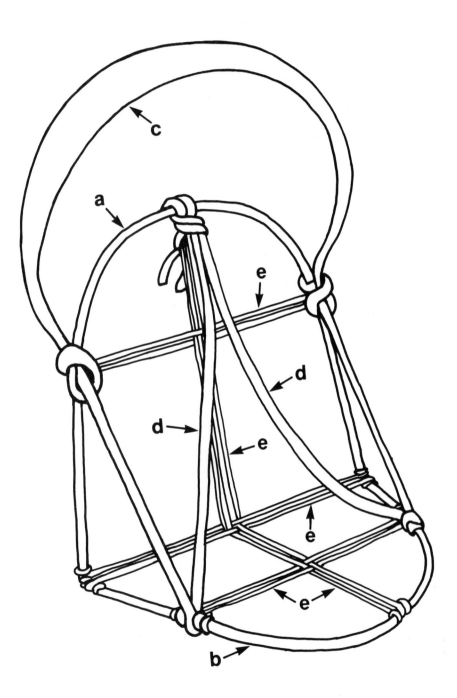

Figure 10.2 *Burden frame: (a) vertical support, (b) horizontal support, (c) center pad of tumpline, (d) long lines of tumpline, (e) fiber supports*

support so that the diameter of the ends of the vertical support is one-half the diameter of the ends of the horizontal support. Bend the vertical and horizontal supports and slide the whittled ends of the vertical support into the holes in the horizontal support. Secure the supports together with basswood ties.

• As shown in Figure 10.2, lash the five fiber supports across the wood supports and attach the center pad section of the tumpline to the vertical support. As the figure shows, the tumpline is knotted at the junctions of fiber support *e* with horizontal support *b* and vertical support *a*. It is tied off at the top of the vertical support.

• To use the frame, load the burden on the horizontal support and tie it in place with the tumpline. Place the frame on your back and pass the center pad of the tumpline over your head and rest it across your chest. For especially heavy loads two lines can be used, one against the chest and the other against the forehead. When the frame is comfortably in place, adjust the line so that it fits snugly.

Using Your Head

In the modern world we are used to carrying heavy burdens on our backs or shoulders. We rarely think about using our heads in carrying. Failure to use our heads is at odds with the practices of most tribal peoples in the world. Many tribal peoples carry heavy burdens on top of their heads, while numerous others use a tumpline across their forehead to support burdens on their backs.

Carrying directly on the head is worth trying if the load is contained in baskets or water vessels. Head carrying, especially of water containers, is used in rural Ireland, North America, the Caribbean, Africa, and Asia. Obviously, it takes some practice to master the technique, especially if you're traveling over hilly, rough terrain. There are several techniques you can try: (1) Carry the load directly on your head without the aid of arm or head pad support; (2) balance the load on your head with one or both arms; (3) balance the load with one forearm; (4) place a pad between your head and the load (head pads can be made from cloth, grass, or leather and are typically donut-shaped); or (5) carry a container that is convex at the bottom so that it conforms to the shape of the head. Use any combination of the above to suit the burden you are carrying and provide comfort.

11
Tree Climbing

Climbing a beech tree with its many alternating branches is often little more difficult than climbing a ladder. But climbing trees like palms or cedars with their long, straight, branchless trunks is another matter.

The Maori people of New Zealand developed their own methods and equipment for scaling tall, branchless trees centuries ago. They use a method of climbing called *topeke* to reach treetops 100 feet in the air, where they spear and snare birds and gather berries. People on some Polynesian islands use a similar technique to scale palm trees to collect coconuts. The term *topeke* is the Maori word for foot-loop (see Figure 11.1), which is the one essential piece of climbing equipment. A foot-loop is a length of braided or twisted bark or fiber cord twisted and tied to form two loops joined by a center strand. In an emergency, a length of inner bark can be quickly twisted and tied to form a rough loop.

A hand-cord (see Figure 11.2) may be used along with the foot-loop. Like the loop, the cord should be made from braided, durable cord with round sticks or dowels added at the ends for easier gripping. The length of the cord depends on the girth of the tree. The cord is most useful for climbing trees with a wide girth and smooth bark that is difficult to grasp with the hands and arms. A more elaborate cord can be made in the style used by Native Americans of the northwest coast. These people tied a rectangular block of wood beveled along one side to the center of the cord to act as a cleat, digging into the trunk as the climber's weight was put on it.

If you decide to try *topeke* climbing, make the foot loops wide enough so that your ankles fit in them comfortably. The length of the loop will have to be adjusted to fit the girth of the tree. As with the hand-cord, the broader the tree, the longer the loop. In the *topeke* method the loops are placed around your ankles with your feet placed on opposite sides of the tree and your knees angled out. When pulled tight between your feet the loop will allow your feet to act as a vise, gripping the trunk tightly from two directions, while leaving your hands and arms free for grasping and pulling your body up. Using the *topeke* method, the Maori were among the most adept tree climbers of all time.

The actual climbing process is fairly simple. Begin by facing and standing close to the tree. If you're using a hand-cord, place the cord around the tree on the ground. Slip your feet through the loops, and set yourself in a comfortable starting position. Pick up the cord, place it around the tree slightly above your head and lean back, allowing the cord to support your weight. Place your feet in a comfortable position on opposite sides of the tree trunk, with the loop pulled tight and your knees angled out. The loop should be tight enough so that your feet support your body without slipping down the trunk. Climb by pulling up with your arms and hands and then rapidly raising your feet and setting them in position higher up the trunk. Climb rapidly, until you reach the top. To descend the tree, reverse the procedure.

Figure 11.1 *Foot-loop*

Figure 11.2 *Hand-cord*

Even though they are expert climbers, Maori men are always fearful of the dangers, as shown by the following saying: ''A tree climbing expert shall be food for roots—sooner or later the sure-footed one will omit or fail in some precautionary measure and then . . . fall into the spirit world from which none return to the upper world of life.''

PART III
Crafts

12
Decorative Techniques

Many of the objects you can make with instructions provided in this book—baskets, moccasins, clothing, tumplines, etc.—look more attractive when decorated. In this chapter we describe three ancient decorative techniques used throughout North America by Native Americans. We have picked these three particular techniques because of the striking, brilliantly colored decorative art they produce. A trip to an art gallery or museum will quickly convince you of the beauty of these decorative styles. Don't be put off by the high prices these craft items command; by following the instructions in this chapter, you can decorate craft items for a fraction of the cost.

Instructions are given here for beadwork, quillwork and ribbon applique. Native Americans used these three materials and techniques for adding colored designs to practically everything they owned. Before you start a decorating project, select the design and colors that you will use. When selecting a design, try to find a clear, color photograph of the design to use as a guide. The *American Indian Art Magazine* is a good place to look for design motifs. Most Native American designs are either geometric like the Sioux designs in Figure 12.16 or curvilinear like the Potawatomi designs in figure 12.17.

Buy your beads! Don't make them! Everyone laughs when they hear that the Canarsee Indians sold Manhattan Island to the Dutch for 24 dollars' worth of trinkets and beads. But if you've ever tried to make even one bead from shell or wood, you'd know that the Indians got the better deal. An arduous, slow, boring task, beadmaking was abandoned by the Indians the day they discovered they could get them from the European settlers.

Beadwork

Beadwork is the best-known Native American decorative technique. The key to successful beadwork decoration is laying out the design properly. The best way to do this is to draw the design on a piece of graph paper. Use colored pencils, matching the colors you plan to use in the design, letting each square on the graph paper equal one bead. Color in the entire design and then trace the outline of all figures in the design directly on to the item to be decorated. Remember to adjust the scale if the squares on the graph paper are a different size from your beads.

You can sew the beads directly to the item to be decorated, or you can sew them to a piece of cloth backing which is then sewn to the article. Most Native Americans prefer black cloth as backing, especially black velvet. When sewing the beads to cloth carry the stitches through the material from front to back as you would do in most sewing. When sewing the beads to leather bring the stitches just under the surface without passing the needle through to the other side.

The two basic stitches used in sewing beads to cloth or leather are the

Beadwork Materials
graph paper
colored pencils
colored glass beads
linen thread
beadwork needles

44

spot stitch (or overlaid stitch) and the *lazy stitch.* Both are quite simple but require some care and patience.

Spot Stitch. With this technique, a thread of strung beads is attached to the article being decorated by another thread sewn across it, as shown in Figure 12.1. We will call the two threads shown in Figure 12.1 the bead thread and the sewing thread. Attach the bead thread to the material with

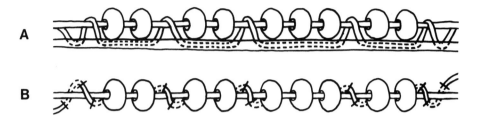

Figure 12.1 *Spot stitch: (a) cross-section, (b) top view*

a knot and string it with two or three beads. Then attach the sewing thread to the material next to the bead thread and sew it across the bead thread at a right angle, securing the bead thread to the material. String a few more beads on the bead thread, bring the sewing thread through the leather or under the cloth, and again sew across the bead thread. Repeat these steps, adding beads as the design demands.

Lazy Stitch. The lazy stitch is the favorite beadwork technique of Plains Indian tribes. With this technique, the beads are applied to the material in a series of transverse strings, with four to ten beads on each string, as shown in Figure 12.2. Using only a single needle and thread, thread the needle, knot the end of the thread, and take a stitch through the material at the edge of the design. String on the thread a row of four to ten beads, lay the threaded beads on the material according to the pattern, and take a second stitch at the end of the row. String another row of beads on the thread, lay them alongside the first row, and take another stitch in the material. Repeat the process until you reach the opposite end of the design, then start over again with a new row of beads.

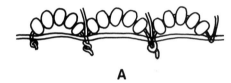

A

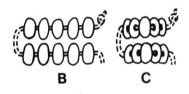

B **C**

Figure 12.2 *Lazy stitch: (a) cross-section, (b) top view, (c) top view, thread pulled tight*

Although both are popular, these two beadwork techniques serve different purposes. Being more durable, the spot stitch is better suited for decorating items that will receive heavy wear. It is also the best stitch for doing curvilinear designs, as shown by the floral design in Figure 12.3. The figures in the design are beaded first, the background is filled in second.

Figure 12.3 *Spot stitch design*

The lazy stitch, though not quite as resistant to wear and tear, is the best stitch to use when covering large areas with beadwork. The Plains Indians used it often in their geometric designs, as shown by the pipebag decoration shown in Figure 12.4. Unlike the spot stitch, the figure and background are beaded at the same time—notice how the successive bands of beadwork combine to form the design.

Figure 12.4 *Lazy stitch design*

Porcupine Quillwork

Quillwork Materials
graph paper
colored pencils
natural dyes
porcupine quills
sewing needle
linen or sinew thread

When done correctly, porcupine quillwork is more attractive, and certainly more exotic, than beadwork. Native Americans sewed flattened, dyed quills of the porcupine (*Erathizon dorsatus*) to the article being decorated. Designs were created by using quills dyed different colors. Expertise in this technique is rapidly disappearing, although it was thoroughly described by anthropologists working at the turn of the century.

Porcupines range throughout most of the northern part of our continent. Sluggish and nearsighted, they were easy prey for Indian hunters armed with clubs. You can obtain quills from an animal lying dead at the roadside, or you can buy them at any sporting goods store which carries fly-tying materials. Quills are hollow tubes about the size of a toothpick with a barbed point at one end. They are creamy white in color, turning a brownish-gray at the barbed end.

Begin by sorting the quills into three sizes. The largest quills come from the tail of the porcupine, the next largest from the back, and the smallest from the belly. The smallest quills are needed only in the finest work. After they are sorted, wash the quills in hot, soapy water, rinse thoroughly, and dye them the colors to be used in the design. Indians preferred red, black, yellow, blue, and natural white in their quillwork designs. Some recipes for natural quill dyes can be found in the margin of this chapter, and others that will also work can be found in Chapter 7.

Natural Quill Dyes
These dyes require no mordant. Simply boil the quills in the dye solution until the desired color takes.
Red: buffalo berry (Lepargyraea) or squaw berry (Virburnum)
Yellow: wild sunflower (Ratibida columnaris) or cone flower petals boiled with pieces of decayed oak bark or cattail roots
Black: wild grapes (Vitis sp.), hickory nuts (Hicoria ovate), or black walnuts (Juglans nigra). Gather the nuts when the shells are soft and place in the sun and sprinkle with water until they turn black.

Different quillwork techniques are used for different types of decoration. Wrapping is used to decorate fringe, edging is used to decorate edges of leather clothing and moccasins, and sewing, or bandwork, is used to cover large, flat surfaces. Since quills will split if penetrated by a needle, they are attached to leather by sewing over rather than through them. Before you use the dyed quills, hold them in your mouth or soak them in a pan of water to soften them. Flatten them using your front teeth or fingernails before you sew them to the leather. As they dry, they will harden into the shape they were when wet.

Bandwork. Bandwork is done by fastening quills to a leather article by sewing over the quills with thread or sinew. Three bandwork techniques are shown in Figure 12.5. In Figure 12.5A the quills are attached by a series of stitches taken with a single sewing thread. In Figure 12.5B the quills are

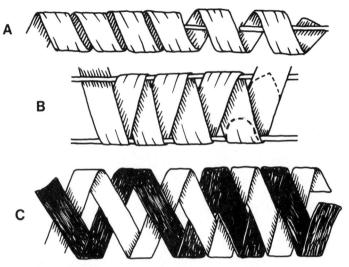

Figure 12.5 *Porcupine quill bandwork techniques*

sewn to the leather with two parallel rows of stitches. This technique requires two sewing threads. Attach the two threads to the leather about one-quarter of an inch apart. Take a stitch over the end of a flattened, moistened quill with one thread, then fold the quill back on itself and take a stitch over it with the other thread. Continue this process until you reach the end of the quill, making sure that the two rows of stitches are parallel. The dotted line in Figure 12.5B shows the best way to splice the quills. When you reach the end of one, lay the end of another quill on top of the first one and take a stitch across the overlapping ends. Figure 12.5C shows the results produced with this technique when two quills of different colors are used simultaneously. The two colors make for a more striking design, but it is a little more difficult to sew.

The spot stitch shown in Figure 12.6 is the best stitch for fastening quills. As quillwork is always done on leather and never on cloth, the

Figure 12.6 *Spot stitch*

stitches should pass just under the surface but never completely through to the other side. Figure 12.7 shows a Sioux design using the technique shown in Figure 12.5B.

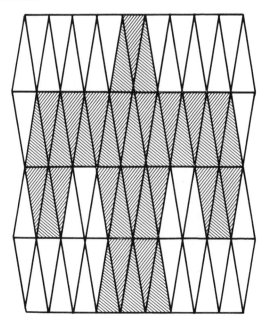

Figure 12.7 *Quillwork design*

Decorative Techniques

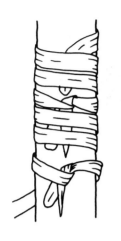

Figure 12.8 *Quillwork fringe wrapping*

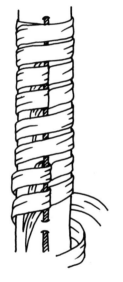

Figure 12.9 *Sewn quillwork fringe wrapping*

Appliqué Materials
pencil
cardboard
scissors
sewing needle
silk thread
silk ribbon

Wrapping. To enhance the beauty of leather fringe, you can wrap the individual strands with dyed quills. Fringe can be made from a piece of deerskin by cutting it into narrow strips from two to twenty inches long and then attaching the entire piece to a shirt, jacket, handbag, etc. The strands can be covered with quills of one color for their entire length, or different colored quills can be used for a banded design. The simplest method is shown in Figure 12.8. No thread is needed. Begin by laying the quill on a strand of fringe and wrapping it over itself as you work down the strand. When you near the end of one quill, add another by twisting the ends together and then wrapping over them. Another method, requiring somewhat wider fringe, is shown in Figure 12.9. Starting at the top of the strand, take a stitch over the end of the quill and wrap it around both thread and fringe until you reach the other end of the quill. Take another stitch, tuck the end of the quill underneath, and continue with a new quill.

Edging. Quills can be attached to the flaps of moccasins and the bottoms of shirts. Two edging techniques are shown in Figure 12.10. In both techniques the quills are folded over a running series of stitches which pass completely through the leather. If you take your time and fold the quills correctly, no stitches will show. The technique shown in Figure 12.10B is the better one to use if you want to decorate both sides of the edge.

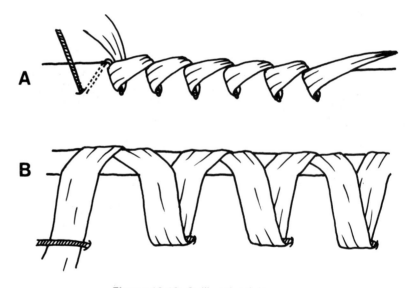

Figure 12.10 *Quillwork edging:*
(a) sawtooth technique,
(b) front-to-back technique

Ribbon Appliqué

Native Americans developed the technique of ribbon appliqué, or cut-ribbon work, quite recently. In regular appliqué, geometric designs are cut from silk ribbon of one color and sewn to a strip of ribbon of a contrasting color which serves as a background. In reverse appliqué, designs are cut from one piece of ribbon which is then sewn to another piece so that the color of the bottom ribbon shows through. In both techniques, the strips are sewn side-by-side to a piece of cloth which is then sewn to a shirt, pants, blanket, etc. Ribbon appliqué requires some patience, but the results are well worth the wait. When working with silk ribbon, remember that needle marks are visible, so plan your stitches carefully and avoid ripping them out. It's best to start over if you make a mistake.

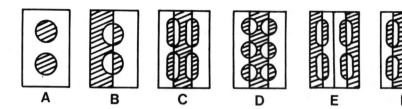

Several different appliqué designs are shown in Figure 12.11. You can use these or others of your own choosing. Before you start, choose a design and determine the length of the piece to be decorated. For the following instructions, assume that you are using the design in Figure 12.11A to make a strip 12 inches long.

Regular Appliqué. Start by cutting a 12-inch piece of ribbon of the background color. Cut a small circle out of cardboard to use as a pattern and trace enough circles on the design color ribbon that you will need to fill the background ribbon. Cut the circles from the design ribbon, leaving ⅛ inch extra material all around.

Sew the circles to the background ribbon to form the design. Fold the edge of each circle under and sew it to the background ribbon using the hemming stitch shown in Figure 12.12. You will find sewing easier if you cut ⅛-inch slits around the circles, as shown in Figure 12.13.

Figure 12.12 *Hemming stitch*

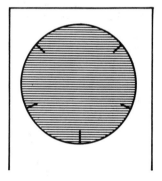

Figure 12.13 *Regular applique*

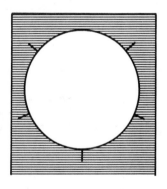

Figure 12.14 *Reverse applique*

Reverse Appliqué. Cut two 12-inch strips of ribbon, one in the design color and the other in the background color. Baste them together carefully along the edges. Cut a circle pattern out of cardboard and trace it on the design color ribbon. Then cut the design out of the top ribbon, an inch at a time, leaving about ⅛ inch extra on the inside. Fold the edge under as shown in Figure 12.14 and sew the top ribbon to the bottom one with the hemming stitch. By cutting and sewing as you work along, the ribbon will neither slip nor fray. The background color will show through in the shape of the design.

You can sew ribbons of reverse or regular appliqué (or both) together to form wide, decorative panels. Fold the edge of one strip under and sew it to a piece of muslin. Fold the edge of another strip, place it overlapping the previous strip, and sew in place as shown in Figure 12.15. Continue this process until you have a panel of the desired width.

Figure 12.15 *Panel sewing technique, cross-section*

12.16 *Sioux moccasin designs*

12.17 *Potawatomi tobacco pouch designs*

Decorating Eggs

Throughout the world, eggs have long been associated with the creation of life. Ancient Egyptians hung eggs in their temples to symbolize fertility. The Romans gave pregnant women eggs to carry to ward off evil and foretell the sex of their unborn children when chickens or goslings hatched from the eggs. In China, eggs are used as religious offerings, and modern Jews roast eggs on the *seder* plate as part of the celebration of Passover.

Because of their symbolic importance, many people have developed the custom of decorating eggs. Christians decorate eggs and give them as Easter gifts. Eggs are painted red in the Greek Orthodox church to stand for birth, blood, and rebirth. The Bavarians paint eggs with watercolors, the Ukranians decorate their *Pysanky* eggs with thin lines of dye using a penlike stylus called a *kistka*, and Mexicans fill hollow eggs with confetti to celebrate the New Year. From the simplest designs of children to the work of Petero Carl Fabergé, whose first eggs were presented by Tsar Alexander III to his Tsarina, eggs have been decorated for centuries.

Materials

Peacocks, chickens, geese, turkeys, quail, emus, rheas, and ostriches all produce eggs, and all have been decorated. Chicken eggs are the easiest to get and extra-large white eggs are the best for decorating.

Elmer's glue, commercial or vegetable dyes, trimmings, beads, pearls, scraps of paper or fabric for appliqué, Testor's paints, watercolors or goache, and varnish will be needed for decorating.

For some projects, paraffin, beeswax, candles, cords or twine for hanging, sparkle or glitter, and cardboard for bases may also come in handy. Use old cans or containers to hold wax, varnish, or paint, because they can be disposed of afterwards with no cleanup.

Getting Started

- **Empty the egg first.** Poke a hole in each end of the egg using a large needle, making one slightly bigger than the other. Blow into the small hole, forcing the contents out of the larger hole and into a saucer. If you have trouble, it may be necessary to break the yolk inside the egg with a needle. When you finish, dribble water into the egg and blow it out, to remove all the contents.

- **Dyes.** Commercial dyes can be used, or you can try natural dyes by boiling flowers, vegetables, or vegetable skins in several cups of water. Use daffodils, crocuses, or onions for yellow; carrots, red cabbage, or beets for red, spinach or broccoli for green; blueberries for blue; and plums, red onions, or coffee for brown.

- **Marbleizing.** Marbleizing makes a good background for découpage, or you may simply prefer to display a marbleized egg without further decoration. Fill a small bowl three-quarters full with lukewarm water. Empty several small bottles of Testor's or other enamel paint into the bowl and stir gently. Carefully dip the egg into the mixture, turning it slowly. Remove the egg and allow to dry.

- **Porcelain.** Make your egg look like porcelain by first dyeing it in the desired color, then applying six or seven coats of Elmer's glue, thinned slightly with water. Allow the egg to dry between coats. Finish off with a coat of clear lacquer.

Decorating Techniques

Many different techniques have been used to decorate eggs the world over. Here, we describe only a few. Remember to work carefully and take your time, allowing paints and glues to dry between steps.

- **Appliqué.** Popular in Europe, appliqué involves gluing scraps of paper or fabric, braid, sequins, tassels, felt, lace, dried plant material, flower petals, feathers, or almost anything else to the surface of the egg. Keep the pieces small, in scale with the egg, and apply the glue to the eggshell, not the appliqué. In Poland, stiff colored paper is cut and glued to the egg to make it look like a small pitcher, with a base, handle, and pouring spout. South American Indians sometimes covered eggs with feathers, imitating the breast of the bird of their origin—pheasant or quail feathers are readily available and work especially well. You may also coat the entire egg with glue and roll it in sand, rice, or small beads for an interesting effect.

Figure 12.18 Polish Egg "Pitcher"

- **Batik.** Batik is used in Indonesia to dye cloth, and the Slovaks find batik also works well in decorating eggs. First, coat part of the egg with wax to resist dye. Paraffin is effective, and you can buy it any supermarket.

51

Heat it in a double boiler, to avoid splatters and smoking. Dip the egg by running a wire through the holes used to blow the egg and lowering it into the wax. When it is cool, draw a design by cutting into the wax with a darning needle. Dip the egg into dye of the desired color, and when it dries, into boiling water to remove the wax. Repeat the process to add a new color each time. To finish off the egg, polish it with a soft cloth and vegetable oil for a shiny surface.

- **Découpage.** Venetian artisans of the eighteenth century perfected the art of découpage by transferring elaborate designs cut from engravings to furniture by gluing them to the wood and embedding them under many coats of varnish. Through the centuries, they have applied the technique to many other objects, including eggs.

  To try découpage yourself, first cut out the picture you want to use. Paint or dye the egg if you like and let it dry thoroughly. Coat the back of the picture with Elmer's glue thinned with water and press it to the egg. If the picture is large, you may have to nip the edges with scissors to make it lie flat. When the glue dries, apply six to ten coats of varnish or urethane, allowing the egg to dry between coats. Painting or varnishing is easier if you run a wire or cord through the holes in the egg and tie the ends to the sides of a shoe box.

- **Pysanky.** Pysanky, which comes from the Ukrainian word *pysaty*, "to write," is similar to batik. The Ukrainians use a special stylus called a *kistka*, but a broad-tipped artist's pen will work just as well. Divide your egg into four equal parts using rubber bands. Heat beeswax over the stove or in a double boiler and use it like ink to trace a design on the egg. The design in all four quadrants should be the same. Dip the egg in yellow dye, let dry, and add to your design, covering any part that is to remain yellow. Finally, dip the egg in blue or red dye and allow to dry. Dip the egg into boiling water for a few seconds to remove any wax remaining. Try different color combinations.

- **Bases.** You will want to display your finished eggs, and bases or stands can be made from many materials. Use driftwood, napkin rings, candle holders, stones, or any other object that strikes your fancy.

Fish (ancient symbol of Christ)

Flower (love, charity)

Endless Line (eternity)

Figure 12.19 *Ukrainian egg designs and their meanings*

Sun (good fortune)

Fir Tree (eternal youth, health)

Triangle (air, fire, water, Holy Trinity)

8-Pointed Star (ancient Sun God)

13
Outrigger Canoe

Outrigger canoes, sometimes wrongly called catamarans, are used by the island peoples of the Indian and Pacific oceans. The simplest outrigger canoe is nothing more than a hollowed-out tree trunk or dugout, with one or two outriggers attached. The outrigger works much like bicycle training wheels, giving the tipsy dugout enough stability so that it is seaworthy even in the roughest waters. Outrigger canoes can be paddled or sailed; the instructions we give here will tell you how to do both. Like many products of tribal technology, outriggers have a number of advantages over more recent inventions. Compared to other watercraft, outriggers are light, sturdy, inexpensive to build, and easy to maintain.

The expert canoe builders of the Samoan Islands use the type of outrigger canoe described here for fishing or traveling in lagoons and on the open ocean. This Samoan-style outrigger has two basic parts, the hull and the outrigger. The hull, 10 to 20 feet long and 1 to 2 feet wide, is open, without decking or thwarts. The outrigger consists of a float and two booms which connect the float to the hull. The outrigger is about two-thirds the length and one-quarter the width of the hull. The exact dimensions for the outrigger described here are given in Figures 13.1 and 13.2.

Although outriggers are often called catamarans, a catamaran is an entirely different type of watercraft. The word comes from the Tamil language of South India where log rafts were called kattu-maran, literally, tied logs.

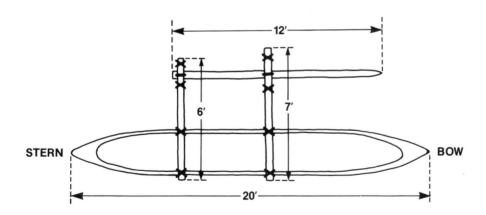

Figure 13.1 *Top view of outrigger canoe*

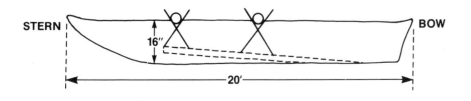

Figure 13.2 *Side view of outrigger canoe*

Materials

The basic material for an outrigger canoe is a large tree, which supplies the wood for the hull, booms, and float. Samoans make their outriggers from the wood of the breadfruit tree (*Artocarpus communus*), which is soft, light, and easily worked yet durable and split resistant. As the breadfruit grows no further north than south Florida, you may want to follow the examples of the Choctaw of the southeastern United States who used the black gum (*Nyssa sylvatica*) for their dugouts; the Iroquois of New York who used pine (*Pinus* sp.), oak (*Quercus* sp.), or chestnut (*Castanea dentata*); or the Hupa of California who used redwood (*Sequoia sempervirens*). Bamboo is the best wood to use for the outrigger float. You'll need a piece 12 feet long by 4 or 5 inches in diameter. The only other material you'll need is cord to lash the parts of the canoe together. The Samoans use coir rope made from the husk fibers of the sennit coconut (see Chapter 5), but you can substitute nylon cord or twine. If you wish to add a sail, you'll also need a piece of light canvas or sailcloth. For tools, you'll need a knife, hatchet, axe or saw, mallet or hammer, a broad wood chisel or gouge, a spokeshave, and a brace with a selection of bits.

Shaping the Hull

The most difficult and time-consuming part of building an outrigger canoe is hollowing and shaping the hull. Figure that this process will take at least one week.

• Select and cut down a suitable tree. Ideally, the tree trunk should have a constant diameter of 18 inches for a straight run of 20 feet and be free of large knots. Trim all branches off flush to the trunk and set them aside. Select the 20-foot length to be used as the hull, cut it from the trunk, and roll or haul it to a flat, open building site.

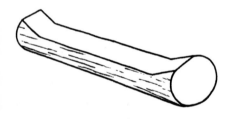

Figure 13.3 *Log with top hewn flat*

• Next, debark the trunk with the axe or a drawknife. Hew one side of the log to the shape shown in Figure 13.3. Hew 4 inches off the center length, tapering to about 1 inch at each end.

• Draw the pattern for the hull on the trunk in the following manner. Roll the trunk over so the flat side rests on the ground. Cut a piece of twine equal to the length of the log. Find the mid-point of the log by doubling the twine and measuring that distance from one end; mark the mid-point. Redouble the twine, giving you a length equal to one-quarter the length of the log, and measure this distance off from each end and mark. Draw the hull shape shown in Figure 13.4, using chalk to mark lines AB, DF, FE, and CA. Distances BD and CE must be exactly the same to insure a symmetrical hull. Lines BD and CE are almost straight, while lines AB, DF, FE, and CA curve inward toward the bow and stern. A cross-section of the finished hull is shown in Figure 13.5 and a side view in Figure 13.2.

Figure 13.4 *Pattern for hull*

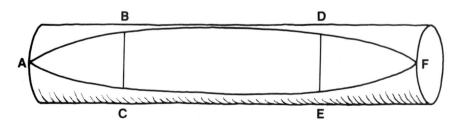

• Hew the bottom of the hull to the shape shown in Figures 13.2, 13.4, and 13.5. Study and follow these drawings carefully. The bottom should be straight except toward the stern. The sides are nearly vertical, sloping gently inward at the top, so that, if the beam of the canoe is 15 inches, the width at the waterline will be 17 inches and the depth of the hull about 16 inches. Hew the sides carefully, using the hatchet. As the chalk guide lines are chipped off, mark new ones following the procedure outlined above. After roughing out the outside of the hull, finish it with a spokeshave.

Figure 13.5 *Cross-section of outrigger canoe*

• To hollow out the inside of the hull, roll the canoe over so that the flat side is up and prop it into position with stones or logs. Every 12 inches along the length of the canoe draw a chalk line across the flat surface. At 3- or 4-inch intervals along each line punch 2-inch holes with the awl. You can make the holes of uniform depth by using a piece of cloth tied 2 inches up from the point of the awl as a guide. Using the hammer and chisel, chisel out sections 5 inches wide along each of the lines to the depth of the awl holes. Remove the wood remaining between the gouged sections with the hatchet. Make sure to leave 2 inches of wood along the sides. Mark new lines at 12-inch intervals, punch new guide holes, and continue chiseling and chopping out the hull until you reach 2 inches from the bottom. As you chop, leave inward projecting flanges along the gunwhales on each side to strengthen them. The outrigger booms will be attached at these points. Again, make sure to leave the sides and bottom 2 inches thick.

Assembling and Attaching the Outrigger

Because the hull of the canoe is so narrow, an outrigger must be added for stability. The outrigger consists of a float, two booms, and stanchions or supports. The booms are tied to the hull and connected to the float with two pairs of supports and rope lashing.

• Cut the two booms from two round, straight branches cut from the log used as the hull. The booms should be about equal in diameter, with one 6 feet long and the other 7 feet long. Debark them and set aside.

• For the float use either a length of bamboo or a round, straight branch 10 to 11 feet long and 2 to 5 inches in diameter. Cut one end of the float to a chisel edge with the hatchet, beginning the cut about 3 feet from the end. This beveled edge is the bottom of the fore end of the float and enables the outrigger to cut through rather than plow through the water. If you are using bamboo, make sure that the hatchet is extremely sharp and take care not to split the float down the middle.

• For the supports cut eight sticks 18 inches long by 1 inch in diameter and debark them. Since they will be set into holes drilled in the float it is important that all the support sticks have the same diameter. If finding eight such sticks is difficult, use 1-inch dowels purchased at a lumberyard.

• You are now ready to assemble the outrigger. Figures 13.1 and 13.2 show the outrigger attached to the canoe. With the hull propped up as it would sit in the water, lay the float on the ground parallel to the hull, 3 feet off the side and 3 feet back from the tip of the hull. The beveled end should be flush with the ground and the aft end raised up about 6 inches by placing a log under it.

Outrigger Canoe

DON'T USE NAILS! The Samoans build sturdy, flexible outrigger canoes by using coir rope lashing instead of nails and screws. Since an outrigger must be able to ride over the waves, a rigid one held together by nails and screws would break up in rough seas.

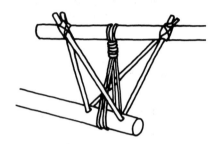

Figure 13.6 *Stanchions*

Figure 13.7 *Paddle*

- Bore a 1-inch hole on each side of the hull 8 feet back from the bow and 2 inches down from the gunwhales with the brace and bit. Rest the longer boom across the gunwhales and lash it to the hull by passing rope through the holes and around the boom, as shown in Figure 13.1. Bore two more holes 5 feet back from the first set and lash the shorter boom to the hull.

- Attach the booms to the float with the stanchions. Use two pairs of stanchions for each boom, as shown in Figure 13.6. Bore four 1-inch holes in the float beneath each boom in which to set the stanchions. Drill the holes at an angle so that the stanchions cross each other at the height of the boom, forming a cradle for the boom to sit in. The stanchions should also flare out slightly from the center line of the float so that each pair forms a V with the pair on the opposite side of the float. Lash the upper ends of each pair to the boom with the rope and tie off with a few half-hitches. For extra strength, you can add a rope brace by taking a few turns of rope around the float and the boom and then wrapping the rope around the vertical cords and tying it off. Your canoe should now look like the one in Figure 13.1.

- For paddles use spruce or white cedar. Cut and split two pieces for the blades, each 18 inches long by 6 inches wide by 1 inch thick. Carve the blades to the shape shown in Figure 13.7. For handles, use poles 6 feet long, flattened on one side. Attach them to the blades with screws or nails.

Adding a Sail

Most outrigger canoes have a simple sail consisting of a mast, sail boom, and the sail itself, as shown in Figure 13.8. The mast is supported by a plank across the gunwhales called the mast step. A list of materials required for the sail is given in the margin of this chapter.

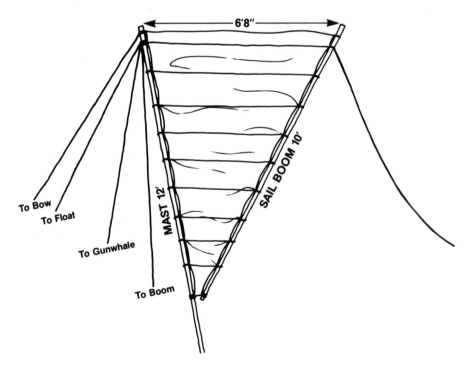

Figure 13.8 *Sail*

• Debark two saplings, the longer one for the mast and the shorter one for the boom. Use wood that is light yet strong. Bamboo is best, but spruce makes a good substitute.

• Lay the plank for the mast step across the hull just ahead of the fore outrigger boom. Secure it in place by lashing it as you did with the outrigger booms or by nailing it to the gunwhales. Drill a 1½-inch hole through the center of the mast step. Then drill a hole exactly ¾ inch deep in the bottom of the hull, directly beneath the hole in the mast step. Don't drill any deeper, as you're liable to go clear through the hull. The mast will be dropped through the hole in the mast step so that it rests in the hole in the hull.

• Lay the mast on the ground and attach the sail boom about 2 feet up from the base of the mast with leather and twine or thin wire as shown in Figure 13.9. The leather is lashed to the poles where they meet, forming a supple, secure joint. The sail boom keeps the sail outstretched.

• Spread the canvas or muslin on the ground and cut it to the triangular shape shown in Figure 13.8. Using a heavy needle and some waxed thread, sew a ½-inch hem around all three sides of the sail. The hem will prevent it from splitting, raveling or stretching out of shape. Starting at the base of the sail, sew a series of parallel lengths of cord across the sail at 6-inch intervals, as shown in Figure 13.8. Tie loops in all the cords except the topmost about 2 inches in diameter along the edge of the sail. A bowline is the best knot to use. Leave enough extra at each end of the topmost cord so that you can tie it to the boom and the mast. Run the mast and sail boom through the loops on the sail and tie the sail to them using the ends of the topmost cord. Tie four 18-foot lengths of cord to the top of the mast to serve as stays. Tie one 30-foot length of cord to the sail boom.

• Raise the sail by mounting the mast on the mast step. Place the butt end of the mast through the hole in the mast step and into the hole in the bottom of the hull. Tie one mast stay each to the tip of bow, the fore end of the float, the far end of the far outrigger boom above the float, and the edge of the mast step where it meets the starboard gunwhale. You can add screw eyes or small cleats at each of these four points to secure the stays.

Using the Canoe

You can either sail or paddle the canoe, which will carry two or three people comfortably. When paddling, the paddlers sit on the inboard ends of the outrigger booms. To sail the canoe, sit on the stern section of the hull and control the sail with the line running from the sail boom. Steer with the paddle, as you would in any canoe.

When not in use, lash the sail and boom to the mast or remove the rig entirely. The canoe should be stored out of water to prevent waterlogging.

Sail Materials
1 sapling 10' long by 1'' in diameter
1 sapling 12' long by 1½'' in diameter
1 piece of light weight canvas or
   muslin, 10' by 7'
100' of strong nylon cord
1 small piece of leather (tongue of an
   old shoe)
1 heavy sewing needle
1 spool of heavy, waxed thread
1 ball of twine or spool of thin wire
4 screw eyes or small cleats

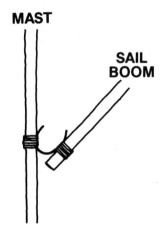

MAST

SAIL BOOM

Figure 13.9 *Mast and sail boom rigging*

14
Baskets

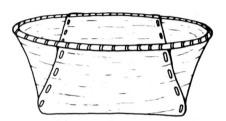

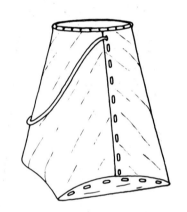

Figure 14.1 *Birchbark basket and bowl*

For centuries, Native Americans in the United States and Canada used canoes, bowls, pots, pans, buckets, and baskets made from birchbark. They did so with good reason, as birchbark is not only plentiful in northern forests but is also a durable and pliable material.

The instructions given here are for the type of basket used by the Penobscot of Maine. This particular basket is a model of simple, efficient design. It is also easy to make; the only materials needed are birchbark, spruce root, and a sharp pocket knife. With a little practice, anyone can learn to make them at the rate of two or three per day. Because of its simple design, the basket can also be made on the spot in the woods as needed. If you ever stumble across a thick berry patch in the woods and need a container, think of the birch bark basket, or even a crude fascimile of it.

Figure 14.1 shows a Penobscot style basket and a bowl. Here we give instructions only for the basket, although the procedure is essentially the same for both.

Materials

You will need birchbark, spruce root, and a small, supple sapling. Gather the birchbark (paper birch, *Betula papyrifera*) in early spring as soon as the snow starts to melt or in late autumn well after the first frost. Bark gathered in the summer may separate into layers and shreds, and bark gathered in the winter will be dificult to peel. The trunk of the birch tree should be at least 6 inches around and relatively free of black splotches or "eyes." Cut the bark from below the first branches but above the maximum height the snow reaches in the winter.

To remove the bark make one vertical 3-foot cut on the trunk of the tree. A quick, slashing cut is best; if you hold the blade square to the tree, the knife will jump and the cut will have a ragged edge. Since the grain of the bark runs horizontally around the tree, you need not cut in this direction. Carefully pry one edge of the bark away from the trunk with the knife blade. Work slowly while prying the bark loose all the way around the trunk, taking care not to split it. The orange inner rind or cambium layer of the bark should adhere to the outer layer if you plan on decorating the basket, so make sure that your vertical cut is deep enough so that you can peel the rind easily. Once the bark is removed, roll it tightly against the grain and tie it with a length of twine. Try to use the bark immediately. If you need to store it for more than a few days, you can restore its flexibility by soaking it in warm water.

You will also need spruce root to sew the basket together. The best root for this type of sewing is that of the black spruce (*Picea mariana*), which grows in much the same environmental regions as the paper birch.

The black spruce has roots of small diameter (about that of a pencil), which are also long and durable and run close to the ground so that you can easily dig them up with a stick. You'll need four or five 6-foot lengths.

To prepare the roots for lacing, you must first split them. Peel the bark off with the knife, then place the roots on a hard, flat surface and pound the thicker end with a stone until the fibers start to separate. When the root starts to fray at the end, split it evenly down the middle with your fingernail. Holding one end between your teeth and the other between the thumb and forefinger of your right hand, pull slowly on both ends so that the root splits evenly in half. If the split starts to run off to one side, bend the root away from the direction of the run and use your left thumbnail or the knife to guide the split back to the center. Follow this procedure to split all the roots in half. As with the bark, try to use the roots immediately. If you can't and they start to dry out, you can restore their flexibility by boiling or soaking them in water.

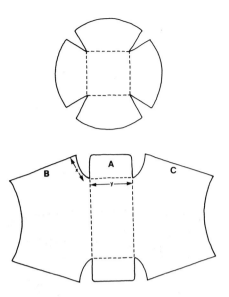

Construction

Construction is a two-step operation. First, cut the bark into the appropriate shape. Second, lace the bark together to form the basket. Patterns for the basket and for a birchbark dish are provided in Figure 14.2. Here, we give instructions only for the carrying basket. Except for the difference in design, the technique involved in making the bowl is exactly the same.

Figure 14.2 *Bowl and basket patterns*

● Trace the pattern on a piece of paper and cut out. When cutting the pattern, remember that distance x must be ½ to ¼ inch longer than half of distance y. Baskets can be made in all sizes, depending on the size of the birchbark sheet available. A piece of bark 30 inches long by 18 inches wide will give you a basket about 10 inches high.

● Place the pattern on the birchbark sheet and transfer it by tracing with a pencil or awl. The outside of the bark must be the inside of the basket if you plan to decorate the basket. Cut the bark to the pattern using a sharp knife or shears.

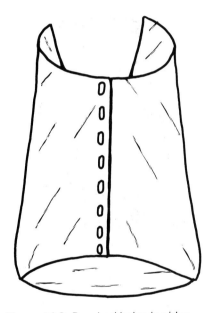

● Lay the bark flat, with the white, outer surface facing up. Fold flap A in and take ends B and C and bring them together to form one side of the basket, making sure that they overlap about ½ inch. The ends can be held temporarily with a clothespin.

Use an awl to punch a series of evenly-spaced holes about ⅜ inch apart along a line where the two ends overlap, as shown in Figure 14.3. Make sure to punch the holes where the ends overlap so that both ends are pierced. Lace the ends together with spruce root using the over-and-under stitch shown in Figure 14.4. Lacing will be easier if the root is sharpened at both ends. The root is not knotted but is tucked back under the first few stitches.

Figure 14.3 *Punched holes in sides*

● Punch a row of holes along the edge of the flap where it meets the two ends, as shown in Figure 14.5. Then lace the flap to the ends with the spruce root using the over-and-under stitch. Repeat the above for the other side of the basket. If the top of the basket is uneven, you can trim it with the knife or shears when the lacing is finished. Use either spruce root or a thin, green sapling for the hoop around the top. Punch an evenly spaced series of holes around the rim about ½ inch down from the top and ⅜ inch apart from one another. Then lace the loop to the top of the basket using

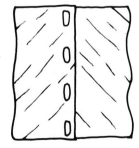

Figure 14.4 *Over-and-under stitch*

the spiral stitch shown in Figure 14.6. You can add a handle for easier carrying by running a leather thong through the top holes on each side and knotting the ends of the thong on the inside of the basket. The basket is now finished.

Decoration

You can etch a design on the orange inner layer of bark, which forms the outside of the basket, with an awl or sharp stick. Scratch the outer layer until the lighter-colored inner layer shows through. Try to etch while the bark is still fresh, otherwise you'll have to soak the basket in warm water until it softens.

The Penobscot usually etched their designs in outline. Characteristic decorations included elaborate patterns made up of dots; straight, zigzag, and curved lines; triangles; diamonds; and half-moons. Figure 14.7 shows the decoration on a Penobscot basket displayed at the American Museum of Natural History in New York City.

The basket can be given a rich, deep red hue by using a natural dye made by boiling shredded bark of the alder *(Alnus incana)* in water. Rub the dye on the basket with a soft rag. Grease or oil (mink oil works especially well) may be rubbed on to further enhance the appearance.

Figure 14.5 *Jointing the flap and ends*

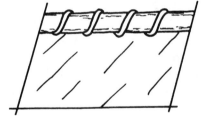

Figure 14.6 *Spiral stitch for the rim*

Figure 14.7 *Penobscot designs*

Shaker Berry Basket

The Shakers are a Protestant religious sect named for the trembling movements which overtake them during their church services. The founders of the sect came to America from England in 1774 and set up a small commune near Watervliet, New York. By the middle of the last century there were over 5,000 Shakers, although their numbers are dwindling today due to one of the primary tenants of their faith, celibacy. The Shakers were known for their handicrafts, especially their basketry. The characteristic Shaker berry basket is a collector's item found in museum and antique shops around the country.

Materials

The Shakers use black ash or maple splints to make their baskets. As these are hard to obtain, you'll be better off using reeds, which are easy to work with and can be purchased from basketry and chair-caning supply houses everywhere. You will need reeds of the following sizes:

10 flat reeds ½ inch wide by 24 inches long for the stakes
6 or 8 flat oval reeds ¼ inch wide by 24 inches long for the weavers
2 flat oval reeds (flat on one side and oval on the other) ½ inch wide by 26
    inches long for the rim
1 flat reed ¼ inch wide by 12 feet long for the rim
1 size 9 round reed 16 inches long for the handle

With these materials you can make a basket 5 inches high with a bottom 7 inches square. In addition to the reeds, you'll need an awl, a small ruler, a few clip-type clothespins, a pair of strong scissors, and a sharp knife.

Construction

Before you begin, soak all the reeds in warm water for about thirty minutes. If they start to dry out as you are weaving the basket, resoak them or wet them with a sponge. Every reed has a smooth side and a rough side. They should be woven so that the smooth side is on the outside of the basket.

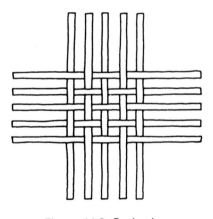

Figure 14.8 *Basket base*

• To make the base of the basket, lay out five stakes side by side about ⅝ inch apart. This is the warp. Take another five stakes and weave them one at a time over and under the warp stakes at right angles, again leaving ⅝ inch between the stakes. The base should now look like the one shown in Figure 14.8. The checkerboard is the bottom of the basket and the stakes are folded up later to form the sides.

• Take one of the flat oval reeds that is ¼ inch wide (hereafter called the "weaver") and cut one end on a diagonal with the scissors. It is a good idea to use the longest reed you have as the beginning weaver. Slip the square end of the weaver under the first reed on the lower right-hand corner of the base, with the smooth side of the reed down. Weave it under and over the reeds of the base, working diagonally across to the upper left-hand corner.

61

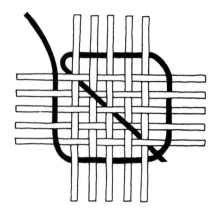

Figure 14.9 *Starting the Weaver*

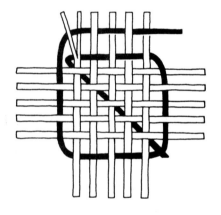

Figure 14.10 *Split stake*

● Turn the weaver to the right and begin weaving the sides. To start, pass the weaver around the outside of the first stake, as shown in Figure 14.9. Weave over and under the stakes, keeping the work flat at this point. After you have completed the first round, split the first stake down the middle from its end down to where it meets the weaver and treat the split reed as two individual stakes (see Figure 14.10).

● Continue weaving until you have completed three rounds. After you finish the third round, fold the sides of the basket upright. Holding a ruler against the stakes on each side as you make the fold will make the folding easier. Make sure that all three rounds of weaving are visible on the outside of all four sides. If the reeds are becoming dry, soak them or wet them with a sponge before you fold up the sides. Dry reeds have a tendency to split when bent.

● At this point, if the weaver seems too loose, carefully pull it tighter, beginning at the first turn. When one weaver is used up, add another by overlapping it with the previous weaver through two stakes. Continue weaving from the outside of the basket, remembering to keep the smooth side of the weaver facing out and taking care not to twist it. Keep the weavers tight against one another as you work up the sides, as shown in Figure 14.11. Use the awl to push the weavers down. After the fourth round with the weavers, begin tightening up the corners by pulling the weaver firmly to give the basket its characteristic shape (see Figure 14.15).

● When the sides of the basket measure about 4½ inches high, cut the weaver so that its end is hidden behind a stake. Cut all of the stakes on the *inside* of the basket even with the top weaver. Cut the stakes on the *outside* at a diagonal so that they project about 1½ inches above the top of the weaver, as shown in Figure 14.12. Fold the outside stakes down to the inside of the basket, and use the awl to tuck them into the third weaver round down.

● You are now ready to make the handle. Take the size 9 round reed and stick the ends into the basket so that they touch the third weaver round down. If the handle is too long, trim it to size with the scissors. Now make pencil marks on each end of the reed above and below where it touches the top weaver round on each side. Remove the reed from the basket and make two small notches on the insides of the handle where you made the pencil marks. Taper the ends of the handle by shaving them below the bottom mark, but don't make them too thin or they'll break. To attach the handle,

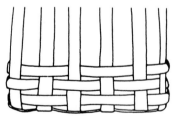

Figure 14.11 *Forming the base*

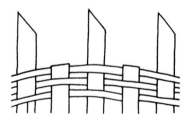

Figure 14.12 *Outside stakes*

slip each end under three weavers on the inside of the basket so that the top weaver on each side fits into the notches that you have made in the handle, as shown in Figure 14.13.

● To finish the basket you must add rims around the top edge. Take one of the two ½-inch flat oval reeds, run it around the inside of the top of the basket and trim one end so that it overlaps 1½ inches with the other end. Measure, run, and trim the other reed, this time around the outside of the top of the basket. Now attach these two reeds to the top of the basket, using clothespins to hold them in place. Make sure that the ends of the reeds don't overlap near the handle. Take the flat reed that is ¼ inch wide by 12 feet long, cut one end at a diagonal, and slip it between the rims, anchoring it under several weavers. Bring this reed over and under around the top of the basket, weaving it so that it encircles the top weaver together with the two rims, as shown in Figure 14.14.

● When you get to a handle, make an X by weaving across the handle and then back through on the other side. After you have gone all the way around the rim back to where you started, cut the flat reed at a diagonal and tuck it down between the two rims. Secure the end by slipping it under several weaver rounds.

Figure 14.13 *Attaching the handle*

Figure 14.15 *Shaker berry basket*

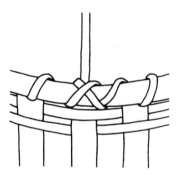

Figure 14.14 *Top rim*

63

15
Sandpainting

Sandpainting (or drypainting, as it is sometimes more accurately called) is a form of artistic and religious expression in a number of cultures around the world. But nowhere is it so endowed with the aesthetic and ceremonial richness as among the Navajos of the southwestern United States.

Today, sandpainting has evolved into an art form, with hundreds of Navajo sandpainters producing permanent sandpaintings as works of art rather than as part of religious ceremonials. High-quality commercial sandpaintings rely on the same materials and techniques as ceremonial paintings. They also often depict similar scenes or figures, although most sandpainters make changes in the commercial versions that render them useless ceremonially. This is done both to preserve the secrecy associated with ceremonial sandpaintings and to protect the painters themselves from supernatural sanction.

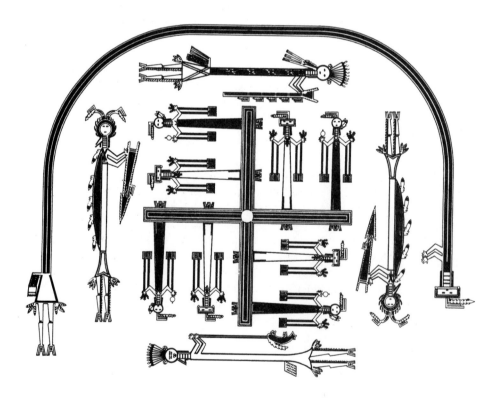

Figure 15.1 *Black crossbars represent pine logs; the circle water. Figures of gods with their wives (goddesses) sit upon the logs. Round heads denote male; rectangular heads, female. Rattles and piñon sprigs bring male and female rains which bring forth vegetation. Arching over all is the rainbow goddess upon which the gods travel.*

Traditional Sandpainting

Sandpainting is part of most major Navajo ceremonies. Designs exist in the memories of the sandpainters. About 500 different ones are known to outsiders; the actual number known to the Navajos is uncertain. Sandpaintings depict supernatural beings and are a major component of rituals designed to cure illness or reverse misfortune. The rituals are usually conducted in a hogan (the traditional octagon-shaped Navajo dwelling) by a male ritual specialist called a *hatathli* or "singer." The sandpaintings are made on the earthen floor of the hogan and average from three to six feet in diameter although some can be large as 20 feet in diameter. Leland Wyman describes the basic religious elements of Navajo sandpainting:

> In summary, the purpose of the drypainted pictures of Holy People and their activities is, first, to attract these [supernatural] beings (for they enjoy seeing their portraits made) so that they may help cure the patient. Secondly, the sacred pictures are used to identify the patient with the Holy people by seating him on the figures and applying their sands to his body. Finally, this procedure provides a two-way path (between the patient and the symbols in the sand) for the exchange of good and evil, health and sickness, immunity and susceptibility; thus, man is enabled to partake of the nature of the divinity.

The composition and design of the paintings are fixed, and to be effective, each painting must be made without major change. At the close of the ceremony, the sand is collected, taken outside the hogan, and thrown into the wind. Themes inherent in Navajo culture such as movement, repetition, balance, harmony, and emotional control are reflected in the designs. Key design components include the use of five basic colors (white, black, blue, yellow, and red), symmetry, and opening on the east side, and particular meanings associated with the use and alignment of colors and figures.

As a central component of the Navajo religion, sandpaintings cannot be truly understood by outsiders as a symbolic religious act or object.

Commercial Sandpainting

Commercial or permanent sandpainting began among the Navajos in the late 1940s. It has now grown into a distinctive art form with top quality paintings selling for as much as $1000. They are made by Navajo artists on boards with the sand applied to glue which holds it in place when dry. The paintings are then framed and sold. Commercial designs are usually based on traditional ones, although they are often altered so as to both protect the secrecy of the original and to protect the artists from supernatural sanction. As this art form evolves, one can see the emergence of distinctive styles associated with particular artists, which tend to diverge more and more from tradition.

Making a Sandpainting

Making a good quality sandpainting requires practice, patience, and correct materials. Although it is possible for amateurs to make traditional Navajo-style paintings, they are extremely difficult to make well. (Keep in mind that Navajo sandpainters begin learning their craft as children by working alongside already accomplished artists.) For beginners, it makes more sense to start with simpler designs you already know. It also helps to keep details such as narrow straight lines, dots, etc. to a minimum.

Materials

½-inch- or ⅜-inch-thick sheet of particle-board
   or finished plywood PVC water-soluble glue
nongloss spray wood sealant
sandpaper
2-inch paintbrush
small paintbrushes
pigments—sand or other minerals of various colors
sifter or fine-meshed screening
hand saw
pencil
ruler

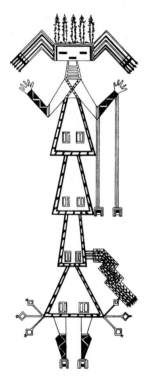

Figure 15.2

Figures 15.2–4 *Navajo, Arizona–New Mexico. Patterns and figures from dry paintings of Dśilyidje-Qácal. The Mountain Chant. Washington Matthews, Fifth Annual Report Bureau of Ethnology, 1887.*

Preparation of the Pigment

• The five sacred colors used in sandpaintings are white, blue, black, yellow, and red (which is used in various shadings). Sometimes gray and brown are used, and green was used in the past. The chart below lists the colors and the traditional sources of the pigments.

Color	Source
white	white sandstone, cornmeal, pollen
yellow	yellow sandstone, cornmeal, pollen
blue	cornmeal, lupine or larkspur petals, charcoal from the root of the rock oak mixed with white sand
black	charcoal
red	red sandstone, cornmeal, pollen, red berries, rosehips
gray	charcoal and white sand
pink	red and white sand

• Once the stones, charcoal, or other materials are obtained, they must be ground into pigment. The first step is to dry the materials fully in the sun. Large stones should be broken into smaller pieces before drying. If they are not thoroughly dry, they may not grind correctly or may change color later. When thoroughly dry grind the material into sand, using a traditional *mano* and *metate* (see Figure 34.2), mortar and pestle, or a hand-cranked coffee mill. Sift the sand to move large particles and then sift at least three times to yield grains of different degrees of fineness. Discard any material reduced to powder as they are difficult to apply correctly.

Preparing the Board

• Cut a board to size (large enough for the painting plus framing). Sand it smooth, including the sides. Wipe off all dust. With the paint brush, coat the board with a layer of glue.

• You may want to thin the glue with water, and some experimentation may be necessary until you get the right consistency. Spread the glue in a thin layer, using a thin, straight-edged rule or board. Let the glue dry thoroughly. Sand the glued surface lightly to remove any bumps or lumps.

Making the Sandpainting

Making the painting involves three steps: (1) marking the design on the board, (2) applying the glue, (3) applying the pigment.

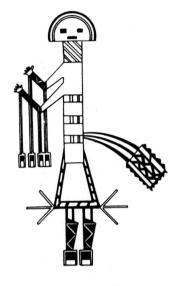

- Although sandpainting artists work entirely from memory or mark only a few guide lines, you will find it much easier to draw the design in pencil on the board. You can draw freehand, with a ruler, or even transfer a template. As part of drawing the design, you should either mark on the design or on a separate copy the colors you plan to apply. This is important, as you will apply the pigment in stages, one color at a time.

- When the design is marked, begin applying the glue with a thin paintbrush. The glue should be applied only to one section of the painting at a time. Apply it carefully to create a smooth, even layer. If it is too thick the sand will be raised too much; if it is uneven, the sand will be uneven. Again, some trial and error will be needed here. Within the section, glue should be applied only to areas of the same color, to prevent mixing of colors when you apply the sand.

Figure 15.3

- While the glue is wet, apply the pigment. Although techniques vary, this is generally done by holding a bit of sand in the palm of your hand and letting it trickle down over the index finger, controlling the flow with your thumb. Keep the flow steady and apply an even layer of sand. Again, trial and error is in order until you find the technique that works best for you. Work on the painting section by section and color by color until it is complete. It may take days or even weeks to complete the painting as you must wait for the glue to dry completely before applying adjacent colors.

- When the painting is done, you will need to fill in the background with sand. Again, apply the glue and then the sand. You should use a very fine sand and apply a thin coat so that the design stands out. After the entire painting is dry (this will take a day or two after the last color is applied), you may apply a light coat of nongloss spray wood sealant to hold the top layer of sand securely. Do this very carefully, as too much sealant will appear glossy and ruin the painting. Practice applying a thin, even coat on a piece of wood before applying it to the painting. The painting may then be matted and framed.

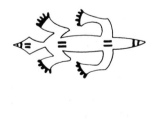

Figure 15.4

67

16
Moccasins

Trapper's Mocs
Many trappers in the 1800s made their moccasins from heavy (10 or 12 ounce) canvas duck. To make them waterproof, the fabric was rubbed with paraffin wax and a warm iron passed over it. In cold weather they stuffed the moccasins with deer hair, pine needles, or dried leaves to keep their feet warm. As one old trapper put it, "Mocs are like cracker jacks; the more you eat, the more you want, or the more you wear Mocs, the more you will."

The first moccasins were probably little more than pieces of animal hide wrapped around the feet to protect them from the cold and from thorns and rocks along the trail. But by the time the first explorers arrived in the New World, there was a dizzying array of designs and styles worn by the Native Americans already living there, with each style adapted to the particular terrain of the people who wore them.

There are two basic kinds of moccasins. In the soft-sole style the soles and uppers are formed from a single piece of leather. In the hard-sole style the soles are cut separately from a stiff piece of rawhide. Native Americans living in the eastern woodlands made one-piece moccasins from soft, supple deerskin and found them well suited for silent travel through the forest and for use in canoes. Native Americans living in the western Plains preferred the two-piece moccasin, which is better suited for rocky terrain. For contemporary use, the two-piece moccasin is better suited for wear on pavement, concrete, asphalt, etc. Instructions for making both types are provided here.

Materials

For both the soft- and hard-soled styles you will need a piece of medium-weight leather 18 inches long by 36 inches wide. For the hard-soled style you will also need a piece of heavy rawhide for the soles and a leather thong for the ties. As for tools and equipment, you'll need an awl, a triangular-pointed glovers needle, shears, a ball of sinew or heavy waxed linen thread, a piece of chalk or pencil, and an old sheet or piece of muslin. The moccasins can be decorated with the materials and techniques described in Chapter 12.

Hard-Soled Moccasins

Hard-soled moccasins were worn by Native Americans of the High Plains, including the Crow, Blackfoot, Arapaho, and Teton Sioux.

• To make them, first draw the pattern for the sole by placing one foot on the piece of cloth and tracing around the foot, leaving an extra ½ inch on all sides. Cut out the pattern, trace or pin it to the rawhide, and cut the two soles. You will find that by flipping the pattern over you can use one pattern for both your right and left feet.

● Draw the pattern for the uppers using Figure 16.1b as a guide. The upper will be sewn to the sole along ABCDE so that point C is at the toe

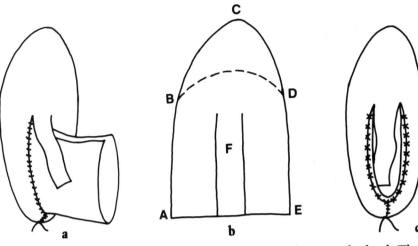

Figure 16.1 *Hard-soled moccasins*

and points AE meet in back with a slight overlap, forming the heel. The distance from B to D should be equal to the distance around your instep plus ½ inch. Cut the slits for the tongue, F, about 1½ inches apart, beginning just past the point above the ball of your foot. At this point you may want to pin the pattern to the sole and slide your foot in to check the fit. When you're satisfied with the fit, transfer the pattern to the leather and cut the left upper. Flip the pattern over and cut out the right upper.

● Sew the moccasins inside out so that the seams are not visible when turned right-side out. Sew the upper to the sole, beginning at point A, using the overhand stitch shown in Figure 16.2. With the awl punch six or eight holes in the sole about ¼ inch in from the edge and ¼ inch apart from one another. Punch matching holes in the upper. Take your time sewing; make sure the stitches are even and pull firmly on the thread or sinew after taking each stitch. Repeat this process until the upper and sole are joined all the way around to point E. Sew up the heel seam and trim off any excess leather. Turn the moccasins right-side out.

● There are two ways to finish off the moccasin at the ankle. You can trim it with a piece of red cloth or ribbon, folded around the edge of the leather and sewn with a fancy cross-stitch as shown in Figure 16.1c. Run a length of leather thong through the fold to serve as a tie. Or, you can add ankle flaps. Cut them from scrap leather and sew them to the inside edge of the uppers as shown in Figure 16.1a. Add the thongs by running them through slits cut in the leather as shown in Figure 16.3.

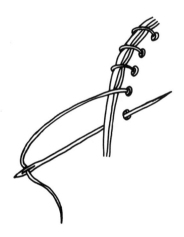

Figure 16.2 *Sewing the upper to the sole*

Figure 16.3 *Thongs*

69

Soft-Soled Moccasins

This one-piece design is used by forest-dwelling Native Americans such as the Iroquois and Shawnee. They are easier to make than the hard-soled type, if the pattern is cut correctly.

- First, draw the pattern by placing your foot on a piece of cloth and tracing around it. Then draw the form shown in Figure 16.4 around the outline of your foot. Points A and B will be sewn together down to G to form the toe, and C and D will be sewn up in back to form the heel. Points A and B should be far enough apart so that when brought up over the foot they overlap about ¼ inch. Slits E and F are ¾ inch long and 1½ inches apart. They should just touch your heel. The triangular cut at G is 2 inches long and ¾ inch wide. Cut out the pattern and check the fit. Transfer it to the leather and cut out two identical pieces—the same pattern serves for both feet.

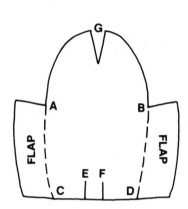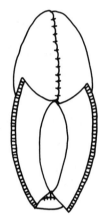

Figure 16.4 *Soft-soled moccasin*

- Sew the moccasins inside out. Sew the toe first, beginning at the point of triangular cut G. As you sew take in the leather between each stitch slightly to form a series of small, neat gathers or "puckers." Inserting a piece of leather between the two sides of the toe which are puckered will make it easier to sew them up.

- Turn the moccasin right-side out. Slip your toe in and mark the leather in back at the point where it meets your heel. Trim off the excess leather, leaving about ¼ inch for the seam. To finish the heel, sew C and D together down to slits E and F and sew the flap up against the heel. The edges of the flaps may be rounded first, as shown in Figure 16.5. Trim the edges of the side flaps with brightly colored ribbon or cloth. The finished moccasin should look like the one in Figure 16.4c.

- Shape the moccasins to your feet by wetting them thoroughly and wearing them until they dry. Oiling the leather regularly will help keep them water resistant.

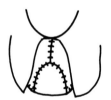

Figure 16.5 *Sewing the heel*

17
Snow Goggles

Snow blindness is a potentially serious problem for anyone living or traveling in the far north or at high altitudes. Snow blindness is usually a temporary impairment of vision caused by exposure of the eyes to ultraviolet rays of the sun reflected off the snow. Symptoms include a gritty sensation in the eyes, swelling of the eyelids, and a partial or complete loss of sight. Snow blindness is especially common in the spring months when the sun shines brightly and snow is still on the ground. Darkness is the only cure for snow blindness, although the condition can be easily prevented by wearing snow goggles or sunglasses.

If sunglasses are not available, you can fashion snow goggles from natural materials found in northern climates. People in Greenland, Canada, Alaska, Siberia, and Tibet make snow goggles from wood, deer antlers, animal hides, metal, birchbark, and braided horsehair. Most of the goggles look more or less like those made by the Ingalik people of Alaska shown in Figure 17.1.

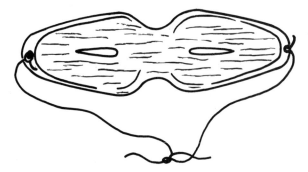

Figure 17.1 *Snow goggles*

Variations on this basic style include goggles with projecting brow pieces or hoods, goggles with ventilation holes cut above the eye slits, and double goggles made from two eye cups joined by a hide strip. Perhaps the most elaborate goggles are made by the Samoyed people of Siberia, who use brass plates sewn into ornamental suede. Sometimes the goggles are blackened around the eye slits by smoking or rubbing with charcoal to reduce the glare. The goggles described below are the basic wooden style used by the Ingalik people in Alaska. You can expect to get two years' wear out of them.

Materials

Cut the goggles from one piece of spruce wood about 7 inches long, 2 inches wide, and 1½ inches thick. The goggles are held in place with a length of babiche (rawhide) line, as described in Chapter 5. Tools you'll need are a handsaw, chisel, gouge, drill with small bits, and sandpaper. The goggles should be cut and carved to fit your face and eye sockets. The eye slits should be about ¾ inch long and ³/₁₆ inch wide.

Construction

- Cut, split, and trim a piece of green, long-grained spruce wood to size. Burn, chisel, and gouge out the two concave eye cups to fit your eye sockets. Burn by pressing a heated stone against the wood. When the cups are gouged to size, finish with fine sandpaper. Trim the goggles to shape with the chisel or carve with a sharp knife, then fine-sand.

- Chisel an eye slit about ¾ inch long and ³/₁₆ inch wide in each eye cup and fine-sand the edges. Drill a hole at each end of the goggles and string a length of babiche line through each hole, securing with a knot. Wear the goggles by tying the lines together behind your head.

18
Fingerweaving a Belt

Fingerweaving is an ancient craft of Native Americans of North and South America used to make garters, headbands, bags, belts, and sashes. It is an unusual form of weaving because the same set of threads serve as both the warp and weft and because no loom or shuttle is used. All you need to fingerweave are fiber, a smooth stick, scissors, and your fingers, which form the sheds and act as the shuttles.

Native Americans living near the Great Lakes gather and process milkweed (*Asclepias syriaca*) into fiber cord for use in fingerweaving. The Tupi peoples of the Brazilian Amazon use sheep's wool, which they spin into yarn for their weaving. You, of course, can use commercial yarn, which is easier to obtain and provides equally pleasing results.

Milkweed Cordage

In case you want to fingerweave in an entirely traditional manner, here are instructions for making milkweed fiber weaving cordage. Gather the milkweed (see Figure 18.1) when its flowers are bright purple and fully opened. Cut the plants off at the base of their stalks and remove the leaves. With a sharp knife carefully peel off the bark in long strips and hang the strips to dry in a sunny spot indoors. When the strips are thoroughly dry (in about six months) they are ready for use. Soak them in water for five days and then strip into threads. The threads will be very fine and must be corded for use in fingerweaving. To cord, take several threads together and roll them on your bare thigh. The natural oil of the skin helps the threads adhere to one another. Roll them only in one direction; for example, away from your body. Then add a little more thread to make the cord longer by overlapping a little and rolling in the opposite direction. This reverse rolling is what "locks in" the twist. The cord can be dyed naturally by following the instructions in Chapter 7.

Figure 18.1 *Milkweed pods*

The Weaving Method

Before attempting to weave a sash or belt it is a good idea to first practice the fundamentals of fingerweaving. For practice, choose four different-colored yarns, which we will call A, B, C, and D. A heavy worsted like "Aunt Lydia's Rug Yarn" is the ideal weight of yarn to use. Cut eight strands of each color about 36 inches long. Be careful when cutting the yarn not to stretch it. Stretching will become an important consideration when you are making a belt or band of a specific length later on.

After measuring and cutting, gather the yarn in your hand and tie a loose overhand knot in one end to keep it all together. Tie the knotted end of the yarn to the back of a chair with another loose knot, so that you will be able to exert pressure on the yarn by pulling it toward yourself while weaving. Find a smooth, 12-inch-long stick about the diameter of your finger or use a knitting needle.

• Sit in front of the yarn tied to the chair and hold the stick in your left hand up close to the knot of yarn. Arrange the strands of yarn on the stick. Bring a strand of color A over the stick towards yourself, then loop it around the stick and let it hang down (see Figure 18.2). Repeat this process working from the right to the left of the stick, first arranging all eight strands of color A, then all color B, and so on, until all the strands are looped around the stick. Push the strands gently together. The yarn hanging below the stick is what you will weave.

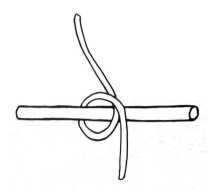

Figure 18.2 *Looping the yarn*

• Separate the yarn: Beginning with the first strand on your left, bring every other strand forward and let the others fall back. Transfer all of the yarn to your right hand. Hold the back strands between your first and second fingers and the forward strands between your thumb and first finger. Make sure to keep all the colors in their proper order.

• Weave the yarn with your left hand. Take the first forward strand on the left and bring it underneath the rest of the forward strands all the way over to the right. This strand is called the weaver. Loop it over the stick to keep it out of the way (see Figure 18.3). Then, beginning with the first strand on your left, bring the back strands forward one by one with your left hand, passing them through the forward strands which are left to fall back. When you get to the end, unloop the weaver and let it fall—it should always end up in the back. With your right hand pull down on the back strands to even up the weave. Transfer the yarn to your right hand, as described above, and repeat the process with a new weaver.

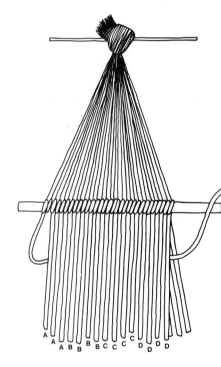

Figure 18.3 *Arrangement of yarn*

This is the fingerweaving process. Practice until you have the hang of it. Be careful not to twist the yarn and to keep the colors in order (the strands in the back will give you the most trouble). Correct any mistakes as they occur. They will not right themselves later on, as is the case in some crafts, and the rest of the work will not fall into place properly. Weaving is easier if you maintain a constant, slight tension on the ends of the strands. After a little practice, you should be ready to make a belt.

Fingerweaving a Belt

A great variety of patterns can be used in fingerweaving a belt. Because the diagonal weave is the easiest, the instructions given here are for that pattern (see Figure 18.4).

• Using four colors of yarn, cut eight strands of each color to a length that is 3 times the size of your waist plus 18 inches. This amount of yarn will give a belt that is 2¼ inches wide, but any *even* number of strands may be used, depending on the width of the belt desired. If you want a wider belt, for example, add two more strands of each color yarn.

• Gather all the strands together and tie a knot in the middle. You will be fingerweaving half of the belt at a time. Attach the knot in the middle of the yarn to a chair as you did while practicing and proceed with the first step (looping the strands over the stick) of the weaving instructions. After weaving half the length of the belt, pull out the stick, turn the unworked side toward you and weave the remaining half.

The belt can be finished in several ways:

The Divided Weaving Method. At one end of the belt divide the yarn in half. With just sixteen strands, begin again the weaving process. That is, separate the strands by bringing every other one forward and letting the others fall behind and then weave just those sixteen strands for 4 inches. Tie the ends in a knot or series of knots and leave some fringe for decoration. Repeat this process with the remaining sixteen strands, and finish the other end in the same way.

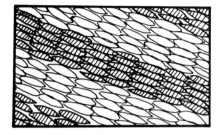

The Herringbone Braid. Divide the ends of the strands in half and hold them flat in your hand. Braid them by bringing the outside strand to the center—first the left strand and then the right, continuing until you have the length desired. Knot the ends. You can also use the divided weaving method followed by the herringbone braid to finish the belt.

Among the many detailed designs that can be fingerwoven are the lightening and chevron patterns. These are fairly complicated, however, and it is best to gain some skill with the diagonal pattern before attempting other designs.

Figure 18.4 *The weave*

19
Yugoslavian Peasant Blouse

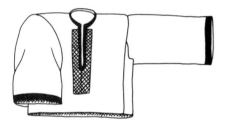

Figure 19.1 *Yugoslavian peasant blouse*

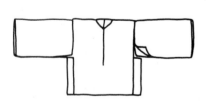

Figure 19.2 *Blouse pattern*

Peasant garments are made to last. They have to be, as peasant men and women work hard in the fields and at home, leaving little time for mending or sewing clothing. Although European peasant embroidered garments are widely admired for their design and detail, for a peasant the embroidery serves the more practical purpose of strengthening the garment cloth. It is no accident that the parts of clothing most often embroidered are those most likely to fray—the collar, wrists, and front opening.

The instructions given here are for the everyday blouse worn by farm women in the Bosnia region of central Yugoslavia. It is a plain, functional garment, consisting of rectangular sleeves and body panels, with embroidery along the sleeves and embroidered panels sewn to the neck, wrists, and front opening, as shown in Figure 19.1. Although we present the instructions for sewing the blouse first, keep in mind that the sleeves should be embroidered before they are seamed and sewn to the body.

Blouse

As shown in Figure 19.2, the blouse is constructed from six panels of cloth: two for the body, two for the sleeves, and two for the body side panels. The embroidered collar is added later. Neither the body nor the sleeves are gathered or tapered in any way. The body should hang loosely to the waist, the sleeves to mid-forearm. As the embroidery is sewn with cross-stitches, a counted-thread technique, you should use even-weave fabric. Yugoslavian women preferred good-quality calico or linen, although cotton broadcloth will do nicely. To sew the blouse you'll need the usual assortment of sewing supplies—needles, pins, thread, facing tape, scissors, a tape measure, and a large piece of paper or a pattern board.

• Lay out a pattern like that shown in Figure 19.2. Cut out the four rectangular body and side body panels, the two square sleeve panels, and the strips for the wrists, collar, and front opening embroidery. Cut the strip for the collar 1 inch longer than the neck opening and 4 inches wide. Cut the strips for the front opening embroidery so that they will run halfway down the front of the shirt. These two strips should each be 2½ inches wide. The strips for the wrists should be 2¼ inches wide and long enough to go all the way around the wrist openings.

• Next, cut the openings for the neck and arms and the front opening in the body panels. Sew the rear and front body panels together across the shoulders and neck using a ½-inch seam. Finish the seam either by overcasting or by turning the edges under ⅛ inch. Sew the two sleeve squares to form the two sleeves and finish. Remember that the sleeves should be embroidered before they are sewn. Sew the sleeves to the body and finish. Note that the underarms are left open, as there are no gussets joining the sleeves and the body. Sew the side panels, joining the front and rear body panels. Hem the bottom, wrists, and underarms. Sew the embroidered strips to the wrists and along the front opening, then sew the embroidered collar to the neck. This strip should be 4 inches wide with only 1⅜ inch embroidered. Fold the strip in half lengthwise and sew it to the neck with the embroidery facing out.

Embroidery

The three different motifs which decorate the front opening, wrists and collar, and sleeves are shown in Figures 19.4, 19.5, and 19.6. Only the right-side motifs are shown for the front panel and sleeves; they should be reversed for the left side. If the embroidery is done on broadcloth it will be necessary to use scrim, a textile grid resembling penelope needlepoint canvas, in order to keep the stitches even. Baste the scrim to the fabric to be embroidered and embroider over the scrim. To remove the scrim when the embroidery is completed, wet the piece of cloth and then pull the scrim out, thread by thread.

The embroidery motifs given here are figured for 14 stitches to the inch. At this rate, the sleeve motif will measure 2 inches by 2 inches, the wrist and collar motif 1⅜ inches by 1⅜ inches, and the front opening motif 1⅝ inches by 1⅝ inches. Be sure that the pieces of cloth to be embroidered are large enough to seam. Traditionally, the cross-stitch (see Figure 19.3) was generally used for all embroidery, although half-cross, stroke, and slanting stem stitches were sometimes used for edging work. In place of the traditional homespun goat's wool or linen, our embroidery consultant recommends six-strand cotton embroidery floss sewn with a tapestry needle.

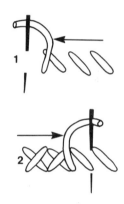

Figure 19.3 *Cross-stitch*

Figure 19.4
Front panel motif

Figure 19.5
Wrist and collar motif

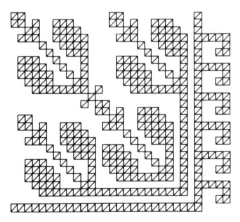

Figure 19.6
Sleeve motif

20
Food Bowl

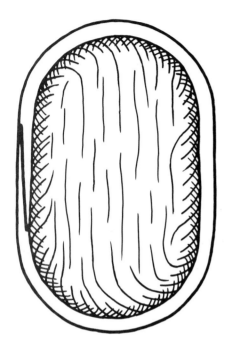

Figure 20.1 *Top view of food bowl*

Figure 20.2 *Side view of food bowl: (a) side hoop, (b) bottom, (c) spruce root line, (d) wooden pegs*

Most bowls are little more than hollowed-out round or oblong pieces of wood, stone, bark, clay, or metal. The bowl described in this chapter is unique, as it is made from two pieces of wood snapped together to form the bowl shown in Figures 20.1 and 20.2. This particular style of bowl was made and valued by Native Americans and Eskimos living in Alaska and western Canada. Because of its value, it was widely traded among groups living in the area. Its value was based in part on the craftsmanship that went into carving the bowl. It was no easy task to carve the two pieces with a beaver-tooth chisel so that they fit together tightly.

The bowl is always oblong in shape, but the size can vary depending on its use. The instructions given here are for a bowl 15 inches long, 8 inches wide and 4 inches deep. The side hoop is made from spruce wood, the bottom from spruce root. The side hoop is stitched with spruce root line. For tools, you'll need an axe, saw, plane, chisel, hammer, knife, awl or drill and bit, and sandpaper. It will take about two days to make the bowl.

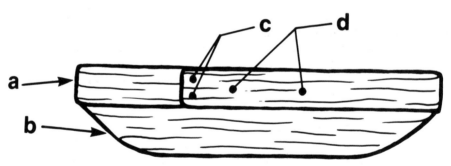

Construction

The two parts of the bowl—the side hoop and bottom— are made separately and then snapped together to form the bowl. As you work on the two parts, keep in mind that they must be snapped together tightly at the end.

Side Hoop. Make the side hoop from a single length of green spruce wood about 55 inches long by 2 inches wide by ½ inch thick. Cut the wood for the hoop from a spruce sapling or branch. The wood should be green and as pliable as you can find. Split, whittle, and sand the wood to form a flat board 55 inches long by 2 inches wide. Plane the sides so that the board is thicker at what will be the top (about ¾ inch) than at the bottom (about ½ inch). If you're making a bowl with different dimensions than we're using here, make sure that the hoop board is at least 5 inches longer than the planed circumference of the finished bowl. Bevel the opposing sides of the board so they can be overlapped and joined as shown in Figure 20.1.

• Bend the board around your knee and bring the beveled edges together to form a hoop. Test the fit of the two ends and make sure that the board does not split. To make the board pliable so that it doesn't split while you bend it, soak it in hot water before trying to bend it. If it still splits after soaking, try a new piece of wood from a different tree. Once you're sure that the board won't split and that the ends overlap neatly, join the overlapped ends together with the wooden pegs and spruce root line as follows (see Figure 20.2):

• Bend the board so that the ends overlap and temporarily secure with a tie line wrapped around the ends. Drill two holes dividing the overlapped ends in thirds. Drive spruce wood pegs (small bits left from shaping the hoop work well as pegs) through the holes and trim them off flush with the sides. Remove the temporary binding and drill four holes through the overlapped ends 2 inches in from the edge of the overlap. Sew the overlapped ends together with spruce root line. (Instructions for making spruce root line are provided in Chapter 5.) To sew the ends together, push one end of the line through the top hole and wedge it in place with a peg driven from the outside in. Pull the line tight and pass it inward through the second hole, outward through the third hole, and inward through the bottom hole. Pull the line tight and wedge it in the bottom hole with a peg. Trim the two pegs flush with the sides.

• Mark a groove around the inside bottom edge (the ½-inch edge) about ½ inch high and ¼ inch deep. Chisel out the groove and fine sand. Take care to keep the groove as even as possible all around the hoop.

Bottom. The bottom of the bowl is carved from one large piece of spruce root chopped from the base of a large tree. Select and chop out a piece of spruce root at least 3 inches thick and 2 inches wider and longer than the planed circumference of the finished bowl. Keeping in mind that the outside of the bowl will be curved and symmetrical, decide which side of the root will face up and plane that surface flat.

Figure 20.3 *Cross-section of bottom*

• Place the completed side hoop on the flat surface of the bottom piece and trace its inner circumference using the tracing as a guide, hollow out the inside of the bottom with the chisel and smooth with sandpaper. Chisel the outside to the shape shown in Figures 20.2 and 20.3. Note that the bottom of the bowl is rounded at each end and symmetrical and the bottom surface is flat. When completed, the bottom and lower bottom sides should be 1 inch thick and the upper bottom sides about ½ inch thick.

• Carefully whittle and sand the upper edge of the bottom so that it fits tightly in the goove in the side hoop as shown in Figure 20.4. Continually check the fit of the two parts as you whittle. Snap the bottom and side hoop together. Fill the bowl to the top with oil to seal any cracks.

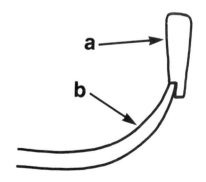

Figure 20.4 *Side and bottom alignment: (a) side hoop, (b) bottom*

21
Living Off the Spruce Tree

Figure 21.1 *Spruce cones and needles*

Figure 21.2 *Maul*

Native people of the north country—the Lapps in Scandinavia, Eskimos in Alaska, Aleuts in the Aleutian Islands, and Athabascan and Algonquian Indians in Canada—meet many of the necessities of life with the spruce tree. If you have a spruce on your property, take a second look at it. It will supply you with raw materials for tools, utensils, dwellings, toys, furniture, and even medicine. Think of the tree like the Indian does: as a storehouse for supplies. In this chapter we describe twelve fairly simple projects based on products of the spruce tree.

About a dozen species of spruce grow in the cooler regions of North America. Most common are the black spruce (*Picea mariana*), red spruce (*P. rubens*), and white spruce (*P. glauca*). Spruce wood is resinous, light in weight, straight grained, and of uniform texture. These properties make it rot resistant and easy to split.

There is more to a spruce tree than the properties of its trunk wood. The roots, bark, needles, branches, and gum also are valuable materials. The long roots of the spruce are quite thick near the base of the trunk and are soft and easy to carve. They quickly taper off to about the size of a pencil, and can easily be split and rolled into cordage which is water and rot resistant. Both hard and soft wood can be found in the trunk of the spruce. Light-colored trunk wood is moderately soft. The red-grained wood on the outer side of a spruce that grows bent over is as hard as birch. Young spruce trees have wood that is harder than the wood of old trees, although the red-grained wood is found only in old trees. Charring spruce wood in a fire will harden it but it will also make it brittle, especially when it gets wet.

The craft projects described here can all be accomplished with a bare minimum of tools. A knife and hatchet are essential, and a saw, brace and bit, drawknife, and plane will come in handy.

Maul and Wedges

Most woodsmen use an axe and metal wedges for splitting firewood or for making planks from trunk wood. A wooden maul and a set of wooden wedges are actually better for the job, as they absorb much of the shock of impact and prevent it from reaching your hands.

• Mauls are carved from trunk wood. They can vary greatly in size, depending on the job to be done and the strength of the person using the maul. They can be made anywhere from 18 inches to 4 feet in length, with the diameter of the head ranging from 3 to 12 inches. The maul shown in Figure 21.2 is 18 inches long by 3 inches in diameter at the head.

To make the maul, select a tree with a trunk the same diameter as you want for the striking head of the maul. Cut a section of the trunk suitable for the maul and debark it. Trim the handle to shape with the knife and hatchet and the maul is finished. Make sure to leave a knob at the end of the handle, so the maul doesn't slip out of your hands when in use. Trim the head of the maul with the axe if it starts to split when you are using it.

- Wedges are best made from red-grained trunk wood, the harder the better. Trim a block to the width of your choice and to a length from 5 to 18 inches, as shown in Figure 21.3. To harden it, spread a little fish or vegetable oil over it and lay it in a small campfire until it is thoroughly charred.

To use, make a ½-inch groove with the hatchet along the splitting plane in the butt end of a log. Insert two wedges into the groove and pound alternately with the maul. The wedges can be sharpened to a blunt point with the hatchet as necessary. You can also use the maul to drive stakes.

Figure 21.3 *Wedges*

Chewing Gum

Spruce gum, which collects in clumps on the bark, makes an excellent chewing gum. Take the gum directly off the tree and chew it. At first it will stick to your cheeks and gums, but by adding a little ice or snow you'll find that you can form it into a ball in your mouth. As you chew, the gum will turn in color from a deep yellow to a light pink. The Ingalik people of southern Alaska say that if girls chew spruce gum they will develop large breasts.

Canoe Paddles

Canoe paddles can be made from a plank of straight-grained trunk wood. The plank should be as wide as the blade of the paddle. The paddle should be as long as the distance from your armpit to the ground. Trace the outline for the paddle onto the plank using Figure 21.4 as a guide. The blade is leaf shaped, with a ridge running the length on each side to give it extra strength. The ridge is actually a continuation of the handle, with the blade tapering out from the ridge on each side. Rough out the paddle with a hatchet and finish with the drawknife or plane.

The handle can be carved either from the same plank as the blade or made separately and then attached to the blade. To make the handle separately, cut a section of branch about 3 inches long by 1½ inches in diameter and debark it. Drill a hole in the center and fit in on the end of the paddle, using a little glue to secure it. Drill another small hole through both the handle and paddle and insert a peg, again using a little glue for added strength. The finished handle is shown in Figure 21.5.

Make sure to sand the paddle smooth with sandpaper, otherwise you are sure to get blisters when using it. You may want to experiment a little with the design of the paddle, depending on its use. Make one with a broad blade for use when transporting heavy loads in a canoe, as it will give you extra pushing power. For fast paddling, as when hunting or fishing from a canoe, make a paddle with a long, narrow blade.

Figure 21.4 *Canoe paddles*

Figure 21.5 *Paddle handles*

Compass

Figure 21.6 *Compass*

An impromptu compass can be made in a jiffy for scribing wood when constructing circular objects such as plates, small spoons, tops, etc. The design for the compass is one used by the Athabascan Indians of northwest North America.

Find or cut to size two sticks that are about 8 inches long and ¼ inch in diameter. Whittle one end of each stick to a point. Lash the two sticks together about three-quarters of the way up their lengths with a thin cord. Then cut a third piece of wood about 1 inch long and ⅜ inch in diameter. Pull the ends of the longer sticks apart so that the two sticks form an X and insert the short plug between the sticks just above the point where they are tied together. Lash the plug in place with a piece of line. The plug will keep the sticks in a secure position a set distance apart. (See Figure 21.6.)

Use as you would any compass. The distance between the sticks can be adjusted by using a wider or narrower plug. Wet the scribing end with a little ink or paint to mark the line.

Bridge

Many of us have been out hiking or hunting only to have our progress blocked by a stream too wide to jump and too deep to ford. A temporary bridge can be made, of course, by dropping a log across the stream. But if you must cross at the same spot often, you may want to make a more permanent bridge, especially if the spot is near your cabin or camp. The Tanaina people of Cook Inlet in Alaska make their bridges from spruce poles.

The bridge is made from poles fastened together to form a series of inverted Vs and then connected together by five poles laid lengthwise, as shown in Figure 21.7. All you need to construct the bridge is a hatchet to cut and trim the poles and twine to lash them together. Cut the lengthwise poles about 3 feet longer than the width of the stream. To cross the stream on the bridge, walk on the bottom lengthwise pole while holding on to the lengthwise pole at the apex of the Vs.

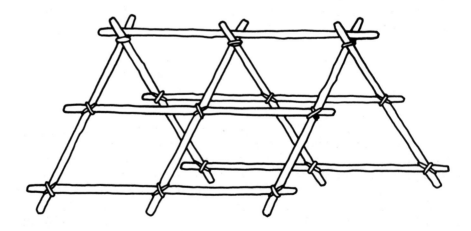

Figure 21.7 *Bridge*

Breath Protector

Breath protectors are used by people in the north country for two purposes: to prevent inhaling scalding steam when taking a sweat bath in the summer, and to avoid directly inhaling frigid arctic air in the winter.

To make one, gather up the spruce shavings left by your drawknife and form them into a sausage-like roll about 4 inches long and 1½ inches in diameter. Squeeze the shavings together to compact them and bind with a piece of cord or leather. Attach a thong to each side and place the breath protector over your mouth, tying the thongs together behind your head.

Figure 21.8 *Breath protector*

Medicine

Athabascan Indians of northwestern North America used various parts of the spruce as medicine to treat a variety of minor ailments. The light yellow sap and resin found on the inner wood of the tree is used as an application for burns and cuts. You can obtain it by splitting green wood and scraping off the sap which gathers on the surface, or by simply cutting away the outer wood layers of a living tree. Prepare the sap by gently heating it until it becomes runny and then apply it to the wound.

To cure a stomach ache, the Indians say, boil a handful of spruce needles in water all day long and give a spoonful of the broth to the patient. To treat a sore throat and head cold, the inner fibers of spruce bark can be boiled in a little water to yield a paste which is applied externally to the chest and neck. When they have a stomach ache caused by overeating, the Indians powder a little charcoal, mix it with water, and drink it.

Funnel

Spruce root is an excellent material for making funnels because it is water resistant. Funnels can be used for transferring any kind of liquid and are always handy around a campsite. Cut a 6-inch section of root near the base of the tree. Drill or bore a hole through the center of the section of root, working from the narrow to the thick end. Use the knife to widen the mouth and to smooth the exterior.

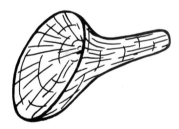

Figure 21.9 *Funnel*

Glue

A waterproof glue of excellent quality can be made from spruce gum. It is widely used in the north country as an adhesive and as a waterproofing for boats and dwellings. The glue is applied to the seams of birchbark canoes, for example, to keep water from seeping in.

You need two types of spruce gum to make the glue: the dark brown type found in clumps on the trunk, and the type which oozes down from the bark of the branches. Melt equal parts of each type in a small pan over low heat (be careful, the gum is flammable), add a couple of teaspoons of fish or vegetable oil, and stir slowly. The oil increases the strength of the glue and makes it less sticky to handle. Use a small wooden paddle or a stick to apply the glue while it is still warm. Wetting your hands with water so that the glue won't stick to or stain them is a good idea.

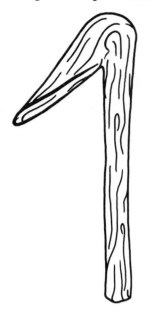

Figure 21.10 *Digging stick*

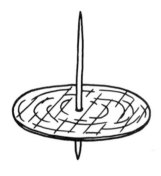

Figure 21.11 *Top*

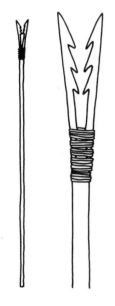

Figure 21.12 *Fish lances*

Digging Stick

The digging stick is used by tribal people the world over for many varying purposes. It can be used as a small hoe in gardening, as an aid in digging up edible roots and tubers, and, most importantly for the northern Indians, as a tool for digging out spruce roots.

You can make a spruce wood digging stick from any piece of wood that has a natural fork in it. Good sections can be found where two branches meet or where two roots enter the trunk. Trim to the shape shown in Figure 21.10 with the hatchet and knife and form a blade by trimming the inner face of the shorter arm so that it tapers off toward the end. Char it in the fire to harden it. Use the digging stick like you would a hoe in weeding a garden.

Top

Tops are a favorite children's toy everywhere. To make a spruce top, cut a section from a branch 3 inches in diameter and ¼ to ⅜ inch thick. Drill a ¼-inch hole through the exact center of the disc (you can use the compass to find the center). Sand the disc smooth and taper the edges. Then cut a spindle that is as long as the diameter of the disc from a stick, trim both ends to a point, and fit the disc onto the spindle about 1 inch up from the end. Add a little glue to hold the disc in place and allow it to dry.

Spin the top by twisting the longer end of the spindle between your thumb and forefinger, or by holding the longer end between your palms and rubbing them together.

Fish Lance

The fish lance is an effective implement for spearing fish in water clear enough so that they can easily be seen from land or from a boat. The lance has three parts: two tines cut from bone and a shaft made from spruce. For the shaft, use a pole about 4 feet long by ¾ inch around. Debark the pole before attaching the tines to it. To attach the tines, cut two grooves, one on each side of the pole, in which to insert the tines. The grooves should be about 2 inches long. To make the tines, find a long, flat piece of bone (rib bones are especially good) and hold it in a vice. Cut out the two tines with a hacksaw. Each tine should have at least three barbs, which should be sharpened with a file. Fit the tines into the grooves in the shaft and wrap with sinew or thin copper wire. If bone is not available to use for the tines, wood can be substituted, although it lacks the flexibility and strength of bone.

To fish with the lance, wait in the water until a fish comes into view. Hold the lance about halfway up the shaft, about shoulder high. When you see a fish, make a quick thrust at it with the lance. The barbs will hold the fish on the lance until you pull it from the water.

Weather Control

The Ingalik say that if a person born on a clear day burns a live, standing spruce tree it will stop raining, but if a person born on a rainy day does the same thing, it will only rain harder.

22
Brickmaking

If you live where clay occurs naturally in the soil you are walking on excellent building material. The Fellahin Arabs of upper Egypt use a simple method for making clay bricks, handed down from one generation to the next since the time of the pharoahs. All you need is suitable clay soil and a few pieces of wood to make a brick mold.

Clay

Clay soil is slippery to the touch when wet. The best soil for brickmaking contains equal parts of clay, silt, and sand, plus some organic matter such as bits of wood, leaves, etc. To test if your soil is suitable for brickmaking, put a handful in a glass jar, fill the jar with water, shake well, and let it sit over night. By the following day the soil should have settled in the jar. The sand will form the bottom layer, the silt the middle layer, and the clay the top layer. If the depth of three layers is about the same, you have soil suitable for brickmaking.

Molding the Bricks

• Fellahin women prepare clay by placing it in a hole in the ground and kneading it with their feet. You can follow their example or mix it in a wheelbarrow. Add a handful of chopped straw and a quart of water to every 50 pounds of soil, kneading until thoroughly mixed. The clay is ready for molding when it has the consistency of loose bread dough.

Figure 22.1 *Brick mold*

• Nail, screw, or peg four 1-inch boards together to form a brick mold like that shown in Figure 22.1. The dimensions of brick molds vary widely, but a good size is 10 by 9 by 3 inches. Cut the board for one side a little long and trim it with a knife to form a handle. If you plan to do a lot of brickmaking, soak the mold in cooking or engine oil for a few days to help preserve the wood.

• To make the bricks, lay the mold on a flat, sandy surface and pack the clay in. Use a flat stick or board to level off the top. Remove the mold. If the clay sticks to the mold, add a little more water; if it loses its shape after removing the mold, add a little more soil. Let the bricks dry for two or three days in the shade. When dry, stand them on edge and cure them in the sun for at least ten days. If it rains, cover them with a waterproof tarp.

Bricks made this way can be used for fences, corrals, sheds, or dwellings. Make mortar by mixing the clay as you did for the bricks, but leave out the straw.

23
Clay Water Jar

The water jar and pottery technique described here is slightly different from the other craft projects in this section in that it is a technique used by one specific craftsman rather than a technique typical of an entire tribal society. The potter, Noor Kahn, worked in the Kafiristan Valley region of northern Pakistan in the early 1970s. His particular technique, which differs somewhat from techniques used by other Pakistani potters, was described in detail by two scientists, Owens Rye and Clifford Evans, who travelled to the valley to study pottery making.

Noor Khan is a member of the Sheik ethnic group, people who were once members of the Kafir ethnic group but have converted to Islam. Noor Kahn made and traded forty to fifty of the water jars described here each year. A completed jar is shown in Figure 23.1. The same technique can be used to make cups, cooking pots, and large grain storage containers. Because of the composition of the natural clay used and the firing technique, the water jar will hold liquids without glazing. You should keep in mind that the clay you use, especially if it is store bought, will probably weep or leak if left unglazed.

Figure 23.1 *Clay water jar*

Materials

* You will need 10 pounds of dry clay, 2¼ pounds of fine sand, and water. The potter gathers his clay from mountainside deposits of weathered slate and removes the impurities by hand and by multiple sievings. Rather than use coarse sand, he prefers to grind the sand himself from quartz rocks collected in dry streambeds.

Equipment consists of a hand-powered turntable, a base, a slate or wooden bat, a water bottle, and a large pan. Tools include large and small modeling tools; a leaf-shaped shaping tool; and a stone, oblong-shaped shaping tool, all shown in Figure 23.2. You'll also need a heavy wooden pestle or baseball bat, a rag, a sieve, and pointed and triangular-tipped decorating tools.

Figure 23.2 *Tools*

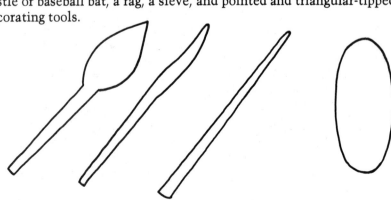

• To fire the jar in the traditional way, you'll need to build a pit-kiln, a slate-lined pit about 3 feet across by 18 inches deep, as shown in Figure 23.3. The sides extend about 6 inches above ground level. The above-ground section of the wall is supported by earth packed against it all around the outside of the pit. To line the entire pit, bottom and sides, you'll need about 100 pieces of slate, each about 6 inches square and 2 inches thick. The kiln is fueled by large pine-bark chips much like those sold at garden centers as ground cover. If you cut your own chips, take them from an old tree with deeply grooved bark rather than from a young tree with smooth bark.

Figure 23.3 *Pit-kiln*

Preparing the Clay

• Dig the clay, remove large impurities such as leaves, stones, or clumps of non-clay soil, and spread on the slate slab to dry. Sieve the dried clay until it is free of impurities and lumps. Spread one pound of sand over an area about 18 inches square, spread the clay over the sand, and form the two into a cone-shaped pile. Pound the clay with the pestle to break up any lumps, frequently turning the clay on the outside of the pile into the center. When the clay is crushed to a powder and mixed with the sand, sieve one last time to remove any lumps.

• You are now ready to mix the clay and water to form the body. Mix on the same stone slab used for the pounding. Pile the clay in the middle of the slab, scooping out a hollow in the center of the pile. Pour water into the hollow and mix the clay by hand, turning the clay on the outside of the pile in and squeezing it through your fingers. Work across the pile of clay, making sure that all of it gets wet. Knead by pushing down and away from your body on the pile with the heels of your hands.

• Roll the clay into a large lump, then flatten the lump in the large pan and work in the sand (one part sand for every seven parts clay) by hand kneading. To keep the clay from sticking to the pan, you can sprinkle some sand in the pan before you flatten the clay in it. Pound the clay and sand mix with the pestle, working the materials from the sides into the center.

Forming the Jar

Figures 23.4 through 23.11 show the jar at various stages of completion. Forming the jar is a three-step process, first, shaping the lower wall; second, adding and shaping the upper wall and rim; and third, shaping the rounded bottom.

• Set the turntable in the base on a level surface and center the wooden bat on the turntable. Sprinkle the bat with sand and clay dust. Form the 3½ pounds of clay into a ball and center it on the bat. Pat the ball flat until it is about 8 inches across by ¾ inch thick around the edge and 2 inches thick in the center, as shown in Figure 23.4. Push the clay from the center of the bottom out to form a 1-inch rim around the edge. The bottom should now be about 14 inches across, with a rim about 1 inch thick, as shown in Figure 23.5.

• Working with both hands, thumbs on the inside, fingers on the outside, thin and lift the rim to form the lower wall, shown in Figure 23.6,

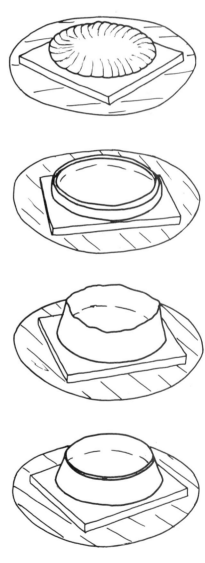

Figures 23.4-23.7 *Shaping the lower wall*

87

in three steps. First, raise the rim to a low, thick wall. Second, raise it to a height of about 3 inches, with a thick band of clay dividing the upper and lower half of the wall. Third, smooth out the band so that the wall is about 3 inches high and evenly thick from top to bottom. The base of the jar should now be about 10 inches across. Use the large modeling tool to smooth the outside wall and, with the sharp edge of the small modeling tool, trim the top edge of the wall even all around to the shape shown in Figure 23.7.

• Form the upper wall from a 6-pound lump of clay, kneaded and coiled. The length of the coil should be slightly less than the circumference of the upper edge of the lower wall, as it will stretch when pinched and smoothed into place. Lay the coil on the upper edge of the lower wall and join the two by smearing the coil clay down over the lower wall as shown in Figure 23.8. When the two sections are thoroughly bonded, smooth the walls and raise the upper wall by pushing and smoothing it in a slightly upper direction with the large modeling tool.

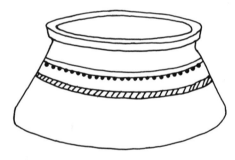

• Raise the rim as shown in Figure 23.9. You should now have a jar with a base 10 inches across, a top opening 6 inches across, and a height of 6 inches. Form the rim, shown in Figure 23.10, using the small modeling tool. Fold the rim out, using your fingers as a guide, and finish the edges. Decorate the outside wall, as shown in Figure 23.10, with the pointed and triangular decorating tools. The triangular tool is used to make the small, vertical slashes, the pointed tool for the horizontal lines.

Figures 23.8, 23.9 *Shaping the upper wall*

• Wrap the bottom of the jar in a wet cloth and set the jar aside until the wall and rim are leather-dry. Finally, round the plastic-hard bottom, shaping the outside with the large modeling tool, while supporting the inside with the oblong-shaped stone tool. Smooth the outside of the rounded bottom with the leaf-shaped tool. The shape of the finished bottom is shown in Figure 23.11. Set the jar aside to dry.

Figure 23.10 *Decoration*

Firing

• The jar must be preheated over an open fireplace before being fired in the pit-kiln. Build a small, circular fireplace out of stones and light a fire. Place pieces of slate over the top of the fire, leaving an opening about 5 inches square in the center. Place the jar top-side down over the opening and let it heat until it is too hot to handle. Remove from the fire and set aside until it is cool enough to handle.

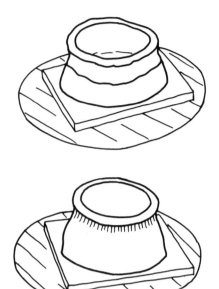

Figure 23.11 *Bottom shape*

• To fire the jar, line the bottom of the pit-kiln with 4 inches of pine bark chips. Lay the jar on the chips with the top facing down at about a 45 degree angle. Pack and cover the jar with pine chips and cover the kiln with slate, leaving small openings on two sides. Insert pieces of burning bark through the two openings to light the kiln. When the fire ignites, cover the openings with slate. Allow the fire to burn for about an hour and forty-five minutes or until the fuel is entirely consumed. Leave the pot to cool in the kiln, then remove and dust off the ash.

PART IV
Food Quest

24
Slash-and-Burn Horticulture

Other Names for Slash-and-Burn Horticulture
forest fallow rotation
fire agriculture
swidden farming
milpa
shifting cultivation

Over two million people around the world eat fruits and vegetables grown by means of slash-and-burn horticulture. Although largely confined to tropical regions north and south of the Equator today, slash-and-burn horticulture was used to clear land and fertilize crops in prehistoric Europe and by settlers in the United States as recently as 100 years ago. With this technique, a garden plot is cleared and its soil enriched by cutting and burning all plant matter growing on the plot. Since the nutrients in the resulting ash last only a few years, garden plots must be rotated between gardening and fallow periods. If you have land overgrown with brush which you would like to farm, you may find slash-and-burn horticulture a useful and ecologically sound technique.

Among its advantages are: (1) it is ecologically sound—what comes from the soil is returned in the form of ash; (2) it allows the land to retain its natural form; (3) it provides a rich supply of plant nutrients including nitrogen, phosphorus, and other minerals; (4) it is a cheap and easy gardening technique; (5) it requires only two tools, a digging stick and a machete; and (6) it enables one to grow a vegetable garden on a treed, rocky terrain. Among the limitations are: (1) only a portion of the land can be farmed at one time, as most of the land will be in the fallow or reforesting stage; (2) a garden plot can be used for only two or three consecutive years; and (3) because the overgrowth is removed, erosion can be a problem, especially in hilly terrain.

If you have a few acres or more of wooded or overgrown land and don't want to clear and level it permanently for farming, but do want to have a good-sized vegetable garden, slash-and-burn horticulture may be the answer. You can slash and burn a plot, crop it for two or three years, and then allow it to reforest while you crop another plot. However, you will need a fair amount of land if you want to use this method continuously over a period of years. You should figure that after the first few years, only about 15 percent of the land will be available for cropping in a given year; the other 85 percent will be in various stages of regrowth. It may take from eight to twenty years for a cleared plot to reforest. If you're not interested in full-blown slash and burn, you may still find that certain aspects of the slash-and-burn approach can be incorporated into the more conventional gardening techniques you now use. For example, you can slash and burn to clear a brush-covered plot you want to use for a garden. The ash will fertilize the garden for two or three years, after which you can switch to commercial fertilizers, manure, or compost. Or you can burn accumulated brush and leaves on your garden plot each spring to add organic matter and nutrients to the soil.

In talking about slash-and-burn horticulture, there are some key technical terms you should be familiar with. A *swidden* is the cleared garden plot. *Cropping* is the process or period of time when the swidden is gardened. *Fallow* is the period of time when the swidden is reforesting.

Slash-and-burn horticulture is a seven-step operation: (1) selecting the plot; (2) clearing the plot; (3) felling the trees; (4) clearing a firebreak; (5) burning the plot; (6) planting; and (7) weeding.

Selecting a Plot

The plot you pick should be large enough (at least 10,000 square feet) to make the work put into clearing it worthwhile. The plot can be on flat or sloping terrain, although a plot on the side of a steep hill will probably erode badly in a year or two. The plot you select should be thoroughly overgrown with bushes, vines, shrubs, weeds, tall grasses, and small trees. A few large trees on the plot are fine, but a heavily treed plot is likely to have little undergrowth, making a successful burn impossible.

Clearing the Plot

Cut the shrubs, grasses, vines, and small trees off at ground level with a machete and spread them evenly across the entire plot. Clearing and spreading is easiest if you begin at one end of the plot and slash through the brush, depositing it on the ground behind you. As the brush piles on the ground will get pretty thick, you want to avoid having to walk through them. If the lot is on a hill, start at the lower end and work up. It is important that the slash be spread evenly over the entire plot. An even spread will help insure a thorough burn and an even distribution of ash and will help control erosion before the burn. If extra brush is available nearby, haul it over and add it to the spread.

Felling the Trees

Fell the larger trees, leaving a 12-inch stump and the roots intact. Again, work across the site, from one end to the other. Chop the smaller branches from the felled trees, cut them into 2- to 3-foot lengths, and spread them over the slash. Remove the larger branches and tree trunks from the plot. If you are in doubt about whether a branch will burn or not, remove it.

Clearing a Firebreak

For safety, you'll need to clear a firebreak at least 10 feet wide around all four sides of the plot. The firebreak should be cleared of all flammable growth. If it is grass covered or has a heavy groundcover, you should turn the soil over. You can actually create a firebreak when you slash the plot by turning the slash from the outer 10 feet into the center of the plot.

Burning the Plot

This is the key step in the slash-and-burn technique. For the burn to be a success, the brush must be left to dry for two or three weeks after being slashed. In addition, the burn should be made only after two or three days of dry weather. Start a fire at one end of the plot and allow it to spread across the entire plot. You may need a second or even third burn to clear off partially burned branches or brush. When the burn is finished the plot should be covered with a thick layer of ash.

Planting

Plant the swidden as soon after the burn as possible. Before planting, the ash should be soaked thoroughly, either by rainfall or watering. Since the ground beneath the ash is left unworked, conventional gardening tools such as hoes, spades, racks, and forks are unnecessary. The only tool you'll need is a dibble or planting stick like that shown in Figure 24.1, used to punch holes in the ground for the seedlings or seeds. Make sure to plant the seeds in the ground beneath the ash. You can plant seeds, seedlings, bushes, and fruit trees in the swidden. To help control erosion, they should be planted haphazardly, not in long, straight rows. Make sure to include some vine plants such as pumpkins, squash, melons, and cucumbers which will spread over the swidden and help control erosion. Root crops will do best if planted away from the roots of the larger tree stumps.

The swidden can be planted for two or three years, depending on the types and amount of plant material burned, the types of vegetables you grow, and the amount of erosion. You can expect a rich harvest the first year. In the second and third year you may want to cut back on heavy feeding crops as there may no longer be sufficient nutrients in the soil to bring them to full growth.

Weeding

Since the wood ash enriches the soil with nitrogen and minerals, weeds will flourish alongside your crops in the swidden. Planting soon after the burn will give your vegetable plants a two-week or so head start on the weeds, but once the weeds appear, you'll have to weed periodically to keep them under control. The pulled weeds can be discarded off to the side of the swidden or thrown onto the swidden to serve as mulch.

Figure 24.1 *Planting stick*

25
Fishing Tips
from the South Seas

There is more than one way to skin a cat, the saying goes, and there is certainly more than one way to catch a fish. The people of the Truk atoll in the South Pacific drug them, spear them, trap them, net them, troll for them, and lately, even use explosives to shock them. Since most of the protein in the Truk diet comes from the fish and shellfish they catch, it is not surprising that the Truk people can teach us something about fishing.

Trukese fishermen show remarkable ingenuity in their fishing methods. They have no fancy tackle, expensive lures, or electronic fish-finding equipment. Using only natural products and relying on their knowledge of fish behavior, the Trukese catch enough fish in a single day to make any modern fisherman green with envy.

The Trukese fish mostly in the lagoon surrounding their islands, although they also travel far offshore in their outrigger canoes (see Chapter 13) on day-long fishing expeditions. The Trukese fishing methods explained here will work equally well in ponds, lakes, bays, and the open ocean. Some of them may not be legal in your state, however, so before trying them be sure to check local and state fishing regulations.

Finding Fish

Before you can catch fish, you have to find them. The Trukese tell us that the birds know where the fish are. Herrings and gulls feed on schools of minnows which are chased to the surface by larger fish below. Floating driftwood is another sign that fish are nearby.

The Trukese fisherman doesn't need a calendar to tell him when to fish. He knows that if the sand washes up on the beach in small piles there will be *rasin motho*—plenty of fish. He also knows that if the starling has smooth feathers, there are fish nearby. If he sees a comet at night, he knows that there is no reason to leave his hut the next morning, as the fishing will be bad.

When Trukese women go fishing for crabs and clams in the shallows of the lagoon they take half a coconut and a mussel shell along with them. If the sea is rough, they use the shell to scrape bits of coconut onto the surface of the water. The oil in the coconut meat smoothes the surface, enabling the women to see their quarry in the rocks and weeds on the ocean floor.

Deep-Water Fishing

Bottom fish are taken with a hand line, hook, and detachable sinker. To make one of these rigs, tie a hook to one end of a line and then weight the line by tying an oblong stone about one foot up from the hook. To make the stone weight detachable, tie it by making a loop, lay the loop on the stone, and take several turns around the stone and the loop with the line. In that way, when you drop the line in the water and it hits bottom, you will be able to jerk the stone free. Then you'll know just where the bottom is, but the sinker won't ruin the "feel" of your line when a fish strikes.

Float Fishing

The Trukese know that the more hooks there are in the water, the better the chance of catching fish will be. Many modern fishermen have thought to fish more than one rod at a time, but Trukese float fishing would enable them to fish many lines at once without using a single rod. To make a float fishing rig, tie a hook to one end of a 2-foot line and tie a large wood or cork float to the other end (the Trukese use hibiscus wood). Working from a boat, bait twenty or thirty of these rigs and set them out in the water. When one of the floats starts to bob, paddle over to it and pull up the fish. You can also use these rigs for surf fishing by tying each rig to a pole, setting the poles in the sand, and placing the rigs a short distance off-shore. Sit on the beach, watch the floats, and when a fish strikes swim out and bring it in.

Catching Turtles

Trukese fishermen have perfected a simple, effective method for catching turtles. When a turtle surfaces near your boat, strike the water wildly with the paddle or oar. The frightened turtle will quickly submerge before having had a chance to breathe. The next time it surfaces, it will be groggy from a lack of oxygen, and you can easily haul it in. This method works because turtles cannot breathe underwater.

Fishing with Drugs

This Trukese fishing method, although clearly illegal in the United States, is included here for curiosity's sake. Octopus and small fish such as anglefish and bass are taken with the help of narcotic plants. The fruit of the *Kuun* tree (*Barringtonia asiatica*) or the roots of the *wuup* vine (*Derris elliptica*) are pounded and then wrapped in a cloth bundle. The fisherman wades into the shallow, still water of the lagoon and wrings the bundle in the water near growths of coral. The drug dissipates in the water and stuns the fish hiding in the coral. They float to the surface and lie there helplessly while the fisherman nets them.

Spearing Lobster

The Trukese fish for lobster at night with a single-point spear. Wade or paddle through the shallow water of a bay or inlet on a night with a full moon and look for lobster crawling along the bottom. When you spot one, cast a shadow over the bottom by holding a small branch with leaves still attached over the surface of the water. The lobster will mistake the shadow for a rock or other hiding place and crawl toward it. By moving the branch slowly toward the spot where you are standing, you can bring the lobster within easy spearing range.

Kite Fishing

No matter how far a fisherman on a beach casts his line, he always wants to get it out a little further. The Trukese method of kite fishing is the answer to this problem. You will need a kite with 500 yards of string, a fishing pole, and a 10-foot length of two-pound test monofilament. Have a companion put the kite a couple of hundred feet in the air. Then, tie one end of the 10-foot monofilament connecting line to the kite string and the other end to your fishing line, 10 feet up from the hook. Drop the baited hook in the water. As your companion releases more kite string, pay out your fishing line along with it. When a fish takes the bait the monofilament connecting line will break, and you can play the fish while your companion brings in the kite. With this method the kite will carry your baited hook over 300 yards offshore while you fish from the beach.

Fishing for Crabs

The Trukese catch rock crabs with a simple method that requires no tackle. Fish at low tide, using a mussel or clam for bait. Crack the mussel or clam shell on a rock and tie it to one end of a long piece of seagrass. Find a clump of seaweed or stones where the crabs are likely to be hiding and lower the bait into the water. Make sure to hold the other end of the seagrass line. When a crab grabs the bait with its claws, gently lift it out of the water and drop it in a bucket or pail. These crabs are usually steamed in seawater and eaten on the spot.

Fishing Weirs

The islands along the Truk lagoon are dotted with the remains of stone fishing weirs, which are used to trap fish along the shoreline as the tide goes out to sea. Three types of weirs (see Figure 25.1) are commonly used. All are constructed from large stones arranged into walls about three feet thick and one foot high. The walls must be high enough so that the tops are above the low-tide water line. All three weirs work on the same principle, to trap fish which have come to shore to feed at high tide between the shore and the stone wall. Small fish like herring and mackerel are scooped from the water into baskets or nets; large fish are speared.

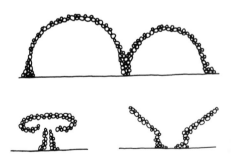

Figure 25.1 *Stone fishing weirs*

The Truk Philosophy

By now you've probably figured out that the Truk approach to fishing is much different from ours. They don't see fishing as a sport, a battle of skill and wits between fish and fisherman. There are no life-like lures or flies or ultralight line used on Truk. Rather, Trukese fisherman seek to give themselves every advantage possible over the fish. Not having to obey state game laws, these include turning fish behavior to their advantage, fishing close to shore, and using methods and equipment that will yield large harvests.

26
Food Preservation

Tribal peoples have discovered seven ways to preserve perishable foods: cooling, freezing, salt-curing, jellying, drying, pickling, and smoking. Each of the four methods described here—drying, pickling, smoking and cooling—has its advantages and disadvantages. Cooling preserves the flavor and nutrient value of the food, but requires a large, immovable storage space. Pickling provides long-term storage but sacrifices taste. Drying saves much of the nutrient value but sacrifices taste and appearance. Smoking enhances the flavor but is time consuming and uncertain, depending on weather conditions.

The instructions and recipes provided here are something of a mix—drying methods from North America, Mexico, and seventeenth-century England; pickling from eighteenth-century England; and smoking and cooling from Native Americans in the United States and Canada.

Drying

Drying is a method best known for preserving fruits and vegetables. Among Native Americans, it was a method used to preserve staple foods in an easily transportable form. Pemmican is the best known of the dried foods.

Pemmican. Pemmican is a mix of dried meat, animal fat, and wild berries. If made correctly, it will keep for up to three years without refrigeration. A staple in the diet of early Native Americans in the United States and Canada, it later became an important part of the diet of trappers, traders, and settlers who moved into the western Plains. There are as many pemmican recipes as there are Native American tribes in central North America. This one is from the Blackfoot tribe of Alberta, Canada:

5 lbs. lean beef
1 lb beef fat (back fat is best)
wild berries (blueberries, raspberries, or walnuts, pecans, etc.)
beef bones
4 peppermint leaves

Cut the beef into thin strips and dry on a rack in the sun. When thoroughly dry, pound the beef into a fine powder. Heat the bones in water in a heavy skillet to melt the marrow. Skim the marrow and save. Pit and crush the berries or nuts. Spread the powdered beef in a 2-inch layer in a cake tin. Cover with the marrow, fat, crushed berries, and peppermint leaves. Mix the ingredients together. Roll the mix into balls and store in a tight container.

Dried Squash. Many fleshy, fibrous vegetables such as squash or pumpkin can be sun-dried for future use. Sun-drying works best in hot, sunny climates with low humidity and good air quality. Halve, peel, and seed the squash. Set in the sun for two to three days. Cut the semidry halves into thin strips and drape the strips over poles or sticks. Hang the sticks in the sun for two weeks or until the squash strips are dry. On damp or rainy days, bring the strips inside. When dry, roll the strips into balls like yarn and store in a cool, dry place. To use, break up the strips and boil for two to three hours.

Dried Artichokes. Boil ripe artichokes in water for 30 minutes. Dry them in a low oven or process in a dehydrator until dry. Store in a dry place. To use, soak in water overnight and then boil until tender.

Apricot Chips. Pare the apricots, cut them into halves, and remove the pits. Cut the halves into strips and sprinkle lightly with confectioner's sugar. Stir-fry gently for 15 minutes. Remove from the heat, cover, and set aside overnight. In the morning stir-fry again for 15 minutes. Remove the chips one by one from the pan and roll in confectioner's sugar. Dry them in the sun or in a low oven, turning them often. Store in a tight box or cookie tin.

Mushroom Powder

1 peck mushrooms	1 tablespoon salt
40 cloves	12 onions
6 bay leaves	½ pint white vinegar
2 teaspoons pepper	1 piece of butter as big as an egg

Wash and rub the mushrooms, but do not remove the skins. Mix all the ingredients in a large pot and boil rapidly. Remove the mushrooms, spread on a cookie sheet and dry in the oven. Remove from the oven and set out to air-dry. When thoroughly dry, pound the mushrooms into a fine powder.

Blackberry Flour. Collect wild blackberries and lay them out in the sun to dry for several days, turning them at least once each day. When dry, pound into a coarse flour. Mix the flour with a little water and knead into a thick paste. Pat the batter into cakes, sun-dry for one day, and store. Fermentation is prevented by drying after picking and then pulverizing. To turn the cakes into jam, pound them into a coarse meal, mix with water, and simmer until thick. Skim the seeds off as they rise to the top of the pot. Use the jam immediately.

Pickling

Pickled Lobsters

fresh, whole lobsters	peppercorns
salt	mace
white wine	bay leaf
cloves	

Boil the lobsters in salted water until cooked (about 11 minutes per pound). Remove the tail and claw meat. Make a pickle consisting of half white wine and half water. Add a handful of cloves, a few peppercorns, mace, and 2 or 3 bay leaves to the pickle. Bring the pickle to a rolling boil and add the lobster meat. Boil the meat for 3 minutes, remove, and set aside to cool. Allow the pickle to boil for an additional 5 minutes, remove from the heat, and set aside to cool. When both the meat and the pickle are cool, add the lobster to the pickle and put in jars. Process the sealed jars for 30 minutes. Serve the lobster cold with oil, vinegar, and lemon.

Pickled Nasturtium Buds

nasturtium buds	ground horseradish
salt	pepper
white wine	cloves
vinegar	mace
shallots	nutmeg

Harvest the nasturtium buds in the fall after the blossoms drop. Soak the buds in cold, salted water for three days, stirring the solution once each day. Make the pickle by combining the white wine, vinegar, shallots, horseradish, pepper, salt, cloves, mace, and nutmeg to suit your taste. Add the buds to the pickle and put in jars. Process for 15 minutes.

Pickled Quince

6 quince
2 lbs. honey

Cut the ripe quince into small pieces and mix with 1 gallon of water and 2 pounds of honey. Boil gently for 30 minutes. Strain the liquid into canning jars. Remove the quince pieces, cool, and wipe clean. Add the quince to the liquid, seal, and process for 30 minutes.

Smoke-Drying Fish

The many tribal peoples who live off fish know that drying and smoking are the best ways to preserve fish for long-term storage. Since tribal peoples often take fish in large quantities (see chapter 25), it is imperative that they preserve them for future use. The best-known fishing societies in North America were those on the northwest coast. In many of these groups fish that were taken during six months of the year supplied enough food for the entire village for the entire year. Thus, it was vital that the fish be properly preserved.

To smoke-dry fish you need fish, a drying rack, and a fire. By smoke-dry we mean drying and preserving the fish through a combination of sun-drying and smoking over an open fire. Not all fish are suitable for smoking. Oily, fleshy fish such as haddock, cod, herring, whitefish, salmon, and sturgeon smoke best. Others, such as trout, eel, or pike, can be smoked but will probably become too dry. The fish must be fresh (the sooner it is dryed and smoked after being caught the better) and should be scaled, gutted, split lengthwise, and boned before smoking. Small fish will be easier to handle if you leave the heads on, but you can remove the heads of larger fish. If the fish are especially large, slash the flesh to allow the smoke to penetrate fully.

Two types of smoking racks are shown in Figures 26.1 and 26.2. The smaller, triangular rack in Figure 26.1 is easy to build and meant for only short-term use. If you plan to dry and smoke a lot of fish over a period of years, you would be wise to invest some time and effort in building the more substantial rack shown in Figure 26.2. Either rack should be constructed from hardwood, with the framework either lashed or nailed together. The fish are draped over the drying poles, flesh up. These poles should be sturdy hardwood poles with the bark left on. The bark will help keep the oily fish from sliding off the pole and falling on the ground or into

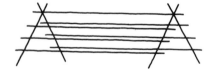

Figure 26.1 *Triangular smoking rack*

the fire below. If the fish slip off despite the bark, slip a clump of grass between the fish and the pole.

Build the fire directly beneath the rack. A low, smoldering fire of freshly cut and rooted hardwood such as oak, ash, maple, or tamarack will give fish a rich, brown color. Softwood, especially pine, should not be used as it will produce "dirty" fish. The smoking time can take from hours to days, depending on how thoroughly you want the fish dryed, the size and type of fish, the type of wood fueling the fire, and the weather. Obviously, the best weather for outdoor drying and smoking is clear, sunny, windless days and nights. In case of wind or rain, you'll have to drape the rack with a canvas tarp.

If you plan to eat the fish in a day or two, eight hours of drying in the sun over a fire followed by additional cooking by broiling or boiling should be sufficient. This method of smoking is called cold-smoking. For long-term preservation, you have to hot-smoke the fish, that is, smoke them for five to eight days. Hot-smoked fish will last for a long time and can be eaten without further cooking. Of course, the meat will be drier and flakier than the meat of cold smoked fish. To test for doneness following hot-smoking, make sure that all of the meat is a rich, brown color and that the skin along the backbone is hard and cracks when twisted.

Cooling

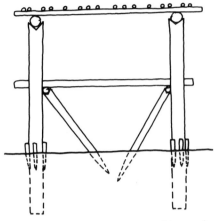

Figure 26.2 *Permanent smoking rack*

Food can be stored by submerging it in cold water, packing it in ice, or storing it underground. Since ice is not always available and storing food in open water makes it tempting to animals, underground storage or caching is often the best alternative. For long-term storage, a concrete or cinder-block root cellar covered with earth is a good investment. For temporary storage, a food cache or pit is both safe and practical. Dig the cache at least 6 feet deep to insure that the food will not freeze in the winter and will remain cool in the summer. The size of the cache will depend on the amount of food you have to store. Nothing is gained by making a pit larger than you need.

After you dig the pit, line the bottom and sides with sheets of birch bark. Then line the bottom with 8 inches of hay or dry grass. Place the food (squash, potatoes, rutabagas, apples, nuts, etc.) in uncovered containers and set the containers in the hay or grass at the bottom of the pit. Fill the spaces between the containers with hay or grass. Cover the containers with a thick layer of hay or grass and pile other containers on top. Fill the pit to within a foot of the top. Fill this last foot with hay and dry leaves and cover with birch-bark sheets. Lay branches or saplings over the pit and cover with an 18-inch-high mound of dirt. This mound will enable you to find the cache when the ground is snow-covered and will keep the deer out.

27
Blowgun

A blowgun is a long, hollow tube through which darts or pellets are forced by a puff of breath. Although similar in design, the blowgun and the familiar toy peashooter are entirely different in effect. The blowgun's ability to send piercing darts coated with deadly curare poison whistling through the air for distances up to 70 yards makes it an extremely effective hunting weapon. The blowgun described here is the type made by the Jivaro, a fierce tribe of people who live in the Ecuadorian Amazon. Famous for their skill at making trophies of the heads of their enemies, the Jivaro are also said to be the best blowgun makers in South America.

The Jivaro hunt birds, squirrels, monkeys, and other small game with the blowgun, but they never use it in warfare. They believe that if the curare on the darts is used to kill people, then all game brought down with curare will taste like human flesh and cannot be eaten. They explain this belief by saying that curare was given to them only to kill game, never to kill men, and to use it on another person would offend the spirits.

The Jivaro blowgun (see Figure 27.1) is made from two lengths of wood which are carefully grooved down the inside center so that when fitted together there is a straight, smooth, cylindrical bore extending from one end of the weapon to the other. The blowgun has a wood or bone mouthpiece at one end and a wild boar tusk serving as a sight at the other end. The typical blowgun is 6 to 10 feet long and round like a shotgun barrel, tapering from 1¼ inches at the mouthpiece end to ¾ inch at the sight end. The diameter of the bore is ¼ inch to ⅜ inch.

Figure 27.1 *Jivaro blowgun*

Wood darts and clay pellets are used as ammunition. The darts are made from wood splinters about 1 foot long with a diameter about the size of a wood matchstick. They are sharpened at one end and dipped in a dark, gummy, poisonous curare mixture made from the vine of the *Strychnus* genus. The efficiency of the blowgun as a hunting weapon depends on the use of curare, as it is the curare, not the dart itself, that kills the prey. The butt end of the dart is wrapped with cotton so that it fits fairly tightly in the bore. Clay pellets with the same diameter as the bore are used for hunting small birds. No curare is applied to them, since the impact of the pellet is enough to kill the bird.

Making the Blowgun

A blowgun is not hard to make and is great fun to use in target shooting. Whether or not it is legal to use in hunting is a matter you should take up with your state game warden. To make a blowgun you have to complete three general steps: (1) split a wood pole in half; (2) carve a groove in the flat side of each split piece; and (3) fit the pieces back together to form a perfect groove which serves as the bore of the weapon. When making the gun, remember that a straight, smooth bore is essential.

• The tools you will need are a hunting knife, a hatchet, a brace or drill with a ½-inch bit, a small, half-round chisel or wood gouge, a yardstick, a pencil, a pan, a small paintbrush, several sheets of medium and extra-fine sandpaper, and a length of ¼-inch dowel.

• The materials you will need are a wood pole for the barrel, wood glue, twine, one pound of paraffin or beeswax, a few black crayons, a wood dowel 1 inch in diameter and 4 inches long for the mouthpiece, and a wild boar tusk or piece of deer antler for the sight.
    For the pole, the Jivaro use *chonta* palm wood (*Guiliema* sp.), found only in South America, but any pole of straight-grained hardwood will work just as well. White ash or Norway maple are especially good. The pole must be absolutely straight, 6 to 10 feet long, with a maximum diameter of 1¼ inches. Two pieces of half-round molding, available at lumberyards, may be used instead.

Construction

• Select a sapling, preferably white ash or Norway maple, for the barrel. Cut it down, debranch and debark it, and let it season for several months. For the greatest range and accuracy, the barrel should be 10 feet long. If the barrel is even the slightest bit warped or curved the weapon will be useless, so it is wiser to make a short, straight blowgun than a long, curved one.

• With the brace and ½-inch bit drill a hole through the larger dowel to form a hollow mouthpiece. This is easiest if the dowel is secured between stones or in a vise. Shape the butt end of the pole with a knife to form a small "tail" 3 inches long and ½ inch in diameter, as shown in Figure 27.2. Slide the mouthpiece over the tail and make sure that it fits snugly. Remove the mouthpiece.

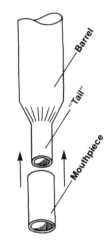

Figure 27.2 *Mouthpiece and tail*

• Split the pole in half lengthwise to make two identical half-round lengths as shown in Figure 27.3. With the medium sandpaper and a sanding block sand the flat surfaces of each length until they are smooth. Finish with the extra-fine sandpaper. Mark the guidelines for the bore down the center of each split length on the flat surfaces. To do this the Jivaro use a device like a chalk line. They place a piece of cotton thread wet with red *manduru* dye (*Bixa orellana*) on each of the flat surfaces, pull it taut, and then snap it, leaving a straight, red line down the center of each split half. You can try their technique or mark the line with a yardstick and pencil.

Figure 27.3 *Section of split pole*

• Carefully following the guidelines, gouge or chisel a groove ⅛ inch deep and ¼ inch wide down the center of each split half, as shown in Figure 27.4. The Jivaro use a wild boar tooth sharpened on stone for this job. A half-round chisel or wood-carving gouge will work as well. After the grooves are chiseled or gouged out, wrap a piece of extra-fine sandpaper around the ¼-inch dowel and sand the grooves until they are smooth. Remember that when the two halves are fitted back together, these grooves will form the bore through which the dart runs.

Figure 27.4 *Section of grooved pole*

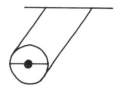

Figure 27.5 *Barrel with bore*

• Glue the two split halves together to form the barrel of the blowgun, as shown in Figure 27.5. Coat each of the flat sides with water-resistant resin wood glue, leaving enough space along the bore grooves so that the glue will not seep into them. Fit the two halves together, wrap with twine or clamp, and set aside to dry. Apply a small amount of glue to the tail at the butt end of the barrel and slide the mouthpiece on. Set aside to dry.

• The Jivaro seal their guns with a natural, black beeswax to prevent air from escaping along the cracks on each side of the barrel. Since black beeswax is not widely available, you can use a mixture of black crayon and beeswax or paraffin. Melt the ingredients in a small pan and spread over the barrel, making sure to fill the two lengthwise cracks. While the mixture is still soft on the barrel, set the boar tooth or deer antler sight at the end. You may have to build up the wax somewhat to attach the sight securely. Your blowgun is now finished and should look like the one in Figure 27.1.

Making Ammunition

The blowgun can shoot either darts or pellets. The darts should look roughly like a knitting needle and should be about 1 foot long and up to ⅛ inch in diameter. A good source of wood for darts is the hardwood splinters that can be found on the ground around any chopping block. Sharpen the ends of the splinters so they will pierce the target. Pellets of clay hardened in the sun also make good ammunition. Their diameter should be slightly less than that of the bore.

Shooting the Blowgun

To shoot the blowgun, take a dart and wrap a small amount of cotton or wool wadding around the butt end so that it fits snugly in the bore. A little saliva will help the wadding stick to the dart. Now place the dart in the mouthpiece end of the gun. Hold the gun with both hands, palms down, bring it up to your mouth with the sight pointing up, and blow into the gun. You'll be amazed at how little air is needed to send the dart out of the barrel at lightning speed. Clay pellets are shot in much the same way, except that wadding is not needed.

Store the blowgun by hanging it on a wall, mouthpiece facing down to prevent warping. And remember, don't shoot at people—you're liable to anger the spirits.

28
Boomerangs

There are seven types of boomerangs. The basic boomerang is little more than a curved stick which will cut through the air quickly and rapidly. Most, though not all, boomerangs can be made to return to their point of origin. The boomerangs shown in the first three figures are Australian boomerangs used mostly to hunt birds or in dueling. These boomerangs are not toys. They are large, heavy, difficult to throw accurately, and hard to catch. But, if properly used, they can be deadly hunting weapons, especially when sent hurtling into a flock of birds. A well-thrown boomerang can soar as high as 150 feet in the air and travel over 100 yards. The boomerangs shown in Figures 28.4 through 28.7 are more recent inventions than the Australian types and are generally used for recreation and entertainment. They are lighter, easier to make, and easier to throw than the Australian types.

The cross-stick (Figure 28.4) is easy to make and easy to fly. It cuts a perfect circle in the air, turning to the left, rising in the air, and then slowly descending as it returns to the thrower. The pinwheel (Figure 28.5) with its six spokes is the steadiest and surest boomerang. It sails gently through the air, returning to the thrower in a series of loops. Boomabirds (Figure 28.6) are heavier than cross-sticks and revolve more slowly through the air, making for an especially long flight. They too can cut a circular pattern with multiple loops, depending on the throwing technique. Tumblesticks (Figure 28.7), with one flat and one convex side, are the most intriguing of all boomerangs. They are very easy to make but difficult to handle. When thrown correctly, they will rise in the air, circle, and descend back to the thrower.

The three types of boomerangs used by aboriginal people of Australia—return, nonreturn, and beaked—are used by different tribes for different purposes. The return type (Figure 28.1) is used by tribes in the southeast part of the continent for hunting and recreation. The larger, nonreturn type (Figure 28.2) is used by people living in the central desert region for hunting and combat. Although not designed to return, the nonreturn boomerang can be made to do so by using a horizontal rather than a vertical throwing motion. When thrown horizontally, it will climb rapidly in the air and descend just as rapidly back at the thrower. The third type of boomerang, the beaked type (Figure 28.3), is used mostly in combat by people living along the northern coast. Both the nonreturn and beaked types are thrown or used as clubs. What advantage is offered by the beak added to what is basically a nonreturn boomerang is unclear. Some Australian natives claim that when an enemy warrior attempts to catch or ward off the beaked boomerang, the beaked end will swing around, striking him in the face or head.

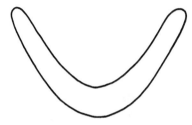

Figure 28.1 *Australian return boomerang*

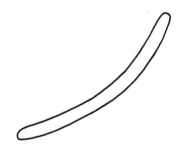

Figure 28.2 *Australian nonreturn boomerang*

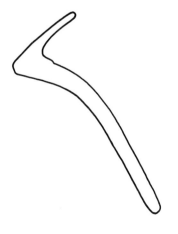

Figure 28.3 *Australian beaked boomerang*

Making A Return Boomerang

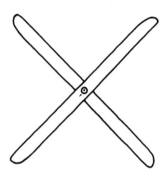

Figure 28.4 *Cross-stick*

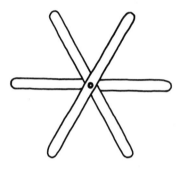

Figure 28.5 *Pinwheel*

Figure 28.6 *Boomabird*

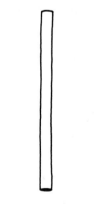

Figure 28.7 *Tumblestick*

Although much is made of the capability of boomerangs to return to the thrower, keep in mind that the goal in using a boomerang for hunting is to hit your prey, not to miss the prey and make the boomerang return to you. Of course, when using a boomerang for recreation, the object is usually to get it to return to you. For whatever reason you use your boomerang, remember that no boomerang will return after striking an object.

Making and throwing a return boomerang is probably the single most difficult project described in this book. Do not let its simple appearance fool you. Unless a boomerang is shaped, bent, and skewed just right and thrown correctly, it will not fly accurately, nor will it return to you.

A hunting boomerang has a blade span of 18 to 36 inches and weighs 8 to 24 ounces. It is about 3 inches wide at the bend and about half that at each end. It is about 2 inches thick, being somewhat thicker in the center than at the ends. The blades should open at a 90-120 degree angle, with an angle between 110 and 120 degrees making for the most accurate throwing. The boomerang must be made from a piece of long-grained hardwood such as maple, ash, hickory, or ironwood. The wood can be either seasoned or green. The basic tool is a sharp carving knife for whittling the boomerang to shape. Other tools you'll likely need are a rasp, hacksaw, keyhole saw, two pairs of pliers, sandpaper, a wood clamp, wood glue, and paper and pencil.

• The first secret to making a return boomerang is to find a branch or tree root with the correct bend. This is no easy job. If your search for the ideal branch or roots proves futile, you can cut the boomerang from a block of seasoned wood. You can either cut the entire boomerang out from the block of wood or you can cut the two blades out separately, as shown in Figure 28.8. The latter approach is strongly recommended by Bernard Mason in his *Boomerangs: How to Make and Throw Them*. Cutting the blades separately and then joining them together provides for a stronger boomerang.

• Cut out the boomerang or the blades. If you cut the blades separately, join them together. First cut a half-lap joint as shown in Figure 28.9. Then fit, glue, and clamp the two blades together until dry. Make sure to use waterproof resin glue. The joint can be reinforced with tacks if necessary. Whittle, rasp, and sand the top surface to the convex shape shown in Figure 28.10.

• The second secret to making a return boomerang is to bend the blades so that the ends are slightly higher than a plane running through the center of the boomerang. Boil the boomerang in water for about 20 minutes until the blades are pliable. While still hot, press a spot on each blade about two-thirds of the way in from the ends against a rock or table edge to bend the blades slightly up. The resulting bend should be so slight that it is not really visible to the eye but is visible if you lay the boomerang on a flat surface.

• The third and final secret to making a return boomerang is skewing the outside edges of the blade tips in opposite directions. In Figure 28.11, you'll see the blade edges labeled a, b, c, and d. One blade end should be skewed so that edge a is above and edge b is below an imaginary plane running through the center of the boomerang. At the other end, edge c should be skewed below and edge d above the plane through the center. One at a time, heat the ends over steam or in boiling water and, when hot, grip with two pairs of pliers, with one pair at the end of the blade and the other about 4 inches in from the end. Twist the pliers in opposite directions to skew the blade about 2 or 3 degrees. Repeat the process with the other blade.

● Now, try to fly the boomerang, using the throwing technique described below. You may have to adjust the bend or the skew to make it fly and return correctly.

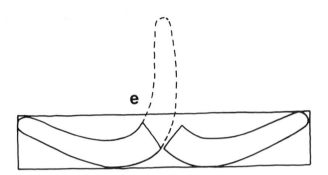

Figure 28.8 *Pattern for two-blade construction*

Decorating the Boomerang

One traditional style of Australian boomerang decoration is shown in Figure 28.12. The deep grooves running the length of the boomerang can be carved with a small gouge. The holes can be dug with an awl or drill. The design at the end of one blade is colored either red or black. Aboriginal peoples used charcoal for black and red ochre for red. The long grooves are left unpainted.

Figure 28.9 *Lap-joint*

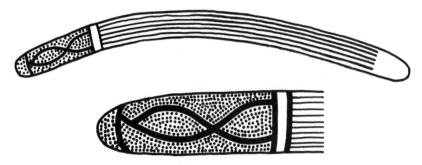

Figure 28.12 *Decorative pattern*

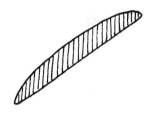

Figure 28.10 *Blade shape*

Throwing the Boomerang

An Australian boomerang is not a toy. It is a deadly hunting weapon. Throw it only in an open field, and make sure there are no other people nearby. Keep your eye on the flying boomerang at all times. Do not attempt to catch it.

Unless you are an expert, the flight pattern is likely to be erratic. Sometimes the boomerang will fly straight for a few yards and then drop to the ground. Other times it will fly straight out, curve to the left, rise in the air, and then gently descend back toward you, or it will rise in the air and then come hurtling right back at you—*so keep your eye on it.*

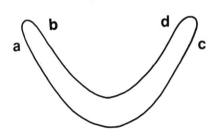

Figure 28.11 *Blade points for skewing*

Boomerangs

Native Americans in the Southwest and southern California used a crude, curved, nonreturn boomerang called a rabbit stick to hunt rabbits and birds. Not nearly as aerodynamic as the Australian return boomerang, the rabbit stick as often struck the prey while bouncing wildly on the ground as through a direct hit.

The goal in throwing the return boomerang is to get it to fly forward for 30 to 50 yards, turn to the left, rise in the air, and then descend slowly back to you. This is more difficult than it sounds. Success depends on the angle, bend, and skew of the boomerang as much as on your throwing technique.

Figure 28.13 shows the correct throwing stance. The boomerang should be held by one blade, perpendicular to the ground. For a right-handed throw, the flat side should face out. For a left-handed throw, the convex side should face out. To throw the boomerang, bring it back past your shoulder, then hurl it forward as hard as you can. When it leaves your hand, your arm should be fully extended. As it leaves your hand, jerk your hand sharply upward. Because no two boomerangs are exactly alike, every one must be thrown slightly differently. These subtle differences can be learned only through trial and error.

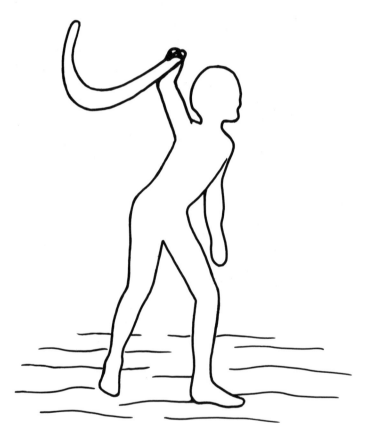

Figure 28.13 *Throwing stance*

29
Crossbow and Hunting Sling

The crossbows in use among the tribal peoples of eastern Burma and adjacent Thailand are formidable weapons. They are accurate enough to drop a squirrel at 20 yards yet powerful enough to be used for hunting deer, tigers, and even elephants. Strongly poisoned arrows shot from crossbows prove deadly in warfare. The only limitation on the power of the bow is the size and strength of the archer, who must be able to draw the bowstring back when shooting. The ancient Chinese used crossbows so powerful that they had to be cocked by three men.

The crossbow looks like a short hunting bow mounted on a gunstock (see Figure 29.1). Its major parts are a stock (a) with a groove (b) to guide the arrow, a bow (c), a recessed trigger (d) with a catch (e), and a bowstring (f). The stock and the trigger mechanism are generally carved from hardwood.

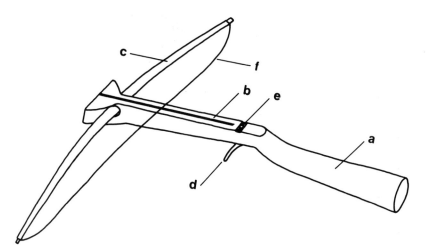

Figure 29.1 *Crossbow*

Tribal peoples use a variety of different materials for their bows, including bamboo and locally available hardwoods. The bowstring might be made of bamboo, twisted hemp, or rattan. Instructions are given here for making the hardwood crossbow used by the Karen people of the Burman hills, who are hunters and slash-and-burn horticulturalists. We have found it to be the crossbow that is the easiest to make and use.

Materials

You will need two blocks of good, firm hardwood, cut with the grain, for the stock and the bow. The Karen use cutch wood (*nya*, the Oriental acacia, *Acacia catechu*) which is difficult to obtain in this country. We suggest that you use maple, ash, or hickory, all of which make excellent substitutes. The piece for the stock should measure 28 inches by 5 inches by 4 inches. You can split a block of this size or buy seasoned wood from a lumberyard. The piece for the bow should measure 55 inches by 2 inches by 1 inch and should be split from green wood. You will also need a length of twisted cordage for the bowstring. Karen bowstrings are made from twisted fibers of the roselle plant (*Hibiscus sabdariffa*), but any of the twisted cords described in Chapter 5 will make an excellent substitute, as will commercially prepared bowstrings available at sporting goods stores.

For tools, you should have a knife, hatchet, spokeshave, wood chisels and a jigsaw handy. A few pieces of sandpaper and some ¾-inch brass tacks will also be needed.

Construction

• Your first task is to cut the stock to the size and shape shown in Figure 29.2. Find the center of one of the 5-inch faces of the block for the stock and draw a line down the middle with a straight edge and a pencil. This will be the top of the stock. Using a hatchet or jigsaw, rough out the approximate shape of the stock and whittle it smooth with the knife and spokeshave. Distance ab in Figure 29.2 is about equal in length to distance bc. When you are satisfied with the general appearance of the stock, sand it down and apply a coat of boiled linseed oil to protect the wood. Don't worry about the trigger mechanism or arrow groove at this stage, as they will be made later on.

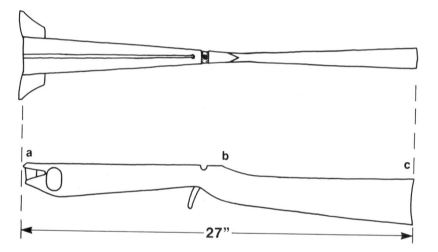

Figure 29.2 *Stock, top and side views*

• Next, trim the wood for the bow to the shape shown in Figure 29.3. Notice that the bow is cut slightly smaller toward the ends and has a profile that is nearly flat. Unlike regular bows, the bow of a crossbow has no grip and is of uniform thickness for its entire length. Cut a pair of notches for the string about 3 inches down from one end and whittle a peg at the other end. Sand until smooth.

Figure 29.3 *Bow*

• The Karen smoke their bows thoroughly before using them. They keep a fire burning constantly in their huts, with no hole in the roof for the smoke to escape through. Above the hearths a platform is hung, and the newly finished bows are left there until dry. The smoke permeates the wood and acts as a preservative, making it resistant to dampness, longer lasting, and considerably tougher. If you do not have a continually burning fire available, set the bow out in the sun to dry. Rub a few drops of linseed oil into the wood every couple of days while it is drying to keep it from splitting.

• You are now ready to make the trigger mechanism, illustrated in Figure 29.4. Cut a notch (a) that is ⅜ inch wide across the top of the stock just above the handgrip. Drill a hole into the center of the notch down through the stock. Turn the stock over and chisel out the hole to form a slot for the trigger housing (b). Cut the trigger (c) from the hardwood, with a little nub just below the far end. Drill a small hole through this nub. To mount the trigger, drive a tack into the side of the stock, making sure that it passes through the hole in the nub of the trigger before piercing the other side of the slot. When you squeeze the trigger, the other end of it should poke out of the hole in the notch on the top of the stock. This will release the bowstring.

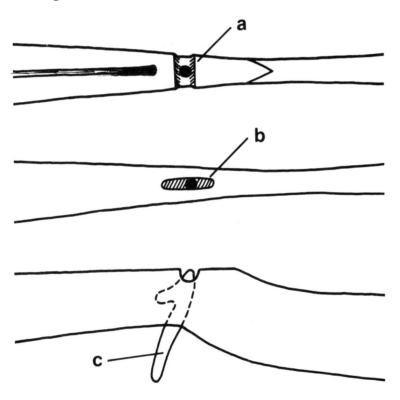

Figure 29.4 *Trigger mechanism*

• Mount the bow on the stock by chiseling out a hole in the end of the stock that is the same diameter as the bow. Slide the bow through the hole, and secure it in place by driving a small wedge of wood into the opening. Chisel out a ¼-inch groove in the top of the stock running from the trigger mechanism down to the end for the arrow to rest in. The crossbow is now finished except for the bowstring, and should look like the one in Figure 29.1.

• Use a 5-foot piece of twisted bast cordage for the bowstring. Tie a bowline knot at each end of the string; if the bow is 50 inches long, the knots should be about 45 inches apart. Trim off the excess cordage. String the bow by slipping one of the loops of the bowstring into the notches at one end of the bow, and resting that end on the ground. Then, force the other end of the bow down with your left hand and slip the other loop of the bowstring around the peg with your right hand. Remember to always unstring the bow when not in use.

Arrow Construction

Karen arrows are straight pieces of bamboo, fletched at one end and sharpened and slightly charred in a fire at the other end (see Figure 29.5). The bamboo used for arrows is cut from young, green shoots about ⅜ inch in diameter and 3 feet long. Any straight piece of hardwood with these dimensions may be substituted if bamboo is unavailable in your area. Trim one end to a conical point and char it in a fire to harden it. At the tip of the opposite end cut a notch for the bowstring. If you are using bamboo, the notch should be cut immediately after one of the internodes, to prevent the arrow from splitting lengthwise. To fletch the arrow, select a few small, straight-quilled feathers from the tail of a small gamebird (chicken feathers are *not* suitable). Split the feathers along the quill with a sharp knife and attach three of them to the arrow shaft by wrapping with silk thread or sinew.

The Karen smear their arrow points with a poisonous gum taken from the Upas tree (*Antiaris ovalfloria*), which is native to Burma. They collect a milky juice from the tree by making incisions in the bark and later dry the juice to form a thick gum. After being smeared with the poison, the arrow is left a short time to dry, but if left for too long the poison will lose its potency.

Enemies of the Karen eat a piece of the hog plum (*Spondius mangifera*) when shot by these arrows, since it is supposedly an antidote for the poison. The Paku tribesmen eat a little of the gum itself, which produces vomiting and apparently helps to counteract the effect of the poison in the wound.

Figure 29.5 *Arrow*

Shooting the Crossbow

Hold the crossbow in the same way that you would hold a rifle or shotgun. Draw the bowstring back and slip it in the notch, which will cause the trigger to move forward. Lay an arrow in the arrow shaft and squeeze the trigger. The bowstring will release, catch the notch at the end of the arrow, and send it speeding away.

Hunting Sling

Slings are both hunting weapons and toys. Men of the Ona tribe of Tierra del Fuego at the southern tip of South America used them to hunt birds. Ona boys used them for target practice and to torment Ona girls by slinging small stones at their feet. The Ona sling is easy to make and easy to use. It can be worn around the neck so that it will be readily accessible when you come across a suitable target. A well-thrown stone is accurate for up to 90 feet.

Materials

You will need a piece of soft, smooth leather, 3½ inches wide by 10 inches long, and two lengths of thin cord, one about 33 inches long, the other about 30 inches long. The Ona made their cord from twisted foreleg tendons of the guanaco. Any light, fairly stiff cord will work as well. You will also need a knife, a sewing needle, and some heavy thread, plus one to three small stones, each about 1 inch in diameter.

Construction

- To make the leather pouch, trim the leather to the shape shown in Figure 29.6. The finished pouch should be about 10 inches long by 3½ inches wide at the center, tapering to a triangular shape at each end. Save the excess leather, as you'll be using it later.
- Tie a square knot at one end of each cord. Stitch the cords to the outside ends of the pouch with two or three cross-stitches. The knots will keep the cord from slipping under the stitches. Take the excess leather from above and crumble it into two small balls. Wrap the ends of the two cords around the balls and tie off. One cord should be about 3 inches longer than the other cord.

Slinging

Place one to three stones in the pouch and hold the pouch shut with the thumb and index finger of your left hand. Grasp the end knot of the shorter cord between the thumb and index finger of your right hand. Slip the longer cord between the middle and ring fingers of your right hand so that the end knot rests in your palm. Raise the sling above your head and swing it around horizontally. Release the pouch from your left hand as you begin swinging the pouch. Swing it hard enough so that the centrifugal force holds the stones in the pouch. After two or three rapid revolutions around your head, let go of the shorter cord. The stones will fly forward rapidly, directly at the target if they are released at just the right moment. Obviously, figuring out just when to release the stones takes some practice. The sling will be held fast by the end knot on the longer cord locked between your ring and middle fingers. Don't be surprised if the sling ends up wrapped around your head after the stones are released.

Figure 29.6 *Sling*

30
Knives and Swords

Knives and swords have been called the oldest, the most universal, the most varied of all weapons, the only ones which have lived through all time. When did swords and knives first develop? In the beginning, technology was devoted to making weapons, the earliest being the spear and the ax. The first knives were probably discarded or broken spear heads. The first swords were likely made from the large bones of animals. Early anthropologists reported Cambodians using the bills of swordfish as daggers and Eskimos using whale ribs as swords. In time, it was discovered that horn makes a far better raw material than bone; it is stronger and harder because it is more dense, and it can also be worked easily with fire and steam, which is not true of bone. Metal, of course, is better yet, since it holds an edge and can be hammered into an infinite variety of forms.

Different shapes, as well as different materials, contribute to the variety of bladed implements. Curved blades, best for cutting or slashing, include the broadsword, backsword, saber, hanger, cutlass, scimitar, dusack, *yataghan*, and *flissa*; straight-bladed varieties, like the claymore espada, dagger, and rapier, are used primarily for thrusting, but can also cut if necessary. Many sword blades are grooved or channeled, the purpose being to let the blood out, thus making it easier to push the blade in and to pull it out. Italian daggers were sometimes grooved and covered with small circular depressions within which poison could be placed. The edge of the blade was almost always a smooth curve or straight line, although the *kris* used by the Malays had a wavy cutting edge, and some Italian bayonets had sawtooth blades.

In this chapter, we will take a look at some of the most "primitive" swords and knives, those made of wood by the Kapauku Papuans of New Guinea. The Kapaukus practice slash-and-burn agriculture and pig husbandry in the rain forest of the western part of New Guinea. You will be surprised at how simple and effective these tools and weapons are and how helpful they are in gardening and other household tasks even when compared to modern metal and plastics.

First, a word about wood as a material for tribal technology. The first rule for utilizing wood is to make sure it is thoroughly seasoned. To understand the need for seasoning wood, you must know something of the material itself. Like all plants, wood is composed of cells. What makes trees unusual is that when they grow, the inner cells die, while the outer cells, in the cambium layer immediately below the bark, continue to grow. As a result, if you cut into a tree of any great age you will find the wood in the middle, or *heartwood*, relatively dry and free of sap, while the wood around the perimeter, or *sapwood*, is moist and sappy. To season wood, you must allow it to dry out, so that the sapwood loses its moisture and becomes more stable and resistant to splitting and checking.

Straight-grained varieties are generally easier to work. Wood can be shaped with a knife, ax, or plane; it can be drilled to make holes; it can be steamed or boiled to make curves or bends; it can be hardened by fire; and it can be decorated by burning, etching, and painting. No wonder it has been such a popular material in the construction of artifacts by the cultures of the world.

The Kapaukus make bamboo knives for butchering animals and carving the meat. Flint knives are used to split the bamboo stalks and to shape the tool. The worker "sharpens" his bamboo knife by using his teeth to detach a splinter from the cutting edge. There are three basic types of knives: the small *dedo duwai bukwa*, five or six inches long with parallel sides and a blunt end, used for cutting pork; the large *dedomai bukwa*, with parallel sides and sharp point, used for butchering the pig; and the *me duwai bukwa*, a surgical or dental instrument par excellence, due to its ready disposability and the facility with which it may be sharpened during a delicate operation by detaching a sliver.

Hardwood knives are used in horticulture. The Kapaukus garden on the floor of the flat and swampy Kamu Valley, which frequently requires the construction of drainage ditches. For this they use a *patau*, or "earth knife," a paddle-shaped tool with a leaf-shaped blade and a handle about three feet long. The gardener stands in the bottom of the ditch and holds the knife with both hands. With the edge of the blade turned towards him, he raises the knife high above his head and thrusts the pointed end deep into the ground, making the cut by drawing the handle downward toward his feet. He cuts first the left side, then the right side of a block of earth. The third and final stroke is made with the blade turned sideways, thus detaching the block and depositing it at the gardener's feet.

Digging ditches is the husband's responsibility, and if a woman undertakes the work, she subjects her husband to great chastisement. Planting and weeding, however, are women's work. Almost everyone is familiar with the simple wooden planting stick, a pointed stick driven into the soft earth to make a hole in which to insert seeds. Weeding is often the first agricultural activity young Kapauku girls learn to perform. As a weeding tool, women use a wooden paddle-shaped implement called a *boo kote*, "weeding tool." Holding it in her right hand, she breaks the ground and severs the roots of grass and weeds, pulling them out with her left hand and placing them in a heap.

Wooden swords and knives had a wide distribution. Captain John Smith found them among the Indians of Virginia; the natives of the Sandwich Islands carried swords of a heavy black wood, probably ebony; and they were also used by the Itonamas, a subtribe of the Moxos in South America. You can have fun by making and using the Kapauku implements described above, or carving replicas of the many types of bladed instruments described in this chapter for use as models.

Root Crop Harvest Stick

Earth Knife

Bamboo Knife

Weeding Stick

Bamboo Carving Knife

Figure 30.1 *Kapauku knives*

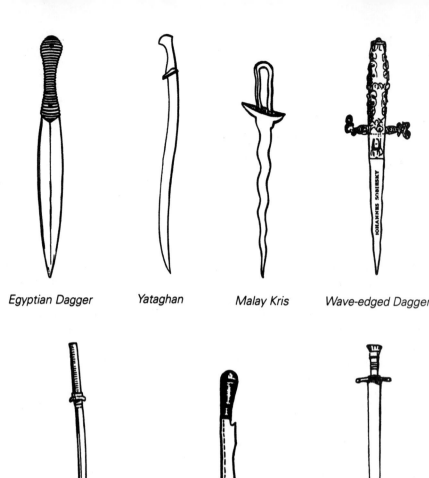

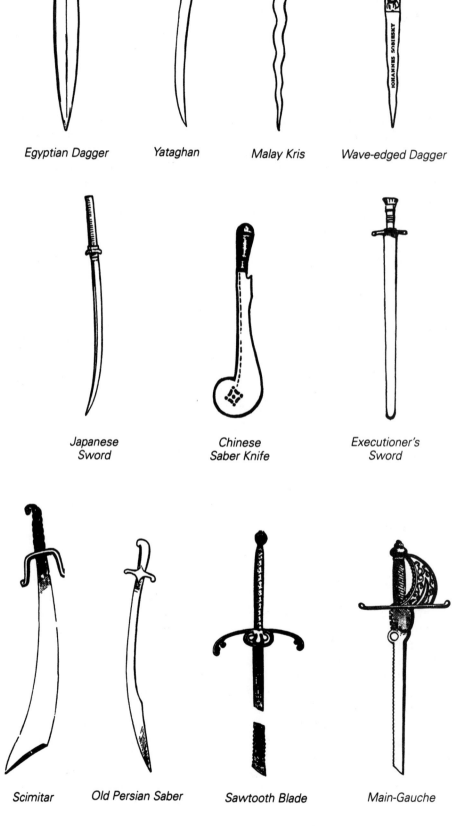

Figure 30.2 *Different types of edged weapons*

Egyptian Dagger *Yataghan* *Malay Kris* *Wave-edged Dagger*

Japanese Sword *Chinese Saber Knife* *Executioner's Sword*

Scimitar *Old Persian Saber* *Sawtooth Blade* *Main-Gauche*

31
Traps, Snares, and Deadfalls

A well-designed trap forces the prey to do the hunter's work. Virtually all tribal peoples use traps in their food quest. Many of these traps are marvels of engineering and design. But the trapper must do more than just set a good trap; he must also entice his prey to its eventual doom. He must learn to imitate the noise made by his quarry, discover the tastes and smells it likes most; and learn to use the animal's instinctive sense of caution to his own advantage. All this requires careful study of the animal's mental life and habits.

A Montagnais Indian, trapping beaver on the edge of the great Mistassini Lake in Labrador, marshals a lifetime of experience and knowledge into his work. Knowing that the beaver will head for deep water when spooked, he fastens a stone sinker to his trap to hold the animal under until it drowns. Knowing that the beaver will will gnaw off its own leg to free itself from the trap, he sets the trap in such a way that those mighty teeth are useless. Knowing that the beaver will approach no area that smells of humans, he soaks the trap in castor and smokes his clothes over the fire to allay suspicion. This intimate knowledge of the animal's ways makes the primitive trapper seem more like a game biologist than the mindless butcher with whom he is sometimes compared.

In this chapter we describe how some of these "primitive" traps work. You may even wish to try a few, if they are permitted by the game laws in your state.

The Deadfall

One of the favorite traps of the Yagua Indians of Peru, hunters of the Amazonian lowlands, is the deadfall, which is designed to drop a heavy weight on an unsuspecting animal, killing it instantly. The deadfall has five parts: the weight, a fixed support and unstable support on which the weight rests, a catch which prevents the weight from falling until the trigger is released, and the trigger.

The Yagua use the deadfall to catch jaguars. They design their traps with the utmost care, often making scale models of them to test their efficiency before setting up full-sized ones in the forest. A semicircular enclosure is made by driving stakes in the ground, and a piece of bait is set in the middle. A large log is then suspended from a nearby tree, with one end resting on the ground and the other connected to the trigger mechanism with two pieces of rope. The trigger consists of a stick across the front of the enclosure where the bait lies, set so that the slightest movement will trip the catch and cause the log to come crashing down (see Figure 31.1). To entice the jaguar into the trap, the Yagua trapper may sprinkle a trail of blood on the ground leading up to the bait.

The Yagua also make a "guillotine" deadfall for trapping smaller animals, such as agutis, anteaters, and racoons. The bait is placed in an

Figure 31.1 *Deadfall*

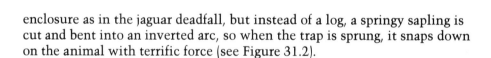

enclosure as in the jaguar deadfall, but instead of a log, a springy sapling is cut and bent into an inverted arc, so when the trap is sprung, it snaps down on the animal with terrific force (see Figure 31.2).

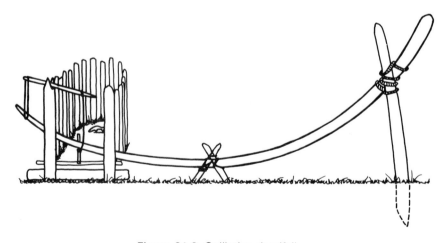

Figure 31.2 *Guillotine deadfall*

116

The noose or snare, a piece of rope or thong looped around itself and tied with a slip-knot, is one of the simplest and most effective and widely used traps. The Ingalik of Alaska use a snare to catch black bears and an occasional grizzly. They call this trap *dethakon*, literally, "fish guts up in the air," after the bear's favorite food, which is used to bait the trap.

The snare is set on a dead tree blown over by the wind that has fallen and lodged itself on the branch of a standing tree so that one end of the fallen tree is high off the ground. High up the windfallen log, a basket full of fish guts, eggs, grease, and innards is tied for bait. Halfway down the log, the Ingalik tie a heavy strip of sea mammal hide and form a noose at the other end, as shown in Figure 31.3. They tie the noose loosely with some willow-bark line to a frame made from two spruce poles. The noose hangs over the log directly in the path the bear must take to get at the bait. The bear smells the bait as he walks by, climbs the log and becomes ensnared in the noose. When he reaches the end of the line connecting the noose to the log, he is jerked off the log by being suddenly stopped, and hangs helplessly until the hunter comes along to dispatch him.

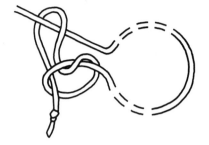

Figure 31.3 *Noose*

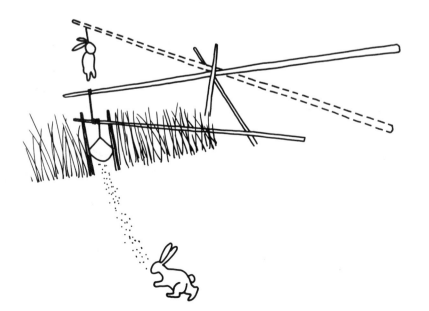

Figure 31.4 *Bear snare*

Another ingenious design used by the Ingalik is the rabbit snare. Finding a rabbit trail, the trapper drives two stakes on either side and lashes another pole on top (see Figure 31.5). This part of the trap does not

Figure 31.5 *Rabbit snare*

117

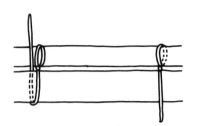

Figure 31.6 *Rabbit snare trigger*

move. He then takes a pole about 10 feet long and balances it in the crotch of two sticks lashed together, so that the small end of the pole will rise in the air if not tied down. He ties a noose in one end of a rope, using the knot shown in Figure 31.3, and ties the other end of the rope to the long pole set in the forked sticks. The trigger of the trap is made by tying the noose line to a small trigger stick with a couple of half-hitches (see Figure 31.6) and then laying the trigger stick on top of the cross-piece of the frame and taking a turn around it with the noose line. A rabbit running along the trail gets caught in the noose, pulls it loose from the cross-piece, and then gets shot up in the air by the weight of the butt end of the pole. His lofty position discourages lynxes and other predators from making a meal of him before the trapper arrives.

The Set-Hook

The set-hook trap works on the same principle as a baited fish hook, except that it is used out of water. A simple form of set-hook is used by the Tarahumara Indians of northern Mexico. To nab the marauding blackbirds who are constantly invading their cornfields, the Tarahumara thread kernels of corn on lengths of agave fiber which are anchored to sticks or rocks. The blackbirds, spotting the free meal, swallow the kernels, and the cord becomes entangled in their esophaguses, holding them to the spot.

The Catapult

The Galela people of northwestern Halmahera in Indonesia set catapult (*bako*) traps along animal trails to capture deer and wild pigs. The catapult is a spring-loaded device which sends a bamboo spear into the animal that sets off the trigger. A long and springy pole is cut down and its butt end is set between the trunks of two trees, as shown in Figure 31.7. The other end is fixed to a crossbar, which rests on two forked sticks driven into the ground, with a trigger stick rigged as shown in Figure 31.7, b and c. A trip line, one end of which is looped around the trigger stick to hold it in place, runs down along the crossbar and across the animal trail and is tied to a tree on the other side. A lance is then made from bamboo, with one end sharpened to a needle point and the other end notched. The pointed end is supported by a forked stick stuck in the ground and the springy pole is set into the notched end. When an animal walks down the trail, it hits the trip line, which frees the trigger stick, which causes the springy pole to snap forward, propelling the lance into the heart of the trapper's quarry. Needless to say, this trap can be hazardous to humans, so if you decide to make one, stick to a scale model.

Figure 31.7 *Catapult*

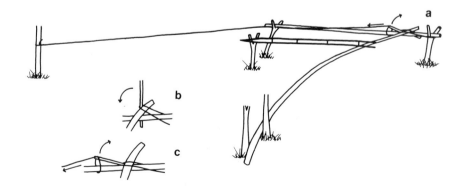

Before the time of horses and guns, the Blackfoot Indians of Montana used a trapping technique on buffalo that they called the *piskun*, or "deep blood kettle." They would first build a large corral at the base of a steep cliff using rocks, brush, or logs—whatever was handy. From the edge of the cliff directly above the corral, two long lines of brush and rocks would be laid out into the prairie, in the form of a huge V, with the opening over the corral being at the angle. On the morning of the hunt, the medicine man would don a buffalo headdress and robe and approach the buffalo herd. Attracting the attention of a few older bulls, he would slowly start to make his way toward the opening of the V-shaped chute. He gradually quickened his pace until the entire herd, following him out of curiosity, was inside the arms of the chute. At this point, the rest of the Blackfoot band, hidden behind the rock and brush walls of the V-chute, would rise up and shout and wave, panicking the buffalo. As the medicine man ducked out, the buffalo would run directly toward the precipice with the arms of the chute directing them to the point just over the corral. Not having the presence of mind to stop at the edge, the animals would go right over the cliff and fall into the corral, where, if not stunned by the fall, they would be killed and butchered by the women waiting below.

Since buffalo will not attempt to break through a wall they cannot see through, the sides of the corral did not need to be very sturdy. Hides were thrown over the rocks and brush that formed the corral so that the animals could not see through to the outside. In winter, to keep the buffalo herd running in the right direction once they were inside the chute, a line of buffalo chips would be set leading to the precipice over the corral. The line stuck out against the white snow, and as it was the only point of reference, the buffalo would always follow it, never veering to the right or left.

The Cage

The cylinder-fall trap made by the Guiana Indians of South America is an excellent example of a cage trap (see Figure 31.8). It is set in shallow rivers to catch small fish and consists of a cylinder made from a length of bamboo. The cylinder is suspended from a crossbar support stuck in the mud of the river bottom. A small piece of bait is tied on one end of a reed and placed inside the cylinder. The other end of the reed is inserted through a hole in a small stick. This stick is ingeniously connected to the cord from which the cylinder hangs so that when a fish pulls on the bait, the cylinder is freed from the crossbar and traps the fish. A branch placed on top of the cylinder acts as a weight, causing the cylinder to sink into the mud slightly when it is released and preventing it from falling over.

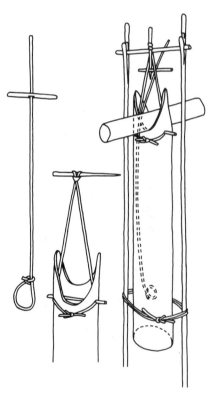

Figure 31.8 *Cage*

32
Atlatl

An atlatl, or spear-thrower, is a device used widely throughout North and South America for propelling spears, harpoons, and darts with great accuracy and force. The term atlatl comes from Nahuatl, the language of the ancient Aztecs, and means, literally, "sling." An atlatl is just that—a rigid sling, which acts as an extension of the arm and enables a hunter or warrior to throw his spear with about 50 percent greater force than if he used his arm alone.

The Aleut people of the Aleutian Islands off the coast of Alaska use the spear-thrower as their primary weapon in hunting and warfare. Although not quite as accurate as a bow and arrow, a spear thrown with a spear-thrower has far greater penetrating power, an important consideration for a people like the Aleut who make their living hunting tough-skinned sea mammals. Another advantage of the spear-thrower is that it can be operated with only one hand and produces no recoil. This is important to the Aleut, too, as they hunt from narrow, tipsy, skin-covered kayaks. The hunter can steady the kayak with a paddle held in his left hand while hurling the spear or harpoon at a seal or walrus from the spear-thrower held in his right hand.

Aleut spear-throwers are made from a variety of hardwoods. Their only decoration is a coat of red paint. They are usually about 16 inches long by 3 inches wide, with a handgrip and a hole for the forefinger at the near end and a groove for the spear on the upper surface at the far end, as shown in Figure 32.1.

Figure 32.1 *Aleut atlatl: (a) top view, (b) bottom view*

To make an Aleut spear-thrower, all you'll need is a block of hardwood (with the grain running long) and a whittling knife. Select a block of birch, oak, maple, or other hardwood that is 1 inch thick, 3 inches wide, and 15 to 20 inches long. If your hand is small, you may want to use a narrower block of wood.

Construction

• Round off the ends and the edges of the block with your knife. Carve out the hand grip. You will want to carve an indentation on one side of the grip to fit the muscles of the lower part of your thumb, and notches on the other side to fit your middle, ring, and little fingers. (Note that the spear-thrower shown in Figure 32.1 is right-handed.)

- Turn the spear-thrower over and, starting at the end opposite the grip, carve a long groove about ½ to ¾ inch wide. It should begin about 2 inches in from the far end and be deep enough to pass through to the wood on the other side. Gradually taper it off near the grip end, until it runs flush with the surface.

- Turn the thrower over again and hollow out a hole for your forefinger at the grip end. Cut a hole completely through the block, coming out on the other side which will hold the spear shaft. The spear-thrower is now finished, unless you want to add a coat of red paint in authentic Aleut style.

Spears

A wide variety of spears, harpoons, and darts can be thrown with a spear-thrower. The Aleut made spears from hardwood poles about 6 feet long and tipped them with ivory or bone points (see Figure 32.2). They also made harpoons with toggle heads. The heads were loosely attached to the shaft with a piece of sinew and connected to a harpoon line. The toggle head would break off from the shaft after it penetrated the animal's gut and lodge there, enabling the hunter to haul the animal in with the harpoon line. The darts used by the Aleut for hunting birds consisted of a wooden shaft with a long, barbed point at the end and three prongs of bone attached about a foot down the shaft. These prongs would entrap the bird, with the weight of the dart dragging the bird down, even if the point of the dart failed to penetrate the flesh (see Figure 32.3).

You can make an exact replica of an Aleut spear using the illustrations in Figures 32.2 and 32.3 as guides, or use any long, narrow pole in your spear-thrower for target practice.

Throwing the Spear

To throw a spear with the spear-thrower, grasp the handgrip and insert your forefinger into the finger hole. Place the butt end of the spear in the groove on the top side of the thrower and slide it back until it fits against the back of the groove. Grasping both the spear and the thrower (see Figure 32.3), raise your hand to shoulder height and throw the spear as if you were throwing a baseball. With a little practice, you'll find that you can throw the spear both accurately and with great force with the help of the spear-thrower.

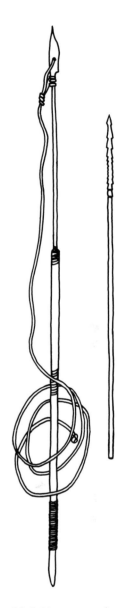

Figure 32.2 *Harpoon and spear*

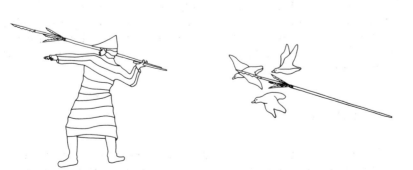

Figure 32.3 *Throwing the bird dart: (a) throwing position, (b) dart in flight*

33
Insects as Food

Although we think of insects as things to be avoided or exterminated, many people in the non-Western world think of them as food. In some places insects are part of the everyday diet, in other places they are considered a delicacy and are eaten in abundance whenever available. Before you dismiss the idea of insects as food, remember that most food preferences and avoidances are learned, and there is considerable variation from one society to another. Additionally, most preferences and avoidances, except for poisonous foods, are not especially rational. For example, two hundred years ago, at the time of the American revolution, tomatoes were thought to be poisonous—so poisonous that they were called the deadly nightshade and were mixed in the food of George Washington in an attempt to assassinate him. Even early in this century tomatoes were viewed with disdain, being referred to as love apples, and not considered suitable for inclusion in the everyday diet. Today tomatoes are one of our most common foods. Although we are not making an argument for the use of insects on a regular basis, it is worth keeping in mind that they can be eaten, and may even prove to be life-savers in emergency situations.

Caterpillars, locusts and grasshoppers, ants, and termites are the four insects eaten most often, owing to their excellent flavor and the relative ease with which they can be collected. Most insects are rich and filling with a sweet, nutty flavor. As the following list shows, there are a great number of insects besides the four mentioned above which are used as food in various parts of the world. The area listed as California refers to Native Americans of the desert regions of southern and western California.

Insect	Area of the World
termite	Africa, Australia, Asia, South America, California, India
ant	Africa, Australia, Philippines, South America, California, India
red ant	Africa, South America
lice	Africa, Australia, South America
grubs (larvae)	Africa, Australia, Asia, South America, California
locust/grasshopper	Africa, Asia, Middle East, Mexico, New Guinea, Philippines, California
cricket	Africa, Asia, Philippines, New Guinea, California
cicada	Australia, Asia, New Guinea
praying mantis	New Guinea
roach	New Guinea
beetles	Asia, South Africa, New Guinea

ant lion	South Africa
earwig	New Guinea
brine fly	Northern California
mayfly	Africa
dragonfly	Philippines, New Guinea
gnat	Africa
wasp	Asia, New Guinea, South America
bee	Asia, South America
waterbugs (back swimmer, water boatman, water strider)	Philippines, New Guinea, China, Mexico
caterpillars	Africa, Australia, New Guinea, Asia, South America, California, Mexico
spiders	New Guinea, South America
scorpions	South America

Insects can be cooked by steaming, roasting, boiling, or frying, although sometimes they are eaten raw. Keep in mind that certain insects are poisonous or dangerous and should not be eaten. Generally, insects lacking bright coloration are safe to eat. It is a good idea to remove the legs, wings, and as much of the tough outer shell as possible. This is especially important for locusts, as the hard bristles on their legs can cause serious intestinal problems if ingested.

Nutritive analyses of insects are relatively rare, although Bodenheimer provides a fair amount of information in his book, *Insects As Human Food: A Chapter in the Ecology of Man*, some of which is summarized below.

Food Source	% Moisture	% Fat	% Ash	% Chitin	Calories/ 100 g.	% Protein
live termite	44.5	28.3	—	—	347	23.2
fried termite	6.0	44.5	6.4	5.1	561	36.0
caterpillar	15.7	13.7	40.0	13.5	268	—
beef	75.2	6.6	1.3	—	127	16.9
dried fish	32.4	3.1	20.8	—	203	43.7

As seen in the chart, the caloric and protein values and fat content of insects compare favorably to those of beef and fish. The chitin is mostly from appendages and skin which should be removed before eating.

Perhaps the major problem in using insects as food is that they are small creatures and therefore relatively difficult to gather in great quantities. Insect-eating peoples have solved this problem by developing a number of collecting techniques that enable them to gather and process large quantities of insects at one time. The Azande people of the Sudan, like many tribal peoples in Africa, are avid consumers of the flying white termites which inhabit tropical regions of the world. The Azande collect termites at night by holding grass torches near the nests. As the termites fly from the nests they are attracted to the light of the burning torch. The Azande then knock them to the ground where they are gathered together in a collection pit. This technique works best on moonless nights, as on bright nights the termites will ignore the torches and fly directly up toward the moon instead.

The Ute Indians of California collected grasshoppers for roasting or grinding into powder. When they located a large field swarming with grasshoppers, they would dig a broad trench down the center of the field. A large group of Utes would then spread themselves around the edges of the field, and with sticks in hand, pound on the ground as they worked their way toward the center pit. The grasshoppers would hop toward and eventually fall into the pit where they would be beaten, burned, or covered with stones.

The Modoc Indians of northern California collected female brine flies. To collect the flies, the Modoc, like all good trappers, took advantage of the predictable behavior of the female flies. The flies would sit in great numbers on the branches overhanging a stream and drop their eggs into the stream. Usually they died there after depositing their eggs. Downstream from the fly-laden branches the Modoc would place logs across the stream and would then shake the flies free from the branches. They would wait for them to flow downstream and get caught on the logs and then would scoop them into baskets.

The Thai people collect female cicada by sitting around a campfire at night and clapping their hands together. The clapping noise attracts the cicada into the camp, making them easy prey.

After you collect insects, you'll want to cook them. Below are recipes for three common insects.

Locust Powder

The Ifugao people in the northern Philippines process dried locusts into flour. Boil the locusts in water, remove the wings and legs, and sun-dry the bodies until they are brittle. Pound the dry bodies into a powder and store in a sealed container. Use the powder in cakes, breads, and gruel.

Termite Oil

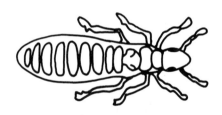

Figure 33.1 *African termite*

The Azande use termite oil pressed from dried termites both for cooking and as a body lotion. Remove the wings and roast the termites on hot coals or stones, then sun-dry until brittle. Heat the dried bodies in water. Strain the water through cheesecloth, retaining the termites in the cloth. Press the termite bodies through a sieve, catching the fluid in a pan below. Boil the liquid to steam off the water, leaving the oil behind. Store the oil in a sealed container and save the crushed bodies for future use. The oil produced this way will equal about 25 percent of the body weight of the live termites.

Roast Grasshopper

Figure 33.2 *Grasshopper*

Native Americans in southern California roasted the grasshoppers they regularly collected. Collect a large quantity of grasshoppers and remove the wings and legs. Dig a pit and line it with rocks heated in a fire. Pile the grasshoppers on the heated rocks and cover with a thick layer of grass. Roast for two hours, remove from the pit and eat. If you are in a region with sandy soil, you can roast the grasshoppers directly on the ground without digging a pit. Build a large fire to heat the ground. Clear the ash and coals from the sand. Pile the grasshoppers on the hot sand and cover with ashes from the fire; cook until done. They can be eaten whole or ground into powder.

34
Cereals, Flours, Breads, and Cakes

Flour ground from cereals, nuts, and seeds serves as the base for the staple foods of most societies around the world. Unleavened and leavened breads, cakes, and gruels are an important part of the diet in most societies. The only major exceptions are people in the extreme north and in some tropical forests who have no cereal or nuts from which to grind flour. Another exception were the Native Americans of the Plains, whose staple food was buffalo meat. They used dried buffalo meat flour, however, to make a jerky-based pemmican (see recipe in Chapter 26).

There are three basic steps in turning cereal or nut kernels into flour. First, you have to hull the seed to remove the kernel. Second, you have to winnow the hulls from the kernels. Third, you have to grind the kernels into flour or a paste.

Steps one and three, hulling and grinding, can almost always be done with two stones; one large and flat or hollowed to serve as a mortar or grinding board, and one round and small to serve as a pestle. You break the hull from the kernel or grind the kernel into flour by crushing the seeds or kernels between the two stones.

Winnowing, the second step, takes some practice. The basic piece of equipment is a large, slightly concave basket. Place the ground hulls and kernels in the basket and shake the basket in a circular motion, causing the hulls and other impurities to rise to the top while leaving the kernels or flour on the bottom. The hulls then can be removed by hand or, if you get really good at it, flipped over the rim of the basket as you shake it.

In this chapter we provide instructions for grinding six different types of flour: acorn, oat, corn, sorghum, rice, and water lily seed. We also provide recipes for turning these flours into gruels, cakes, and wafers. As with all natural foods, it takes some experimentation to figure out exactly how much of each ingredient to use in a recipe; for that reason, we don't always list exact amounts in some of the recipes. Naturally ground flours are often quite bland. To spice up the recipes you might consider adding herbs, fruits, and spices like some of those listed to the right.

blueberries
raspberries
cherries
raisins
mint
anise
nutmeg
walnuts
pecans

Tortillas from Scratch

The availability of *masa harina* on the shelves of many grocery stores has made the grinding of corn flour something of a lost art north of Mexico. *Masa harina* is the dry corn flour used to make tortillas. In Mexican villages, tortillas—flat, round corn cakes—are eaten with every

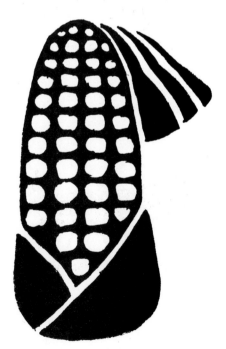

Figure 34.1 *Corn design from ancient Mexico*

125

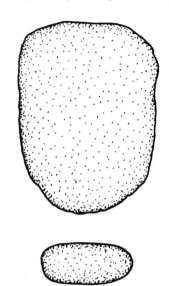

Figure 34.2 *Metate and mano*

Figure 34.3 *Oats (Avena sativa)*

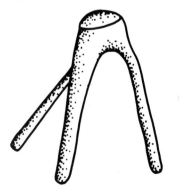

Figure 34.4 *Cranachan*

meal and sometimes between meals as a snack. Mexican peasant women spend a good part of each morning preparing tortillas for the day's meals. Tortillas are made from corn, water, and lime (the mineral, not the citrus fruit).

● First, husk and shell 4½ pounds of sun-dried corn kernels. Clean the kernels by placing them in a clay pot and rinsing them three or four times with hot water. After the final rinse, fill the pot with hot water to cover the kernels. Add a pinch or two of ground lime—just enough to turn the water white. Boil for ½ hour and let sit for 18 hours. Remove the kernels from the water and rinse thoroughly.

● You are now ready to grind the kernels into a paste called *nixtamal*, from which the tortillas are made. For 3,000 years Mexican women ground the moistened kernels on a grinding stone called a *metate* with a stone rolling pin called a *mano* (see Figure 34.2). Today, they more often take the kernels to the village grinding mill for mechanical grinding. Since grinding the kernels by hand is an arduous, back-breaking chore, you'd be wise to follow their example and grind the kernels in a processor or food mill. Any remaining lumps can be flattened with a rolling pin.

● Divide the paste into 24 even lumps. Place a lightly greased heavy iron skillet over medium heat. Mexican women fry the tortillas on a *comal*, a round, slightly concave clay pan. Pat or roll the lumps on an unfloured surface into flat, round cakes about 6 inches across. The cakes should be quite thin, moist, and free of tears, splits, or frayed edges. Place the cakes one at a time in the pan and fry for about 1 minute on each side.

Oatmeal Cakes

In Britain during the seventeenth and eighteenth centuries, oats (see Figure 34.3) were considered a food suitable only for the poor. The landed gentry and urban middle class preferred wheat. The belief that eating oats somehow indicates low social status survives today as the popular belief that oatmeal cookies are the "poor man's" substitute for chocolate chip cookies. Whether they had anything to do with social status or not, oatmeal cakes called *bkocaire* or *blethach* were a staple in the diet of farmers in rural Ireland. Since these cakes would keep for months after baking, they were often taken along for food by Irish emigrants making the long trans-Atlantic voyage to America.

Oatmeal cakes were traditionally baked in front of a fire, propped up against a metal grate or wood stand called a *cranachan*, like that shown in Figure 34.4. A wooden tripod like this can be assembled in a few minutes from sticks or pieces of scrap lumber. The only ingredients for the oatmeal cakes are oatmeal, hot water, and salt. The baked cakes are circular and cut into quarters for eating. They should be about ¼-inch thick when baked.

● Mix the oatmeal, hot water, and salt to form a thick batter. Roll the batter into a thin, circular cake. Mark the cake into quarters so it may be divided easily for serving. Let the cake dry slightly, then prop it up against the tripod in front of a fire and bake, turning it frequently until it is thoroughly dry. Break into quarters and eat.

Mush and gruel made from flour ground from acorn kernels was a staple food in the diet of Native Americans in California. The particular method of grinding acorn flour described here is that of the Yokut people who lived in central California. Both green and ripe acorns from either red (*Quercus rubra*) or white (*Q. alba*) oaks can be used to make flour. Acorns from red oak species contain bitter tannin which must be leached from the flour before it can be eaten. As shown in Figure 34.5, the leaves of most red oaks have pointed lobes with sharp teeth along the edges, and the leaves of white oaks usually have smooth lobes without teeth. In addition, the acorns of red oaks have hair inside the shells, while the acorns of white oaks are hairless.

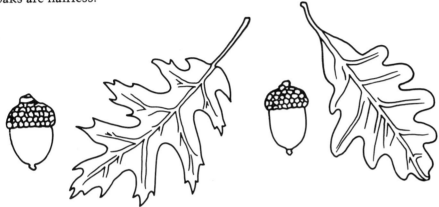

Figure 34.5 *Red oak and white oak leaves and acorns*

The Yokuts harvested acorns from numerous red oak species including the tanbark oak (*Q. densiflora*), black oak (*Q. california*), white oak (*Q. garryana*), and live oak (*Q. chrysdepis*). In addition to the acorns which can be gathered both from the tree and off the ground, you'll need a winnowing basket, sand, grape leaves or cheesecloth, water, a canvas, a kettle, a nutcracker, and a large mortar and pestle. Because leached acorn flour is about the most tasteless food there is, you'll surely want to spice it up with herbs, nuts, or berries.

● Peel (green nuts) or hull (ripe nuts) and remove the membrane covering the acorn kernel. Ripe acorns frequently contain worms. You should remove them unless you want some added protein in the flour. Pound two handfuls of acorn kernels in the mortar and pestle. For a natural mortar and pestle you can use a small hollow in a large stone or boulder as the mortar and a small round stone as the pestle. Winnow the ground flour in the basket to separate out the large unground lumps. Dump these lumps back into the mortar and regrind. Continue grinding and winnowing until all the kernels are reduced to a coarse powder.

● Leach the coarse flour to remove the tannin, if necessary. Dig a hole about 2 feet in diameter by 6 inches deep and line it with clean sand. Cover the sand with the grape leaves or with several layers of cheesecloth. Pour the acorn flour into the hole. Heat 2 quarts of water in a kettle or a pan with a pouring lip. Pour the water slowly over the flour, allowing it to run through the flour rather than forming a pool in it. To insure a gentle flow over the flour, you can pour the water through a fistful of coarse grass stalks held over the hole. Repeat this process several times, tasting the flour after the third time. Continue leaching until all the bitter taste is removed. Cover the hole with the canvas and allow the flour to sit until it hardens into cakes like those shown in Figure 34.6. While the flour hardens keep an eye out for interested squirrels.

• When they are thoroughly dry, remove the cakes from the hole. They can be eaten as they are or turned into mush. To make mush, pulverize the cakes or remove the flour from the leaching hole before it hardens into cakes, add water, and boil to the desired consistency.

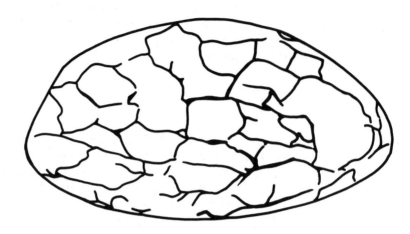

Figure 34.6 *Acorn mush cakes*

Figure 34.7 *Sorghum (Sorghum vulgare)*

Sorghum Wafers

In the United States sorghum is used mostly as livestock feed, but in many other parts of the world it is an important part of the human diet. The recipe given here is for the sorghum wafers called *kisra* made by the Azande people of the Sudan in North Africa.

• Pound the sorghum kernels to loosen the husks and then winnow in a basket. Soak the kernels in water for 12 hours. Grind the moist kernels between two stones or in a mill and set aside for another 12 hours. While they sit, fermentation will begin, giving the flour a slightly sour taste. Next, sun-dry the flour. When dry it will form small lumps. Grind the lumps into dry flour. Add water to the flour, mix, and let the batter sit for two hours.

• Heavily grease an iron griddle and place over high heat. Pour the batter in a thin layer on the pan. Fry for 30 seconds and peel the thin, soft wafer from the pan. Eat as is or sun-dry for storage.

Rice Cakes

Rice is the most important cereal crop in the world. It is a staple food in the diets of a billion people, most of whom live in Asia. Not surprisingly, there are literally hundreds of rice recipes used throughout the world. The recipe we have chosen to include here is for rice cakes called *puto*, a dessert food of people living in northern Luzon Island in the Philippines. These cakes, made with white rice and sugar, are easy to make, gooey, and quite filling. White rice and sugar are the only ingredients. For cooking utensils you'll need a large covered pot, a metal rack, a mixing bowl, a spatula, and muffin tins.

• Cover 2 cups of rice with water and soak until the rice is moist. Drain the water and grind the rice into a thick paste. Add 1 cup of sugar to the rice paste and mix until smooth. Pour the batter into muffin tins, filling each tin ⅔ full. Bring 3 inches of water to a boil in a large pot. Place the muffin tins on a rack over the water and steam covered for 15 minutes. Add more water as needed. The *puto* are ready when a toothpick inserted into the center of a cake comes out clean.

Abraham Maramba, a friend of ours who is a member of the Pangasinense ethnic group of northern Luzon, tells us that Philippinos living in the United States use a different recipe. They find it easier to use 2 cups of Bisquick, 1 cup of milk, 1 cup of sugar, and 2 eggs. The ingredients are mixed and then steamed as described above.

Water Lily Gruel

In late August of each year, Klamath and Modoc Indians of southern Oregon and northern California would paddle their canoes into large marsh areas to collect boatfuls of water lily seed pods (*wokas*), from which they made flour. They collected both ripe and unripe pods, although ripe ones were usually prepared separately as they were thought to be superior both in taste and consistency. The specific water lily you want is the yellow water lily (*Nupher polysepala*), also known as the water chinquepin, American lotus, and yellow nelumbo.

Figure 34.8 *Rice (Oryza sativa)*

• Collect water lily pods in the late summer. Both ripe and unripe pods can be used. Water lilies grow in abundance in ponds, marshes, and quiet backwaters throughout North America. Sun-dry or roast the pods over a fire until dry, turning frequently for even drying. Pound the seeds from the pods by rubbing the pods between two stones with a circular motion. Winnow the seeds from the pods in a basket. Parch the seeds then crack the seed shells open by crushing them between two stones, again using a circular motion. Winnow the hulls from the seed kernels. Grind the kernels into flour or boil in water to form a gruel. The gruel can be eaten as is or flavored with berries or nuts.

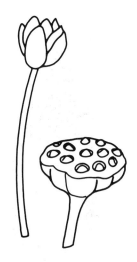

Figure 34.9 *Water lily seed pod and flower*

Fried Bread

Fried bread is a common food at Native American celebrations. Actually, it was never used by Native Americans prior to the arrival of European settlers, as the Indians did not use wheat flour. The ingredients are 3 cups of wheat flour, 1 teaspoon of baking soda, water, and salt to taste. Combine the ingredients and then add enough water to form a thick dough. Knead the dough. Heat oil in a heavy iron pan. Shape the dough into 4-inch cakes and fry until brown on one side. Flip them over and fry until the other side is brown.

35
The New England Clambake

To New Englanders nothing quite matches the taste of clams, lobster, and corn-on-the-cob steamed together in a bed of seaweed and seasoned with the salt of the sea. Add the company of good friends and a sunny day on a New England beach and you have good reason to begin planning your first clambake.

The New England clambake is neither "New England" in origin nor a bake. If accuracy were our only consideration, we would call it a native American clamsteam. It was Native Americans like the Narranganset in Rhode Island who taught English settlers to steam food in a bed of seaweed over hot stones. The advantage of steaming food in the clamback fashion is that the juices from the clams, lobster, corn, and seaweed mix, produces a feast that is of unequalled succulence. The key to a successful clambake, however, is the people, not the food. The more people, the more the preparation and cooking tasks are shared, and the more fun can be had by all.

Materials

The only tools you will need are garden shovels and rakes. You will also need enough hardwood to maintain a fire for four hours, burlap bags or plastic buckets, and a canvas tarp. The amount of food needed depends on the number of people and the size of their appetites. Many different foods can be cooked in a clambake; the traditional ones are lobster and soft-shell crabs (live, of course), clams (quahogs and steamers), flounder, corn-on-the-cob, potatoes, carrots, and onions. People on the West Coast can substitute some other large shellfish, such as king crab, for the lobster. What you choose to cook depends on your personal taste. Experienced "clambakers" report that taking up a collection and buying the food in bulk is the cheapest and most efficient way to procure the food. You will also need butter for the lobster, clams, and potatoes; salt; pepper; plates; napkins; tableware; and cold soda, beer, and wine. For dessert, watermelon and toasted marshmallows are traditional.

Procedure

- Select a site on the beach about 20 yards back from the high tide line. You'll find the pit easier to dig if you can find a spot with a hard-packed sand or dirt base, as loose sand tends to cave in as it is dug. Make sure that there are plenty of fist-sized rocks in the immediate area. For 20 to 25 people, a pit 4 feet square by 2 feet deep will do fine. Dig the pit so that the sides are straight and the bottom flat. Make sure to clear any grass or brush away from the pit. Line the bottom of the pit with fist-sized rocks. Avoid stones with flint or quartz, as they will explode, and avoid sandstone, as it crumbles when hot.

• Set and light the fire. Lay the firewood in a log-cabin style with the kindling in the center. Use only seasoned hardwood such as oak, elm, or birch, as the success of the bake depends on the stones being thoroughly heated. Keep the fire burning for at least four hours, adding more wood as necessary.

• Once the fire is started, begin gathering the seaweed. The best seaweed to use is either rockweed (*Fucus* sp.) or knotted wrack (*Ascophyllum* sp.), both of which contain hundreds of small pockets filled with seawater. Gather about four bushels of the seaweed and store it in the burlap bags or buckets. The seaweed must be kept wet, so either store the bags in shallow water (watch the tide) or fill the buckets with sea water.

• Prepare the food for cooking: peel or scrape the carrots and peel the onions, wash the potatoes, filet the flounder if you wish. Divide up the clams, fish, carrots, and onions into small portions and wrap each portion in cheesecloth. The cheesecloth wraps will keep sand out and make food handling easier. Leave the corn unshucked, place the ears in a burlap bag and soak in seawater for an hour before cooking. If you are using freshly dug clams make sure to clean and de-sand them before cooking.

• After the fire has burned for four hours the stones should be ready. Remove any remaining embers and charcoal from the pit (metal fireplace tongs are handy). Save the coals for melting the butter or toasting marshmallows. Bring the seaweed to the pit and place a 6-inch layer on top of the stones. Work quickly so the stones don't cool off. On top of the seaweed, place the food in three layers. First, the potatoes and cheesecloth packets of clams, fish, carrots and onions. Second, the unhusked corn. Third, the live lobsters. Then cover the entire bake with a 2-inch layer of seaweed and place a potato on the top. When the potato is cooked, you'll know that the bake is ready. Last, place a tarp over the pit and secure it down with stones placed around the edges. The food should be cooked in one to two hours.

PART V
Recreation

36
Board Games

In this chapter we provide instructions for five board games played by tribal peoples around the world. The first four games are games of strategy, the fifth is based solely on chance. All are suitable for play by both adults and children.

The playing boards for these games are traditionally made out of wood, with the playing grid either carved or scratched into the surface. Actually, you don't need a fancy, carved wood board to play any of these games. If you want, you can mark the grid out on a piece of paper (standard size 8½ by 11 inch paper is large enough), or scratch it out in the dirt or sand. All of the games require playing pieces, usually small pebbles, but any small object such as marbles, seashells, beads, pennies, bean or pea seeds, corn kernels, or berries will work as well.

Wari

Wari is a popular board game played in many countries of the world under a variety of names. In Africa, where the game is especially popular, it is called *adji* in Dahomey, *warri* in Nigeria, *en dodo* in Kenya, *chisolo* in Zambia, and *tshuba* in Mozambique. In the Middle East, Egyptians and Syrians play a similar game called *mancala*, in Sri Lanka people play *chanka*, in Haiti it's *caille*, in the Philippines *sungka*, and in the Maldive Islands *naranj*. The particular form of the game described here is played by the Ashanti people of Ghana.

Wari requires a rectangular playing board (see Figure 36.1) and 48 playing pieces. The object of the game is to move pieces around the board in such a way that you can capture more pieces from your opponent's side than he or she can take from your side. *Wari* type games like those mentioned above have been played for hundreds of years, with the earliest recorded reference being to the *mancala* game in Arab religious texts dating to the Middle Ages. The game probably originated in the Middle East and spread from there to Africa.

Figure 36.1 Wari

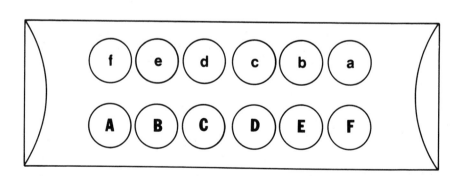

Game Equipment. One playing board and 48 playing pieces. The board is rectangular with 14 cups hollowed out or circles marked on the playing surface. The letters in the cups in Figure 36.1 are not part of the board, we have included them here only for instructional purposes. The cups hold the playing pieces, with the two rows of small cups holding the pieces in play and the two larger cups holding the captured pieces. The only requirement for the playing pieces is that they be small enough so that as many as 15 can fit in a small cup at one time.

To Start the Game. The two players sit on opposite sides of the board and place 4 playing pieces in each of the 6 cups on their side. A coin toss or some other chance procedure decides who goes first.

Object. The object of the game is to capture pieces from your opponent's side of the board while preventing him from capturing pieces from your side. The game ends when all 48 pieces have been removed from the 12 small cups. The person who has captured the most pieces is the winner.

Moving Pieces. Players move pieces from their side around the board in alternating turns. The pieces are moved by a player taking all the pieces from one cup and dealing them around the board counterclockwise, placing one piece in each consecutive small cup until all those pieces are dealt. Pieces can be dealt from only one cup on each turn. The player who is moving the pieces is called the dealer.

At the start of the game the alignment of the pieces is $\frac{444444}{444444}$. As an example of play, let's assume that Player 1 (see Figure 36.1) goes first and deals the 4 pieces from Cup E. At the completion of his deal the alignment will be $\frac{444555}{444405}$. If, on his deal, Player 2 deals the 5 pieces from Cup C, the alignment becomes $\frac{555055}{554405}$. At the end of each player's deal, the cup from which the deal was made must be empty. In cases where enough pieces are dealt so that they are distributed around the board back to the dealing cup, that cup is passed over and the deal continues around the board.

Capturing Pieces. Pieces are captured from the opponent's side of the board when the last piece of a deal falls into an opponent's cup leaving either two or three pieces in that cup. The dealer captures all the pieces in that cup and the pieces in any consecutive cups to the dealer's right of that cup which also contain two or three pieces. For example, Player 1 begins his turn facing the alignment $\frac{403123}{340042}$ and deals the four pieces from Cup E. When the deal is completed the alignment is $\frac{403234}{340003}$, with the last piece dealt going into Cup C. Player 1 then captures the two pieces in Cup C and the three pieces in Cup B. At the end of Player 1's turn the alignment will be $\frac{403004}{340003}$. Captured pieces are stored in the large cup to each player's right. Remember that captures can be made only upon the completion of a deal and only from the opponent's side of the board.

Sometimes near the end of a game one side of the board will have no pieces left. When this happens, the player with pieces left must, on his turn, deal from a cup that will distribute pieces to the other side of the board. For example, facing the alignment $\frac{000000}{013213}$, Player 1 must deal the three pieces from Cup F. If such a deal is not possible, the game ends and the player takes all the pieces left on his side and adds them to his captures.

Main Machan

Main machan is a game similar to checkers played by the Iban people of east Malaysia. The origin of the game is uncertain, although it probably originated in India and was brought to Malaysia centuries ago by traders. The game requires a lined playing board (see Figure 36.2) and 30 playing pieces. It is a game for two people, with the object of the game being somewhat different for each participant. The object for one player is to jump and take her opponent's pieces off the board. The object for the other player is to hem in her opponent's pieces so that they can't be moved around the board. One player starts with 2 pieces, the other with 28 pieces.

Game Equipment. One playing board and 30 pieces. Two pieces should be rectangular or circular pieces of wood, the other 28 should be rectangular and smaller than the first 2. The 2 large pieces are called *endo* (women), the 28 smaller pieces *anak* (children).

To Start the Game. The two players sit on opposite sides of the board. Player 1, who controls the 28 *anak*, places 9 of them on the intersection points in the middle of the board (see Figure 36.2). Player 2, who controls the 2 *endo*, then removes any 3 of the *anak* from the board and places the 2 *endo* on 2 vacant intersection points anywhere on the board.

Object. The object for Player 1 is to hem in Player 2's *endo* so they can neither move nor jump any of her *anak*. The object for Player 2 is to avoid being hemmed in and to position her *endo* so that they jump over and remove from play as many *anak* as possible.

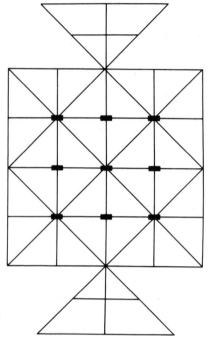

Figure 36.2 Main Machen *(showing initial alignment of* anak*)*

Moving Pieces. Players alternate turns. Player 1 makes the first move after Player 2 places her two *endo* on the board. Player 1's moves consist of placing one *anak* per turn on vacant intersection points anywhere on the board. When all 28 *anak* have been played, those still on the board can be moved around the board like the *endo*, although they cannot remove *endo* from the board. Player 2 moves the *endo* around the board with one move allowed per turn. The *endo* are moved by either moving them to vacant adjacent intersection points or jumping over any odd number of adjacent *anak* and removing them from the board.

End of the Game. Player 1, the player who controls the *anak*, wins when she hems in both *endo* so that they can neither move nor jump any of her *anak*. Player 2, who controls the *endo*, wins when she takes so many *anak* pieces from the board that there are clearly not enough of them left with which to hem in the *endo*.

Shah

Shah is a game of strategy played by the Somali people of Somalia. It is related to and perhaps is a forerunner of the old English game Nine Men's Morris. The game requires a board consisting of lines and circles and 24 playing pieces divided up between 2 players. The game progresses through two distinct stages, with the ultimate goal being the removal of enough of the opponent's pieces so that his position becomes hopeless.

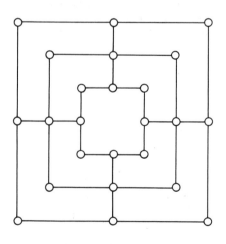

Figure 36.3 Shah

Game Equipment. One board (see Figure 36.3) and 24 playing pieces. The board is a grid of 3 squares aligned inside one another with bisecting lines running from the outer to the inner square on each side. Small cups should be hollowed out or small circles drawn at each of the 24 intersection points. Twelve of the pieces should be one color or shape, the other 12 a clearly different color or shape.

To Start the Game. A coin toss or other chance procedure determines who goes first. The first move and all moves in the first stage of the game consist of placing pieces in vacant circles on the board.

Object. Each of the two stages has its own object. The first stage ends when all 24 pieces have been placed on the board. The object during this stage is to align the pieces so as to form *charri*—3 pieces in a row along any line, as shown in Figure 36.4. If the opponent is able to block any *charri*, the object is then to form an *afarri*—placement of 4 pieces to form a parallelogram, also shown in Figure 36.4. Four *afarri* are possible, 2 on each half of the board.

The second stage begins when all the pieces have been placed on the board. There are two objects in this stage, first, to move the pieces so as to form a *charri* and, especially, to form an *irman*, as shown in Figure 36.5. An *irman* is formed when 5 are aligned so that one piece (piece j in Figure 36.5, for example) can be moved back and forth between two circles to form a *charri* on each turn. Forming a *charri* on each turn is important because it helps you achieve the second object in stage two—removing the opponent's pieces from the board. Each time you form a *charri* you may remove an opponent's piece from the board. Forming an *irman* gives one player a tactical advantage by putting him in a position to remove an opponent's piece on each turn.

Moving Pieces. In stage one, players alternate placing pieces on vacant circles until all pieces are placed. If only one player forms a *charri* in stage one, that player begins stage two by removing one of the opponent's pieces from the board. If neither player has a *charri* at the start of stage two, each player takes one opponent's piece off the board. The player who made the last placement in stage one goes first in stage two. After the start of stage two, pieces are moved around the board in alternating turns with one move per turn. Pieces can only be moved to vacant, adjacent circles along lines. Whenever a *charri* is formed, that player can remove an opponent's piece from the board. If one player's move makes it impossible for his opponent to move, the first player must make an additional move, allowing the opponent to make a move. The first player may not take an opponent's piece if his second move results in a *charri*.

End of the Game. The game ends when one player loses all his pieces or loses enough of them so that his position is hopeless—that is, there is little or no chance that he can remove any opponent's pieces from the board.

The games are played in a set, with five consecutive game victories giving the player a set victory. The method of tallying game victories is unique. When a player wins a game, he places a marker the same color or shape as his playing pieces in the center of the board. As long as he continues to win games, he adds markers to the center pile until he has five, signifying a set victory. But, if he loses a game before winning five in a row, he must remove all his markers from the center and disregard previous victories in the set total. The opponent then places his marker in the center and continues doing so until he wins five in a row or loses before doing so.

Torere

Torere is a simple, quick game played by the Maori people of New Zealand. The playing board (Figure 36.6) represents an octopus, with the eight radials called *kawai*, meaning tentacles of the octopus.

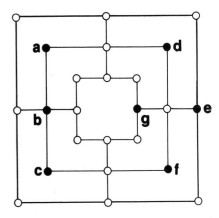

Figure 36.4 Shah (*abc* = charri, *defg* = afarri)

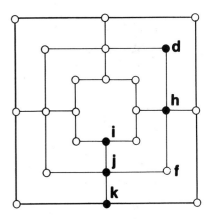

Figure 36.5 Shah (*by moving piece back and forth between j and f you can always form a* charri *dhf or ijk*)

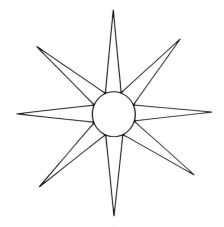

Figure 36.6 Torere

137

Game Equipment. A playing board and 8 playing pieces, 4 of one color or shape and 4 of a different color or shape.

To Start the Game. Each player places 4 pieces on 4 adjacent radials.

Object. The goal is to trap the opponent's pieces so that they can't be moved.

Moving Pieces. Players alternate moves with one move per turn. Pieces can be moved from a radial to the center, from the center to a vacant radial, or from one radial to a vacant adjacent radial. A piece can be moved from a radial to the vacant center only when an adjacent radial is occupied by an opponent's piece.

End of the Game. The game ends when one player is unable to move any of her pieces.

Main Pacheh—The Acheh Game

The *Acheh* game (see Figure 36.7) is one of a number of forms of the *Main Pacheh* game played by the Penang people of Malaya. It is a simplified version of parchesi, based solely on chance rather than on chance and strategy. Because winning is solely a matter of luck, it is a more exciting game for children than for adults. The game can be played by two to four people. The object is to race the pieces around the board and return them to home base faster than your opponents.

Game Equipment. A playing board and 16 playing pieces. Each player uses 4 pieces, different either in color or shape from the opponent's pieces. Seven cowrie shells are used to determine the number of spaces moved on each turn. The center circle on the board is home base. The squares marked with an X are safe squares.

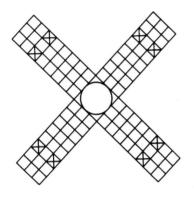

Figure 36.7 Main Pacheh *(The* Acheh *Game)*

To Start the Game. Each player sits at the end of one arm of the board and places her four pieces near the edge of the center circle nearest to her (see Figure 36.8). Highest roll of the cowrie shells determines the order of the moves.

Object. The object is to move all 4 pieces around the board and return them to home base as quickly as possible.

Moving the Pieces. Players move in alternating turns. The number of spaces per move is determined by a roll of seven cowrie shells:

7 shells opening up	=	14 spaces
6 shells opening up	=	30 spaces
5 shells opening up	=	25 spaces
4 shells opening up	=	4 spaces
3 shells opening up	=	3 spaces
2 shells opening up	=	2 spaces
1 shell opening up	=	10 spaces
7 shells opening down	=	7 spaces

Additionally, rolls of 5, 6, or 7 opening up or 7 opening down entitles the player to an extra roll on that turn. After each roll, the player moves any one of her pieces the allotted number of spaces. The roll may not be split between 2 or more pieces. Eighty-four moves are needed to bring one piece all the way around the board and back to home. The pieces must move into home base on an exact count.

If one player lands in a space occupied by another player, she may send the other player's piece back to home base. The 8 squares marked with an X (2 on each arm) are considered safe and can be occupied by more than one player's pieces at the same time. Figure 38.8 shows the course taken by one player's piece around the board.

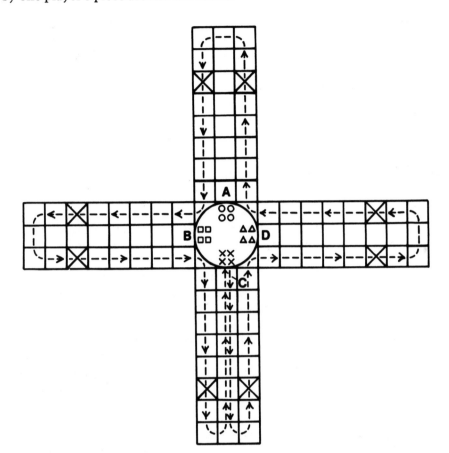

Figure 36.8 Main Pacheh (course around board shown for Player C)

End of the Game. The game ends when one player returns all her pieces to home base.

37
String Figure Games

The string figure game is called many different names by many different peoples. Here are some examples:
English: "Cat's-cradle"
Korean: "Woof-taking"
Japanese: "Woof-pattern string taking"
South Celebes: "Ladder game" (toeka-toeka, from toeka, "steps")
German: "Taking off"
Navaho: "Continuous weaving"
Caroline Islands: "Gagai" (the same word as the name of a pointed stick used for opening coconuts)
Hawaiian: "The net"
Kokoyimidir, Cape Bedford: "Kapan" ("words, letters, writing")

Playing string figure games is a fascinating pastime in which intricate patterns are made by manipulating a piece of string with the fingers. The game is found throughout the world and is played by both tribal and modern peoples. You may recognize it as the familiar "cat's cradle" played by children in the United States.

Some string figures are universal, others are known only to natives of a single locality. The finished figures are almost always named for some phenomenon of nature or some natural or manmade object. In the South Pacific, the string figure game is accompanied by songs and chants, with the figures themselves often representing mythical or religious persons or events. In New Zealand, for example, the game is known as *Maui*, the name of the first human being in the world who supposedly left the New Zealanders the string figure game to amuse themselves with. The Eskimo think that the string figures possess a powerful magical force and must be made only with great care.

In this chapter, we introduce you to four string figures made by tribal peoples, all of which put our humble "cat's cradle" to shame because of their complexity. The instructions and illustrations for these figures are taken, with only a few revisions, from Caroline Furness Jayne's excellent book, *String Figures and How to Make Them*. We have revised them only to make them easier to follow. Jayne spent a lifetime collecting string figures from tribal peoples. Her instructions are accurate and easy to follow because she wrote them out as she watched the figures being made. A few of these figures are difficult and require great skill and dexterity. No special tools are needed; all you need is a loop of string and your fingers to keep yourself and your children amused for hours.

Basics

To make string figures, you will need a piece of string about 6 feet long with the ends tied together to form a loop about 3 feet long. Some Native Americans used a leather thong for the game, and on certain islands in the Pacific a finely plaited cord of coconut fiber or human hair serves as the string. A woven cord is better than a twisted one as it will not kink as easily, but a woven cord cannot be spliced, so the ends must either be knotted with a square knot or laid together and wrapped with thread.

Since the string figure game involves complex movements of all the fingers on both hands, in order to follow the instructions here you must keep a few basic terms in mind: The *usual position* of the hands is with the palms facing each other and the fingers pointing up. In the instructions, we call the fingers of the hand the thumb, index, middle finger, ring finger, and little finger. When we refer to the left and right, we mean your left and right hands or fingers as you see them when they are held in the usual position. As you follow the instructions below, you will find that loops of string run around your fingers. The loops will be named from the fingers on which they are placed as you look at your own hands, for example, "right index loop," "left ring finger loop," etc. The strings of the finger loops which leave the side nearest you are the *near* strings, and those which leave the opposite sides are called the *far* strings. If a finger has two loops around it, they will be called the *upper* and *lower* loops. A string across the palm is called the *palm string*. If you learn these few terms, you should have no trouble following the instructions.

The illustrations in this chapter show the various steps in making string figures as they are seen by the person making the figure. All but the first one can be made by a single person, but it will be helpful to have someone around to turn the pages of this book for you.

The Opening

The first three figures given here all use the same opening or first step. It is best to learn it before attempting any of the figures.

● First, put your little fingers into the loop and separate your hands, holding them in the usual position. Turn your palms away from you and put each thumb into the little finger loop from below. Return your hands to the usual position (Figure 37.1).

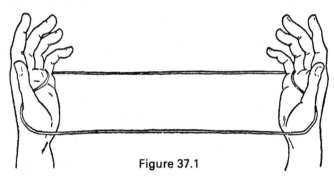

Figure 37.1

● Bring your hands together and put your right index finger under the string which crosses your left palm (Figure 37.2). Draw the loop onto the back of your right index finger and return your hands to the usual position.

● Bring your hands together again and put your left index finger under the part of the string of the right palm that is between the strings on the right index (Figure 37.3). Draw the loop onto the back of your left index and return your hands to the usual position (Figure 37.4). That's all there is to it.

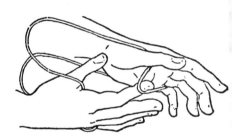

Figure 37.2

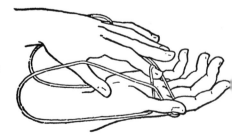

Figure 37.3

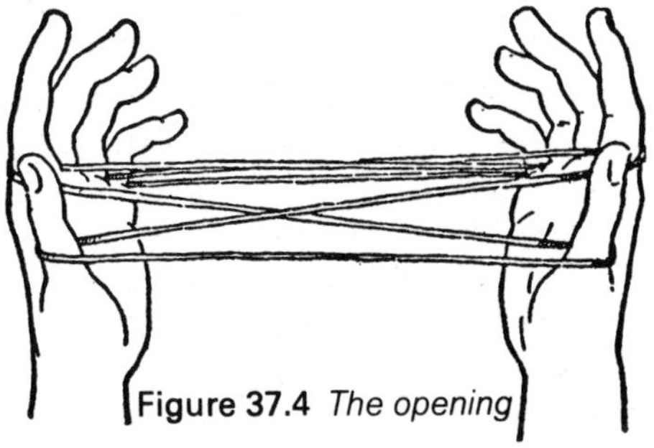

Figure 37.4 *The opening*

The Palm Tree

We will begin with a simple but attractive figure made by the natives of the Torres Straits, located in the Pacific Ocean off the island of New Guinea. Begin with the standard opening. Have a second person catch the middle of the thumb string and draw it away from you over all the other strings, as shown in Figure 37.5.

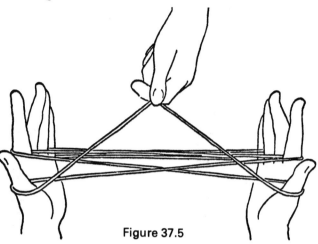

Figure 37.5

- Exchange the loops on your little fingers, passing the right loop over the left loop. Exchange the loops on your index fingers, passing the right loop over the left loop. Draw your hands toward you to pull tight the loop held by the second person, and work the strings to form the crown of the palm tree, shown in Figure 37.6.

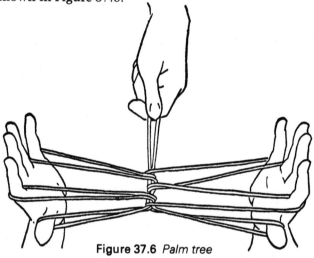

Figure 37.6 *Palm tree*

Circles and Triangles

This next figure is a little more difficult, although it can be done by a person working alone. It comes from Ponape in the Caroline Islands of the South Pacific.

- Begin with the standard opening. Pass each thumb away from you over the far thumb string and the index loop, and pick up from below on the back of the thumb both strings of the little finger loop (Figure 37.7, left hand). Return the thumb to its position (Figure 37.7, right hand).

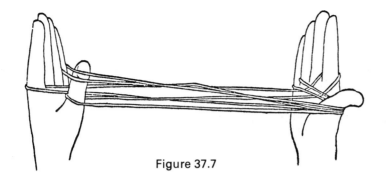

Figure 37.7

● Bend each index finger well down into the original thumb loop, the strings of which pass toward the center of the figure, and move the index away from you by turning the palm away from you as shown in Figure 37.8. Then straighten the index, which then takes upon its back both

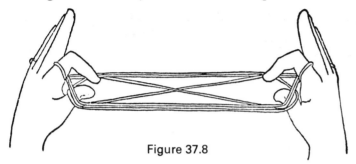

Figure 37.8

strings from the index loop and also the far thumb string (Figure 37.9). Slip your thumbs from their loops and turn your hands so that the palms face

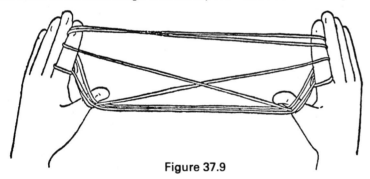

Figure 37.9

each other (Figure 37.10). You now have a loop on each little finger with its strings passing across the palm to the index. On each index there are three near strings; an upper far string passing from side to side, and two strings which may be called the lower far index strings; together they come through a tight loop around the base of the index.

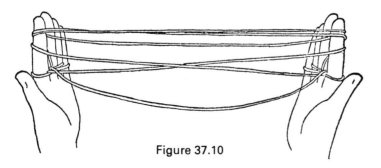

Figure 37.10

• Pass each of your thumbs away from you over these two far index strings and under all the other strings, and, with the tip of your middle finger, press down the upper straight far index string until it is over the back of the thumb. Then catch it on the thumb and bring it back toward you as you return the thumb to its position (Figure 37.11).

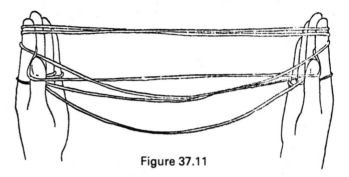

Figure 37.11

• Turn the index down and away from you and let the upper three near index strings slip over its tip. This leaves one loop on the index. Separate your hands. There is now a loop on each thumb, each index, and each little finger, as shown in Figure 37.12. Transfer the thumb loops to the index

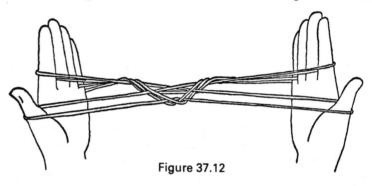

Figure 37.12

fingers by putting each index from below into the thumb loop, withdrawing the thumb, and returning the index to its position (Figure 37.13).

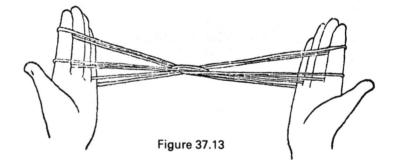

Figure 37.13

• Put each thumb from below into the lower index loop, and, with the back of the middle finger, press down the upper far index until it is over the back of the thumb, when you catch it on the thumb and draw it toward you (Figure 37.14, left hand) as you return the thumb to its position (Figure 37.14, right hand). Withdraw your index fingers from their loops, turn your hands with the fingers pointing away, and extend the figure loosely (Figure 37.15). If you draw the strings too tightly, you will not be able to see the figure, so be careful.

144

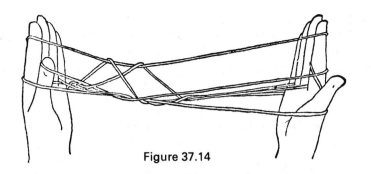

Figure 37.14

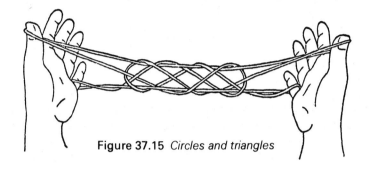

Figure 37.15 *Circles and triangles*

Rabbit

The Klamath Indians in Oregon make a string figure that portrays a rabbit's head quite accurately. It requires about the same level of skill as the preceding figure.

• Begin with the standard opening. Bend each middle finger down toward you into the thumb loop and bend each index down toward you on the near side of the near thumb string (Figure 37.16, left hand). Then, holding this string tightly between those two fingers, straighten the fingers and turn the palms away from you to put the string around the tip of your index (Figure 37.16, right hand). Release the loops from your thumbs.

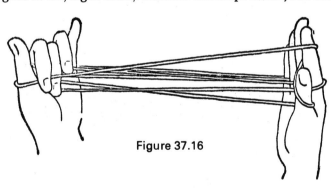

Figure 37.16

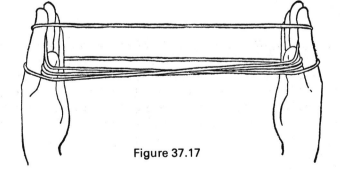

Figure 37.17

145

• Pass each thumb from below into the little finger loop and draw toward you, on the back of the thumb, the near little finger string, the upper far index string, and both strings of the lower index loop (Figure 37.17).

• Pass each thumb up and away from you over the near index string and pull this string down on the ball of your thumb, letting the other strings slip off the thumb (Figure 37.18). Turn your palms away from you and, still holding down the string with your thumbs, pass each thumb away from

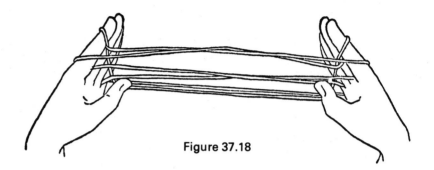

Figure 37.18

you under the far little finger string and draw this string toward you on the back of the thumb. The string that was held down by the thumb will be released by this movement (Figure 37.19).

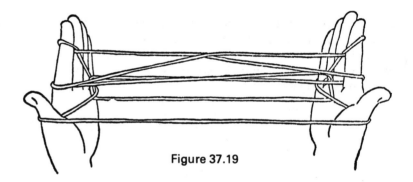

Figure 37.19

• Insert each thumb from below (close to the index) into the small ring-like upper index loop (Figure 37.20, left hand) and draw the upper near index string, on the back of the thumb, down through the thumb loop. This latter loop will slip off your thumb during the movement (Figure 37.20, right hand). Release the upper loop from each index finger (Figure 37.21).

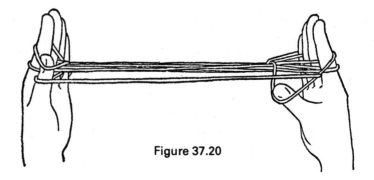

Figure 37.20

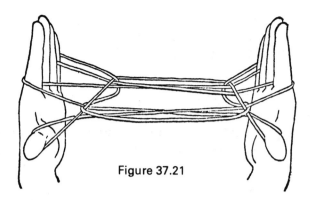

Figure 37.21

- Pass the index, middle and ring fingers of each hand toward you and down into the thumb loop (Figure 37.22). Then gently release the loops from your little fingers and put each little finger toward you in the loop

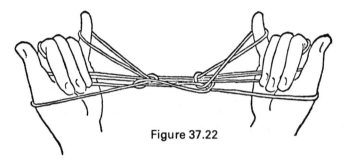

Figure 37.22

with the ring, middle, and index fingers. Hold all four fingers of each hand down on the palm and turn your hands with the palms facing each other. Lift up the near thumb string on the tip of each index and withdraw your thumb. You may have to manipulate the strings a little to make the "rabbit" appear (Figure 37.23).

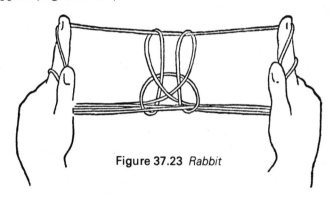

Figure 37.23 *Rabbit*

Breastbone and Ribs

This figure is one of the most complex ever recorded. It was obtained from an Eskimo leader named Chief Zaroff. The native Eskimo term for this string figure is *grut*, meaning "breastbone and ribs." In this figure, the standard opening is not used.

- Lace the string between the fingers of each hand so that it passes behind the thumb, the middle finger and the little finger and across the palmar surface of the index finger and the ring finger. The near thumb string and the far little finger string pass straight from hand to hand (Figure 37.24).

147

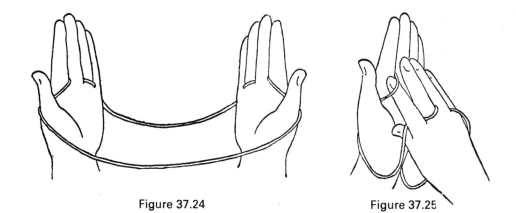

Figure 37.24

Figure 37.25

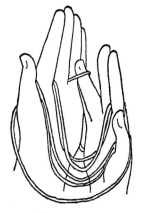

Figure 37.26

● With the right index take up, from below, the string on the palmar surface of the left index (Figure 37.25) and separate your hands. With the left index take up from below, between the strings of the right index loop, the string on the palmar surface of the right index and separate your hands.

● With the right ring finger take up, from below, the string on the palmar surface of the left ring finger (Figure 37.26) and separate your hands.

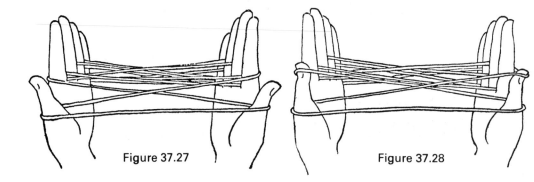

Figure 37.27

Figure 37.28

With your left ring finger take up, from below, between the strings of the right ring finger loop, the string on the palmar surface of the right ring finger and separate your hands. There should now be a loop on every finger of each hand, as shown in Figure 37.27.

● Put each thumb from below into the index loop and separate the thumb from the index (Figure 37.28). With your teeth draw the original thumb loop of each hand in turn up over the loop passing around both thumb and index and, slipping it entirely off the thumb, let it drop on the palmar side (Figure 37.29).

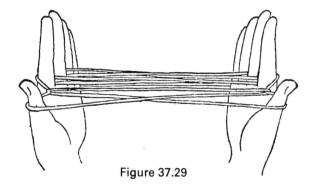

Figure 37.29

• Pass each thumb away from you over the far thumb string and both strings of the index loop and take up from below, on the back of the thumb, the near middle finger string and return the thumb to its position (Figure 37.30). With your teeth, draw the lower thumb loop, each hand in turn, up over the loop just taken on the thumb and, slipping it off the thumb, drop it on the palmar side (Figure 37.31).

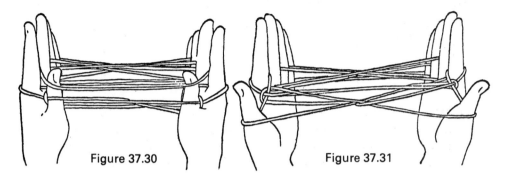

Figure 37.30   Figure 37.31

• Pass each thumb away from you over the thumb, index, and middle finger loops and take up from below on the back of the thumb the near ring finger string and return the thumb to its position (Figure 37.32). With your teeth, draw the lower thumb loop of each hand in turn up over the upper thumb loop (the loop you have just taken on the thumb) and, slipping it off the thumb, drop it on the palmar side (Figure 37.33).

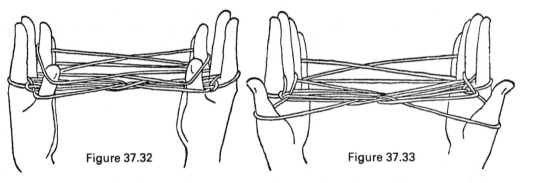

Figure 37.32   Figure 37.33

• Pass each thumb away from you over the thumb, index, middle finger, and ring finger loops and take up from below, on the back of the thumb, the near little finger string and return the thumb to its position (Figure 37.34). With your teeth, draw the lower thumb loop of each hand in turn up over the upper thumb loop (the loop you have just taken on the thumb) and, slipping it off the thumb, drop it on the palmar side (Figure 37.35).

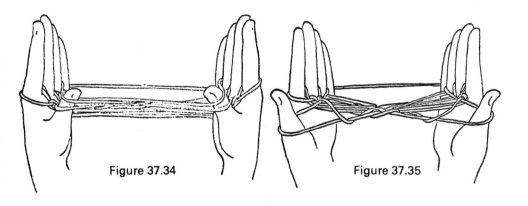

Figure 37.34   Figure 37.35

• Pass each thumb away from you over all the strings except the far little finger string and pick up this far little finger string on the back of the thumb and return the thumb to its position (Figure 37.36). With your teeth, draw the lower thumb loop of each hand in turn up over the upper thumb loop (the loop you have just taken on the thumb) and, slipping it off the thumb, drop it on the palmar side (Figure 37.37).

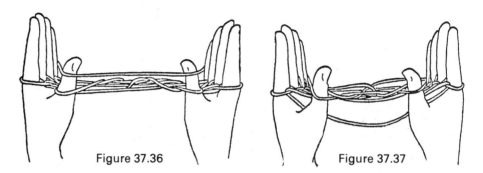

Figure 37.36   Figure 37.37

• Transfer the thumb loops to your little fingers by bending each little finger toward you and putting it from above down into the thumb loop. Then, picking up on the back of the little finger the near thumb string (Figure 37.38, right hand), return the little finger to its position as you withdraw the thumb (Figure 37.38, left hand).

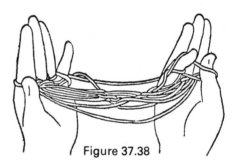

Figure 37.38

• Pick up with your teeth the middle of the nearest straight string which runs from hand to hand (it is usually the one hanging down and is the lower of the two strings which, on each side, form a loop around the near index string). Draw this string toward you and, still keeping the loop between your teeth, extend the figure by drawing your hands away from you, with their palms toward each other and the fingers directed away from you. You may find it more convenient, once you extend the figure, to release the loop held by your teeth and hold it instead between the tips of your extended thumbs (Figure 37.39).

After you have made this figure, you can take the string off your hands without tangling it by releasing the loop held by your teeth or thumbs, removing the upper loop from each little finger, and pulling your hands sharply apart. This will leave a simple loop which you can drop off your fingers.

As you have no doubt figured out by now, some string figures are incredibly complicated and very difficult to describe. It is mind boggling to think that small children in many tribal cultures can remember and demonstrate 50 different string figures without the slightest hesitation or the aid of written instructions.

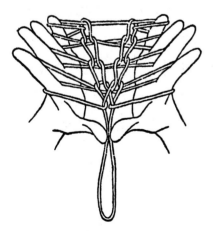

Figure 37.39 *Breast bone and ribs*

38
Tricks and Puzzles

Brainteasing puzzles and magic tricks are favorite pastimes of children all over the world. Recently, with the invention of games like Rubik's Cube, scientists and educators are discovering that puzzles can have educational value as well, with some even requiring a knowledge of algebra and geometry to solve. Since we tend to associate sophisticated tricks and puzzles with our own modern culture, we don't expect to find them among so-called backward or primitive peoples. Surprisingly, though, the Makusi, Wapishana, and Taruma Indians of the Guiana rainforest in South America have invented a great number of tricks and puzzles, a few of which we describe and explain here.

Most of the puzzles described below have a practical purpose for these South American Indians, who believe that their jungle home is inhabited by grotesque, awesome bush spirits who sit waiting to attack innocent human beings out hunting or gathering food in the forest. The puzzles are used as a diversion by the Indian, who always keeps one with him while he is in the forest. He believes that the puzzle will protect him from the spirits, because a spirit will always try to solve the puzzle before attacking the Indian, leaving the Indian enough time to pass through the forest unharmed.

The Indians make their puzzles from natural materials such as wood, leaves, and plant fibers. You can use manufactured materials such as string and cardboard.

The Bowstring Puzzle

The object of the bowstring puzzle shown in Figure 38.1 is to remove the figure from the bowstring without untying or cutting it from the bow. The solution is actually quite simple. As shown in Figure 38.2, just bend the bow so the string loosens, pull the string through the shoulder, and slip out the figure. The Guiana Indians make their figure and shoulder from a green plantain leaf, although you can substitute light cardboard such as that used for file folders. If you don't have a bow handy, cut two figures and two shoulders out of the cardboard and connect them as shown in Figure 38.3.

Figure 38.1 *Bowstring puzzle*

Figure 38.2 *Solution to bowstring puzzle*

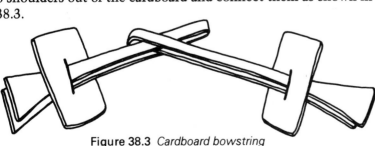

Figure 38.3 *Cardboard bowstring puzzle*

Figure 38.4 *Stringed sticks puzzle*

Figure 38.5 *Solution to stringed sticks puzzle*

Stringed Sticks Puzzle

The stringed sticks puzzle shown in Figure 38.4 is somewhat harder to solve than the bowstring puzzle. The object is to remove the string that has been placed through the three holes in each of the two sticks. To accomplish this, pull the loop of string out from the middle hole of each stick and insert it through the top hole of each stick. Then open the loop up and pass it over the entire other stick and the intervening string and pull it out again through the top hole. The string can now be removed from the two sticks (see Figure 38.5).

This puzzle can be constructed easily with a length of cord and two pieces of wood or leather. Knot or splice the two ends of the cord together and string them on the sticks by reversing the steps given for solving the puzzle. Be sure to cut the holes in the sticks large enough so that the loop of string will pass through when doubled up.

Locked Leaf Strips Puzzle

This is the favorite puzzle of the Wapishana Indians for fooling the bush spirit, as it is extremely difficult to solve. The Indian will be long gone from the forest before the spirit even begins to figure it out. To make the puzzle you will need either a large plantain leaf or light cardboard and a pair of scissors. The only tricky part is to make sure that the slits you cut in the two strips are all the same length and the same distance apart from one another.

To make the puzzle, take two rectangular strips of leaf or cardboard and cut four lengthwise slits in one and five slits in the other (Figure 38.6a). Then lock the two strips together by placing one on top of the other and inserting the cut strips of one into the slits of the other in sequence (Figure 38.6b). This is accomplished easily if you work the strips with the index finger of one hand. When the strips and slits are in place, insert two ends of the strip into the opening made by the finger and pull them through (Figure 38.6c), and then arrange the strips in their final position (Figure 38.6d).

To solve the puzzle—to unlock the two strips—simply reverse the procedure used to put them together.

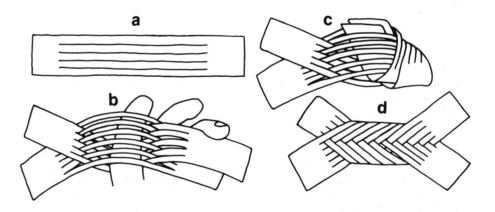

Figure 38.6 *Locked leaf strips puzzle*

In the Wapishana hanging trick you make a loop of string appear to pass through your neck. To perform the trick you will need an 8-foot length of string with the ends tied together to form a loop.

• Hang the loop of string around your neck (Figure 38.7a), then make a second loop around your neck (Figure 38.7b). Cross the left string over the right string in front of you to form upper and lower loops (Figure 38.7c). Insert your right and left thumbs and index fingers into these two loops and hold them in the position shown in Figure 38.7d.

• Raise your hands and drop the lower loop over your head. As you do so, release the strings which form the upper loop and pull down on those forming the lower loop (Figure 38.7e). If all of this is done quickly, the loop of string will appear to pass through your neck.

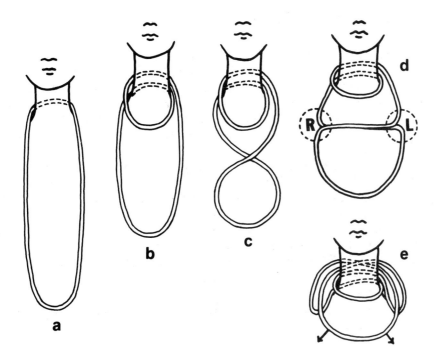

Figure 38.7 *Hanging trick*

Cutting the Fingers

This trick is similar to the hanging trick, except that a string stretched across your palm appears to pass completely through your fingers. For this trick you will need a 6-foot length of string with the ends tied together to form a loop.

• Loop the string around the fingers of your left hand and bring it up from behind over your hand so that strings passes between your index and middle finger and your ring and little finger, forming a loop in the front (Figure 38.8a). Pass the loop around the back of your thumb (Figure 38.8b). Bring the loop in front of your palm, twist it, and loop the end over your little finger (Figure 38.8c).

• Take the upper string from between your ring finger and little finger, twist it, and loop it over your index finger (Figure 38.8d). Insert your right index finger from below into the two loops on your left thumb, take them off the thumb, and let them hang in front of your left palm (Figure 38.8e). Lift the two loops up over the top palm string, pass them through the fingers, and let them fall on the back of your hand (Figure 38.8f). Pull down on the lower palm string quickly, and the upper palm string will appear to pass completely through your fingers.

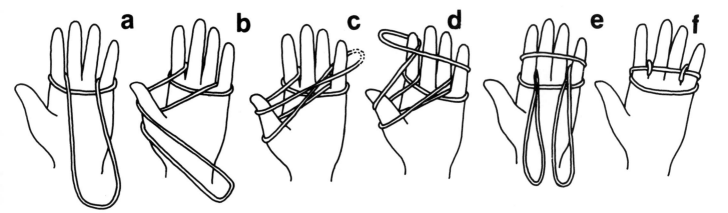

Figure 38.8 *Cutting the fingers trick*

The Sand Flea

The sand flea is the poor man's version of the Mexican jumping bean. The Makusi and other tribes of British Guiana make them from strips of green leaves or green wood shavings. They use the sand flea as a toy to amuse their children. To make a sand flea cut three strips of thick leaf or wood shavings about 8 inches long and connect them together by folding as shown in Figure 38.9. When you press sharply down in the center of the flea where the strips cross one another, the flea will appear to jump.

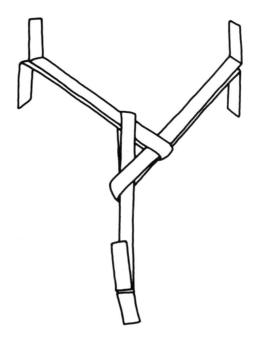

Figure 38.9 *Sand flea*

39
Dental Pictography

Dental pictography is the art of biting impressions into folded pieces of birch bark to produce life forms, geometric patterns, or representative designs. These designs or patterns are sometimes called transparencies because they are especially distinct when held up to the light. Design biting was a common recreational activity of Algonquian and Athapascan Indian women and girls who often turned out designs while sitting around the campfire in the evening. Today, dental pictographs are produced for the Native American craft trade, selling for as much as $25 for a single five-inch square.

The instructions and designs provided here are for the particular methods used by the Chippewa and Montagnais Indians. Once started, design biting can become an addictive activity, as shown in the following Chippewa story recounted by ethnographer Frances Densmore:

> There was once a man who lived with his parents. At sugar-making time he noticed that they were getting old and the work was hard for them, so he brought home a wife to help them. The family were in the sugar camp and he sent his wife to get some birch bark for making dishes as the other women did. She took an ax and was gone all day. When she came home at night she had a great bundle of bark on her back. This made him glad, for he thought she had been very industrious. She opened her bundle and said, "See what I have been doing all day." Then she showed him quantities of patterns and pictures bitten in birch bark. Her bundle was full of them. She had been biting pictures all day instead of making dishes.
>
> The man was so ashamed that he hung his head and died. He could not bear to have people know that he had brought home such a good-for-nothing wife.

Native Americans used design biting in the past for two purposes. First, it was commonly used and probably originally done as a pure art form to produce geometric figures, life forms, and representations of tipis, flowers, canoes, etc. Second, it was done in more recent times as a method for shaping patterns to be used in beadwork. The pattern was heavily indented in the bark, cut out, fastened to the cloth, and then outlined in beads.

Materials

The only material needed is birch bark peeled from the paper birch (*Betula papyfira*) in early spring. (See Chapter 14 for instructions on peeling birch bark). Use only soft, pliable, thin layers of inner bark. The

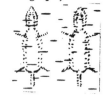

Figure 39.1 *One-fold pattern*

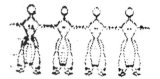

Figure 39.2 *One-fold pattern*

Figure 39.3 *Two-fold pattern*

Figure 39.4 *Two-fold pattern*

Figure 39.5 *Multiple-fold pattern*

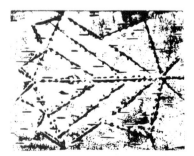

Figure 39.6 *Twelve-fold pattern*

thickness of the bark (the number of layers) depends on the softness of the bark, the pattern you want to indent, the sharpness of your teeth, and the strength of your jaw muscles. The thinner the bark, the more delicate and sharp the indentations will be. In any case, the bark must be soft enough so that it can be folded over two or three times and then unfolded and the fold lines smoothed out. If the bark seems too stiff, soak it in hot water to soften it.

Design biting can also be done on large, thick leaves like those of the straw lily (*Clintonia borealis*), although the results are clearly less rewarding than biting done on birchbark.

The only tools you'll need are your teeth and your fingers. The indentations are usually made with the upper and lower canines on one side of the mouth or with the upper and lower incisors. Obviously, your skill as a dental pictographer will depend greatly on the prominence and sharpness of your teeth. It is reported that the best dental pictographers were elderly women with only one tooth—a single canine—left in their mouths. The bark is rotated between the teeth with your fingers to produce the correct pattern.

Technique

The bark is folded and then bitten to indent the patterns. As described in the following section on patterns, the bark can be folded once, twice, or more; lengthwise, crosswise, or diagonally; or folded, unfolded, and refolded, depending on the complexity of the pattern to be bitten. Learning the biting technique is a matter of practice. It helps at first to practice before a mirror, in order to get a feel for where you should be placing the bark in your mouth. In the end, however, you just have to learn to coordinate the pattern in your head with the movement of your fingers and the bite of your teeth.

Depending on your teeth and the pattern, the bark can either be sharply pricked to produce a small indentation, or ground gently between the teeth to form a longer indentation. In either case, you don't want to bite clear through the bark. You just want to make a clear indentation that is visible to the eye. After the pattern is indented, the bark is unfolded and smoothed flat. If the bark is soft enough, the seams should all but disappear.

Patterns

As shown in Figures 39.1 through 39.6, a variety of patterns can be indented. Among the more popular designs are geometric figures, life forms such as people, animals, trees, and flowers, and representations of everyday objects such as canoes, tipis, or the solar system. There are three basic types of patterns used, which, in order of difficulty, are: one-fold running patterns; two-fold patterns; and multiple-fold or refold patterns.

In running patterns the bark is folded in half and the pattern indented simultaneously on both halves of the bark. The result is matching figures like those shown in Figures 39.1 and 39.2 on either side of the center fold.

In two-fold patterns, the bark is either folded lengthwise and crosswise or lengthwise and diagonally. The result, as shown in Figures 39.3 and 39.4, is matching geometric designs on each half of the bark.

Multiple-fold patterns are far more intricate than either single or two-fold patterns. The pattern shown in Figure 39.5, for example, was formed by first folding the bark crosswise, lengthwise, and diagonally and biting part of the pattern. The bark was then unfolded and refolded and the rest of the pattern bitten. The pattern shown in Figure 39.6 required twelve folds. Obviously, in all patterns, but especially in multiple-fold ones, there is much room for experimentation and creativity.

40
Riddles

A riddle is a puzzling question asked in such a way that the answer is hard to guess. Most often, riddles are told to amuse children or just for fun. In Samoa, riddles are told to boys and girls as part of their education. Sometimes, riddles can take the form of a verbal battle of wits, with the spoils going to the person who can guess the answers. Indo-European mythology is full of stories in which kingdoms rise or fall or fair maidens get rescued or eaten by a dragon depending on the outcome of a riddle. Riddles can also be used to size up a potential enemy: the Fellahin Arabs use riddle-telling to mystify strangers and test their cleverness.

The art of riddling is found in many cultures throughout the world. In this chapter we have included riddles from over 30 different cultures. You'll be able to test your cleverness against a medieval Englishman, an Indian mystic, or an Ila tribesman. Don't be disappointed if you can't guess all the answers—riddles have a way of showing how different people in the world think in entirely different ways. We start with riddles that will seem familiar to you, but we have also included some exotic ones from Africa and Asia that may seem to you to have no logical answer.

As you read through these, you will see that riddles force us to think about similarities between things that at first glance seem quite dissimilar. There are three basic types of riddles. *True riddles* are meant to be guessed and have solutions that always fit the questions asked, no matter how farfetched they may seem. *Conundrums* are riddles whose answers are puns on some word or phrase in the riddle itself. *Puzzles* are short word problems that can require some serious thought to answer. Their solutions often require that you question the obvious and assume nothing.

North Carolina

1. Why is a dirty child like flannel?

2. Why is a dog's tail like the heart of a tree?

3. Old Mother Twitchet had but one eye
    And a very long tail that she let fly
    And every time that she went through a gap
    She left a bit of her tail in a trap.
    Who is she?

4. What is long and slim and slender,
    pokes at where it's tender,
    has no ears, has no nose,
    and tickles where the hair grows?

England (eleventh century)

5. I saw a thing. Its belly was at the bottom mightily swollen. A thane

1. Because they both shrink from washing
2. Because it's farthest from the bark
3. Needle and thread
4. Razor

Riddles

followed after it, a man of strength. And much it suffered when its load flew from its hole. It does not always perish when it has given up its contents to another, but again swells up in strength. Its bloom returns. It creates a son and is its own father. What is it?

6. Wondrously it hangs by a man's thigh,
   under the master's cloak.
   At the front is a hole.
   It is stiff and hard.
   It has a good place when the man
   lifts his own garment over his knee.
   He wants to visit with the head of his hanging piece
   the familiar hole that he often filled before
   with its equal length.
   What is it?

Afghanistan

7. Unless you wet it, make it stiff,
   It will not pass through.

8. Who are those two agreeable friends
   Who are silent while they are together,
   But when they separate from each other,
   O Xaelil, both of them begin to laugh and speak?

Oraon (a tribe of eastern India)

9. Who is the traveller who sees many places in the world, but cannot walk a step?

10. What lives in water but dies at its touch?

11. What bridge connects heaven and earth?

Morocco

12. What is it that crosses the river, sees the water, and gets its feet wet, crosses the river, sees the water, and doesn't get its feet wet, and crosses the river and neither sees the water nor wets its feet?

Samoa

13. Who are the twenty brothers, each with a hat on his head?

14. Who is the man who stands between two ravenous fish?

15. Who is the man who calls out continually all day and night?

16. Who is the man with a white head, always rising to the heavens?

Wolof (a tribe of Senegal)

17. What teaches without speaking?

18. What flies without ever alighting?

19. What has a tail but never moves it?

Scotland

20. Long legs and short thighs
    a little head and no eyes.

21. The man that makes it doesn't need it,
    the man that needs it doesn't see it.

5. *Bellows*
6. *Key, worn hanging from the belt in Anglo-Saxon times*
7. *Needle and thread*
8. *Lips*
9. *Letter*
10. *Salt*
11. *Rainbow*
12. *Pregnant woman with a child on her back*
13. *Fingers and toes (the nails are the hats)*
14. *The tongue, between the teeth*
15. *Surf on the reef*
16. *Smoke rising from a fire*
17. *Book*
18. *Wind*
19. *Spoon*
20. *Pair of tongs*
21. *Coffin*

22. Why is a widow like a turnip?

23. A priest and a friar and a silly old man,
    Sat in the garden where three pair hang,
    They each took one and still two hang,
    How could this be?

24. The beginning of eternity, the end of time and space,
    the beginning of end and the end of every place.
    What is it?

Ireland

25. What's long and thin,
    covered in skin,
    red in parts,
    shoved in tarts?

Fellahin Arab

26. Who rides inside his mother while protecting his father?

27. If one gives three oranges to a boy and his sister, and to a wife and her husband, how can each get a whole orange?

28. Who is the barren person who is pregnant; if she continues to be thirsty she survives with the child that she bears, but if she drinks she dies, and with her dies the child?

Omaha (a tribe of North America)

29. What goes to the water, drinks, and comes back weeping?

Puerto Rico

30. In the middle of the sea I am;
    neither planet nor star,
    nor beautiful moon am I
    Guess what I am;
    I am not of God or of this world
    or of the deep hell;
    In the middle of the sea I am

Yoruba (a tribe of Nigeria)

31. Who is it that drinks maize beer with the king?

32. Who is it that strikes the king?

Indiana

33. What is it that men love more than life,
    Fear more than death or mortal strife;
    That which contented men require,
    The poor possess, the rich require,
    The miser spends, the spendthrift saves,
    And all men carry to their graves?

Mexico

34. They are at your side and you don't see them—what are they?

35. Hairy on top, hairy on the bottom—what is it?

22. *The better half is under ground*
23. *They were all the same person*
24. *Letter "E"*
25. *Rhubarb*
26. *Bullet in a gun*
27. *The sister of the boy is the husband's wife*
28. *Laden boat at sea*
29. *Pail*
30. *Letter "E"*
31. *Fly*
32. *Razor*
33. *Nothing*
34. *Ears*
35. *Eye*

159

Riddles

South Africa

36. Where does a crow fly to when it is seven years old?

37. What walks on its head and what sits on its tail?

Bantu (a tribe of Uganda)

38. Go round this way, and we will meet in the valley.

39. You pass there; I will pass here; let us meet.

40. Pass there; let us meet.

Bagabo (a tribe of the Philippines)

41. A bunch of bananas is the cure for our itch.

42. As that python crawls, it soon bites its own tail.

Argentina

43. What is it? What is it?
    It hits you in the face
    and you don't see it!

44. Many brothers,
    black and white
    sing on top of a long bench.
    What are they?

Tlokwa (a tribe of the transvaal in Botswana)

45. I spread my corn in the open and found it missing the next day.

46. Hlabini's sweet-cane is sometimes sweet and sometimes bitter.

47. Wizards are dancing on the thorn.

Arkansas

48. What is it that gets longer, if you take some off either end?

49. A man had no eyes, but he saw a tree with apples on it; he took no apples off the tree, and left no apples on the tree. How can this be?

50. What can go up a chimney down but can't go down a chimney up?

Panama

51. What swallows but doesn't chew?

52. What chews but doesn't swallow?

53. What animal walks with its legs on the head?

Colombia

54. What is the first thing that a dog makes when he goes out in the sun?

Masai (a tribe of Kenya)

55. What escapes a prairie fire?

56. What is very long, but does not reach up to the belly of a sheep?

57. I have two skins, one to lie on and another to cover myself with. What are they?

36. To its eighth year
37. Bootnail and a dog
38. Skin worn round the waist
39. Girdle
40. Belt
41. Hand
42. Fence
43. Wind
44. Piano keys
45. Stars
46. Sun
47. Rain drops
48. Ditch
49. He had one eye, and there were two apples on the tree; he took one apple and left the other
50. Umbrella
51. Chicken
52. Scissors
53. Louse
54. Shadow
55. A bare spot with no grass
56. Road
57. The ground and the sky

160

58. I saw a strange creature in this land;
    a lifeless one pursuing one who is alive.

59. There are two brothers.
    However much they run,
    They cannot reach each other.

60. An unwoven rug,
    Scattered flowers.
    By God's power
    They are wrought like flowers.

61. Its black is like the grave
    Its tail is like a sword
    It is eager for cheese.

Andhra Pradesh (a state in India)

62. The daughter of a king rolls on poppy seeds
    She has embroidery on her back
    and a lock of golden hair in her stomach.
    Who is she?

Kagaru (a tribe of east central Tanganyika)

63. The small bird fought for the fruits,
    but did not eat any.

64. Grandmother died and left a stench behind.

Ila (a tribe of Zambia)

65. A man travelling with a leopard, a rat, a goat, and a basket of corn
    arrived at a river, and found that the only means of crossing it was a
    very small canoe that would hold only himself and one other thing. He
    put the leopard into the canoe and started off, but as soon as his back
    was turned the rat commenced to eat the corn.
       "This won't do," said he, "I shall have no corn left." He went
    back and took the rat; but the leopard, now left behind, began to eat
    the goat.
       "This won't do," said he, "I shall have no goat left." He headed for
    shore again. But when he came to select his load, he was puzzled.
    should he sacrifice the rat or the leopard? No, they were his children,
    he could not part with them. What, then, did he do?

Chamula (a peasant community of Mexico)

66. My comrade is face-up, my comrade is face-down.
    What is it?

Riyadh Arab (a Libyan Bedouin tribe)

67. A thing.
    Whenever you take away from it, it gets bigger.
    Whenever you add to it, it gets smaller.

68. The cheapest when present
    The most precious when absent.

69. Its setting is red,
    And when it hurts your mother, she wets it.

58. Gun
59. Wheels of a bicycle or night and day
60. Fish scales
61. Crow
62. Melon
63. Hoe
64. Beer
65. He stayed where he was
66. Roof tile
67. Hole
68. Water
69. Ring

161

41
Mankuntu Drum

Tribal peoples of Africa make and play a wider variety of percussion instruments than people in any other region of the world. Different groups of Africans use cylinder, conical, barrel, waisted, goblet, footed, long, friction, and kettle drums. Many groups use more than one type, often in unison. The most elaborate African drums are the footed drums, which are often carved in the shape of a human figure. The most exotic are the friction drums, which are played by moving a stick up and down through a skin membrane covering the top of a hollow cylinder. The simplest drum is the pit drum, nothing more than a hole in the ground covered with an animal skin. Most African drums are carved from wood, although some have ceramic or metal bodies. Drum making is an important, prestigious, and highly skilled occupation in many African societies, with some drum makers specializing in the manufacture of only one type of drum.

The drum described here is a *mankuntu* drum, a cylindrical drum used by the Tonga people of Zambia. The *mankuntu* drum is used traditionally to provide musical accompaniment to the evening dance in the villages. Because each drum has a unique pitch, two or three *mankuntu* drums are often beaten in unison. The drum can be beaten with sticks, with the hands, or with the fists. Larger drums produce their best sounds when beaten with the fists.

The *mankuntu* drum is a hollow cylinder covered at the top end with a skin membrane, as shown in Figure 41.1. The drum is usually decorated by painting, carving, or burning.

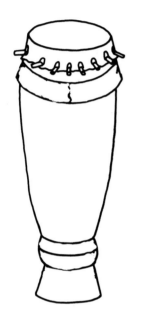

Figure 41.1 *Mankuntu drum*

Materials

First, you need a length of green trunkwood for the cylinder. The length of the log and its diameter can vary depending on the sound you want the drum to make. Larger drums have a lower pitch. The diameter of the log you use should be about the same for the entire length of the log. You can use either hardwood or softwood. Hardwood is less likely to crack, but softwood is easier to work. Tonga drum makers prefer hardwoods such as ebony (*Diospyros mesiliformis*) or wild fig (*Ficus sycamorus*).

You also need 14 to 16 hardwood pegs, each about 2 inches long by ¼ inch in diameter; a piece of fresh animal skin or rawhide, at least 4 inches wider than the diameter of the top of the log; two wooden sticks to serve as drumsticks; a length of cord or a leather thong to attach to the drum as a carrying strap; wood oil or a penetrating stain or a sealant; and beeswax.

For tools, you will need: saw, hatchet, chisel, wood gouge, scrapers, drawknife, knife, drill and bit, hammer, sandpaper. The only specialized tool you'll need is a long-handled chisel to hollow out the inside of the log. Tonga drum makers make a long-handled chisel by attaching a thin chisel blade to the end of a 3- or 4-foot pole. They work the chisel by driving it into the wood with two hands.

Construction

Making the drum involves a combination of hard, tedious chopping and chiseling and delicate carving and smoothing. Hollowing out the log to form a cylinder requires the chopping and chiseling. Shaping the outside requires the careful carving and smoothing. Attaching the skin membrane requires careful measurement and patience.

Hollowing Out the Cylinder. Cut a log of the desired length from the trunk of a standing tree. An entire tree will have to be sacrificed to make one drum, although a large tree might yield enough straight trunkwood to make three or four small drums.

● Move the log to a clear, flat work area and stand it on one end. Begin hollowing out the top end by chopping first with the hatchet and then using the chisel or gouge. As you work down into the log you'll understand why you need a long-handled chisel. The opening for the top end should run about two-thirds of the depth of the log, as shown in Figure 41.2. After the opening is roughed out, scrape and sand it smooth.

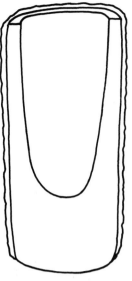

Figure 41.2 *Top opening*

● Turn the log over and hollow out the bottom end to the shape shown in Figure 41.3. This opening should be as narrow as you can comfortably make it. The idea is to have a cylinder with a deeper, wider opening at the top than at the bottom.

Shaping the Sides. Debark the outside of the log and chisel and carve the bottom (the end with the smaller opening) to form the base shown in Figure 41.4. Continue shaping the bottom half of the log to form the base and collar shown in Figure 41.5. The collar should circle the outside of the log at the height where the two inside hollows meet. Measure this point off carefully before shaping the collar.

● Shape the upper half of the log to form the upper collar, also shown in Figure 41.5. Leave two side extensions on the upper collar. The carrying cord will be attached to them later on. Scrape and sand the outside of the cylinder smooth to the shape shown in Figure 41.5. Rub the entire cylinder (inside and out) with wood oil or stain it with a stain-sealant to retard cracking.

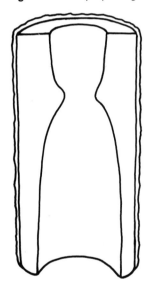

Figure 41.3 *Top and bottom openings (upside down view)*

Attaching the Membrane. Set the cylinder top-side up. Drill or burn 14 to 16 holes around the top of the cylinder, just below the upper rim as shown in Figure 41.6. As the pegs must fit tightly in these holes, make sure that they are slightly smaller than the diameter of the pegs. Drill or burn one hole through each of the two side extensions on the upper collar. Seal the upper and lower rims by singeing them with a hot hatchet blade.

● Cut the membrane to size—at least 4 inches wider than the diameter of the upper rim—and attach. This is a crucial step. The goal is to get the membrane pulled as tight as possible across the top rim, as shown in Figure 41.7. This is accomplished by cutting vertical slits near the edge of the skin and slipping the slits over the pegs. Begin by hammering one peg in place, slit the skin and slip it over the peg. Then hammer a second in place opposite the first one, slit the skin, and slide it over the peg. Hammer a third peg in place, one-quarter turn around the drum from the second peg, slit the skin, and slide it over this peg. Hammer a fourth peg in place, opposite the third one, slit the skin, and slip it over the peg.

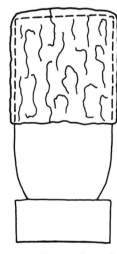

Figure 41.4 *Shape of roughed-out base*

163

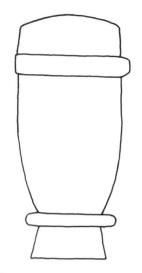

Figure 41.5 *Outside shape*

Figure 41.6 *Peg holes for membrane*

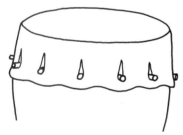

Figure 41.7 *Membrane pegged in place*

Continue placing the pegs, slitting the skin and setting it over the pegs until all the pegs are placed and the skin is tightly secured all around. As you pull the skin in place over each peg, make sure that you pull it as tightly as possible. When the skin is in place, scrape the hair off and leave it to dry.

- The skin can be further tightened if you think it necessary (it often is for larger drums) by lashing around the pegs with a length of cord as shown in Figure 41.8a or by attaching loops of skin or cord as shown in Figure 41.8b. When a skin loosens up, it can be tightened by repegging, or it may have to be replaced.

Figure 41.8a *Continuous lashing*

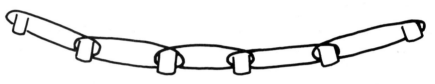

Figure 41.8b *Loop lashing*

- Rub the outside of the drum head with beeswax or oil. The Tonga use oil from the wild fig (*Ficus sycamorus*) or oil from the seeds of the mahogany (*Trichilia roka*) or castor bean (*Ricinus communis*). Thread the carrying cord through the holes in the upper collar extensions and tie off.

Decoration

Geometric patterns like those shown in Figure 41.1 can be burnt, carved, or painted on the drum. The patterns are traditionally added around the upper and lower collars and on the lower base. Red and white are the traditional colors if the drum is painted.

42
Zithers

Zithers are the most popular folk instruments in the world. They have been played by tribal peoples in all regions of the world for thousands of years. A zither is a musical instrument with a string or strings running along the entire length of a sounding board which acts as a resonator.

Zithers can be very simple or quite elaborate. Violins, guitars, and even pianos are examples of modern, sophisticated zithers. There are at least nine major types of zithers found around the world: ground, trough, tube, raft, stick, vinas, long, board, and dulcimers. Ground zithers are the simplest type, being nothing more than a string stretched taut between two posts over a skin- or bark-covered hole. Trough zithers have a string or strings stretched over a hollowed-out length of wood. Tube zithers have strings stretched along the length of a hollow tube such as a piece of sugar cane, rattan, or bamboo. Raft zithers are made by binding several single-string tube zithers side by side to form a broad, flat instrument. Because the tubes often differ from one another in length and diameter, each produces a slightly different sound. Stick zithers look like the bow of a bow and arrow, with a single string stretched across a curved stick. Sometimes a hollow gourd is lashed to the underside of the stick to serve as a resonator. Vinas are elaborate stick zithers used in India. They are often elaborately carved, with a wide body, narrow neck, multiple strings, and gourd or wood resonators.

Long zithers, as their name suggests, have strings stretched along the length of long tubes or arched planks. Bridges are often added at each end to raise the strings above the tube or plank surface. They, too, are often elaborately decorated, with the bridges sometimes made adjustable or tuning pegs added for tuning the strings. Especially popular in Asia, long zithers are called *koto* in Japan, *ch'in* in China, *chakay* in Thailand, and *kachapi* in Java. Board zithers are the European version of Asian long zithers. They have strings stretched across a flat board with tuning pegs at one end. Some board zithers are played with a bow rather than by the more common method of plucking with the fingers or picking with a stick. Dulcimers are popular folk instruments in Europe and North America. In the United States, they are most closely associated with Appalachian Mountains folk culture. Dulcimers have strings stretched across a hollow resonator and tuning pegs and are played by striking the strings with a hammer.

Obviously, no matter where in the world you are, you can find the raw materials needed to make some type of zither. The following instructions are for making two relatively simple bamboo tube zithers used by the Semang people of Indonesia. The Semang use these instruments for both individual amusement and for accompanying dances. The zithers can vary in length from 20 inches to 6 feet and be up to 3 inches in diameter. Both types take only minutes to make, with a sharp knife and an awl the only tools you'll need.

The first zither is the simpler of the two. It is made from a single length of green bamboo. The bamboo tube serves as the resonator. Husk fibers peeled from the outside of the tube serve as the strings.

• To make the zither, first cut a length of bamboo, leaving closed internodes at each end. Pierce one of the internodes with the awl. Using the sharp knife, carefully pry two or three strands of husk fiber loose along the length of the bamboo tube, but leave the fibers attached to the tube at each end. The strands should run the length of the tube, parallel and close to one another. Secure the ends of these strings to the tube by wrapping them with rattan fibers, thread, or thin wire.

• Cut two small blocks of wood to serve as bridges, one at each end of the tube. Gently wedge each bridge between the strings and tube at each end. Set the bridges so that the strings are pulled taut for their entire length. Work with care, making sure not to pull the strings loose at the ends. The zither is now finished.

The second type of Semang zither is a more modern, more sophisticated, sturdier version of the first. As shown in Figure 42.1, it, too, consists of a bamboo tube with strings raised above it by wooden bridges at each end. For this zither, however, the strings (two or three of them) are made from rattan or palm leaf fibers.

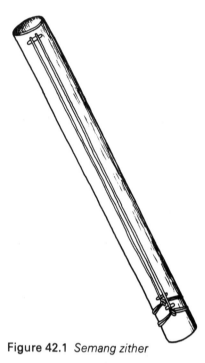

Figure 42.1 *Semang zither*

• Begin by cutting a piece of bamboo tube to the desired length. Cut off the internode at one end and punch a hole through the internode at the other end. As shown in Figure 42.1, punch one small hole for each string near the internode end of the tube.

• Thread the strings into the holes and knot them inside the tubes so that they hold fast. You can also secure the threads to small pieces of wood inside the tube which can be twisted later to tighten the strings as necessary. These wood pieces then serve as primitive tuning pegs.

• At the other end of the tube, wind each string around the tube several times and tie it off with a spiral knot. The strings need to be of different lengths, so that they can be tied off beyond one another.

• Cut small wooden blocks and slide them in place to serve as bridges, as shown in Figure 42.1. The strings at the internode end need only one block for all the strings, while those at the open end need a separate block for each string. The zither is now finished.

You can decorate the zither by carving thin lines or dots around the outside of the tube near the ends and middle. To improve the sound of the zither you can make it with closed internodes at each end and a long slit cut along the length of the tube. If you make it this way, the strings will have to be attached to pegs set in holes drilled in the tube.

Both of these zithers are played either standing or sitting. If you are standing, the zither is held diagonally, with the internode end pointing down. If you are sitting, the zither is laid across one leg. It is played by plucking with the fingers of the right hand or by striking the strings with a thin piece of bamboo.

43
Wine and Beer

People in nearly every tribal culture in the world have discovered at some point that alcoholic beverages can be made by allowing fruits and cereals to ferment. In many cultures this discovery has developed into large-scale wine and beer home industries, with vast quantities produced year round without the aid of elaborate equipment.

We have adapted a number of wine recipes used by English country folk in the early 1700s. We found these recipes in an anonymously written how-to manual published in 1749. For beer fanciers we include recipes for corn beer from the Tarahumara people of northern Mexico and rice beer from the Santal and Gond people of India.

None of these recipes requires the use of any elaborate equipment, although the beers will benefit from brewing in an earthenware or clay pot. You will, of course, need to use the usual wine and beer making equipment: casks, carboys, crocks, or large enamel pots; plastic or glass funnels; a fine-mesh strainer; flannel straining cloth; glass bottles; corks; and stirring and skimming spoons.

One reminder: as with all natural foods and beverages, the taste of the wine and beer will be affected by the time of year you collect the plants, the amount of rainfall during the growing season, the type of soil, and the general condition of the plants. Experimentation and careful study of nature are the only ways to learn to cope with these unpredictable factors. With this in mind, it is a good idea to taste-test your wine and beer at various stages of production to make sure that you're not wasting your time on a bitter, unpalatable beverage. Keep in mind that the beers are brewed for immediate use and should not be stored for future use.

26 Plants Used for Beer and Wine

sugar cane
rice
palm
kava
corn
barley
potato
tea
mulberry
millet
pomegranate
coconut
sweet potato
manioc
banana
mesquite beans
cactus
raspberry
blueberry
mescal
agave
apple
grape
hops
sorghum
plum

Wine Making

Wine results from the fermentation of sugar contained in plant or other matter. It is the action of yeast on sugar that turns the sugar into alcohol. The alcohol content of wine is low because at a certain point in the fermentation process enough alcohol is produced to kill the yeast cells. At this point fermentation stops.

Spiced Mead. Mead is made by fermenting a mix of honey and water. Along with beer and ale, mead is one of the oldest alcoholic beverages consumed in Europe. Its appeal in the past was due to the high sugar content in honey. Consequently, its popularity declined after 1700, when sugar became widely available in Europe.

6 gallons spring water
3 egg whites
10 lbs. unblended, uncooked honey
18 cloves
¼ oz. mace

½ oz. ginger
3 cinnamon sticks
1 sprig rosemary
¾ oz. yeast

167

• Combine the egg whites in the water. Add the honey and boil for one hour, clearing the scum as it rises to the top. Add the spices, then remove from the heat and set aside to cool. When cool add the yeast and cover.

• Set the pot in a warm place and let it work. When it stops working (10 to 24 days), strain, decant, bottle, and cork loosely. Let it stand loosely corked for two months, then cork and seal. Let it stand for six months before using.

Metheglin. Metheglin (also spelled metheglyn) is the Welsh version of mead. It is stronger and spicier than English mead.

16 gallons pure honey (best if collected as it runs from the combs)	¾ oz. cinnamon
	1½ oz. cloves
4 gallons spring water	1¼ oz. mace
1 small egg	1 teaspoon yeast
1½ oz. ginger	

• Combine the honey and water. The mix should be thick enough so that the egg will bob up and down in it but not sink to the bottom. Boil the mixture for one hour. Remove from the heat and let cool, adding coarsely ground spices before it cools. Add the yeast at the same time. Cover and set aside to let it work.

• When it stops working, bottle, cork, and let stand for one month. After the month is up, empty the bottle in a large pot and heat (do not boil) to thicken the wine. Bottle and store in a cool place.

Orange Wine

6 gallons spring water	6 tablespoons yeast
12 lbs. fine sugar	2 quarts Rhine wine
8 eggs	12 lemons
50 Seville oranges	2 lbs. double-refined sugar

• Peel the oranges and juice them, saving the rinds. Juice the lemons, discarding the rinds and seeds but saving the peels. Beat the eggs and combine with the water and fine sugar. Boil for one hour, skimming the scum as it appears on the top. Allow the mixture to cool and then add the orange juice and rinds, the lemon peels, and the yeast. Set aside and let stand for two days.

• Combine the lemon juice, Rhine wine, and double-refined sugar. Mix thoroughly and set aside to stand for ten to twelve hours. Combine the two mixes and let stand for ten to twelve days before bottling and corking.

Milk Punch

1 quart milk	1 quart brandy
2 quarts water	sugar to taste
½ pint lemon juice	

• Combine the milk and water and heat until warm. Do not boil. Add the sugar and lemon juice and stir well. Add the brandy and stir well. Strain through flannel until the liquid is clear. Bottle and use within two weeks.

Shrub. Shrub is an alcoholic beverage made from citrus juice fortified with an alcoholic beverage.

2 quarts brandy	3 pints white wine
5 lemons	1½ lbs. sugar
½ nutmeg	

• Juice the lemons, saving the peels from two of them. Combine the brandy, lemon juice and peels, and nutmeg. Cover or cork and allow the mixture to stand for three days. Add the white wine and sugar. Mix thoroughly and strain through flannel twice. Bottle and serve as a cordial.

Birch Wine. This unusual wine is made from the sap of the birch tree. As the original recipe does not specify the type of birch, we assume that the sap from any birch tree can be used. For this recipe you will need to use a wooden cask.

birch sap	yeast
sugar	1 pint Rhine wine
1 slice toast	

• Collect the sap, boil it, and clear the scum as it rises to the top. Boil for as long as the sap continues to rise. Add 1 lb. of sugar for every gallon of purified sap and boil for ½ hour, clearing any additional scum. Allow the mixture to cool to lukewarm and add the yeast spread on the slice of toast. Let it stand uncovered for five or six days.

• When the mixture has stood long enough, prepare the cask. First, drop a lit, sulfur-tipped match in the cask, cover the cask, and shake it vigorously. Remove the match and dump out the ashes. Then pour the pint of Rhine wine in the cask and slosh it around so that the inside is wet. Pour out the Rhine wine. Fill the cask with the sap mixture, cover, and let sit for six months. Open and, if clear, bottle.

To Recover Wine that Has Turned Sharp. Open the wine bottles and combine the wine in a large pot. Add 1 lb. of oyster shell powder for each 10 gallons of wine. Prepare the powder by first scrubbing the shells clean and then drying them in an oven until they crumble easily. Stir the wine and powder thoroughly. Cover and let stand for two to three days or until the wine is clear. Decant, bottle, and cork.

Lisbon Method of Fining Wine. Fining is the process of removing sediment from a wine after straining. Beat ten egg whites and a handful of salt into a froth. Combine with slightly more than one quart of the wine you want to fine. Add the mix to 20 gallons of the wine to be fined and let it stand for several days, until the wine is clear. Decant and bottle.

Tesguino (Corn Beer)

Tesguino is a sweet-tasting, thick, milky-white beer brewed from corn kernels. The Tarahumara people believe that *tesguino* was given to them by God to help them work and to make them happy. Consequently, whenever a new bottle is opened, they show their appreciation by tossing three small gourdfuls of beer in the four directions of a hanging cross. *Tesguino* is as important to the Tarahumara as wine is to the Italians or French. In other words, *tesguino* is brewed and consumed at all times by all Tarahumarans. It is fed to infants to help prevent illness. It is applied as a salve to superficial cuts and scrapes. It is consumed in great quantities at festivals and celebrations. It is served whenever a guest arrives at the house. It is consumed by men and boys before a hunting trip to bring good luck. When a boy starts brewing his own *tesguino*, it is a sure sign that he has become a man.

The main ingredient in *tesguino* is sprouted corn kernels. Actually, corn is all you need to make a palatable *tesguino*, although other ingredients are often added to enhance the flavor. Brome grass (*Bromus arizonicus*) is the most common additive. It will take from eight to ten days to brew the *tesguino*, depending on the speed of the fermentation process. Since *tesguino* does not keep well, you should brew only as much as can be consumed in eighteen to twenty-four hours after fermentation stops.

The first recipe is a standard *tesguino* recipe followed by the Tarahumarans who live in the hill country where corn and other additives are plentiful. The second recipe is for *patcili*, a type of *tesguino* made from corn stalks. It is considered inferior to pure *tesguino* and is brewed only when the corn crop is poor and the corn must be conserved for food use.

Hill-Country Tesguino

30-60 lbs. corn kernels
1 pint brome grass
1 handful of any of the following seasonings (optional): crushed *kakwara* (*Randia echinocarpa*), ground *foninowa* (*Stevia serrata*) or *tikuwari* (*Datura meteloides*) leaves, crushed lichen (*Usnea subfusca, U. voriolosa*), or moss (*Selaginella cuspidata*).

• If you plan to use brome grass you must collect the stems and seeds in the fall, sun-dry them, and store them in bundles in a dry, ventilated place such as open roof rafters.

• Shell the corn, moisten with water, and store in a clay pot in a warm spot for two or three days. Dig a hole 12 to 18 inches deep in a sunny location and line it with pine needles or grass. Put the moist corn kernels in the hole and cover with grass and flat stones. Leave the kernels in the hole until they sprout. This is a crucial step in *tesguino* making; as the kernels sprout, the enzyme diastase converts the starch into sugar. Add water to keep the kernels moist if necessary. Make sure that the grass and stone covering keeps the rays of the sun off the kernels (kernels that sprout in the sun will be green and bitter).

• When the kernels have sprouted, remove them from the hole and grind them into a thick paste. They can be ground either by hand or with a food mill, as described in the section on tortillas in Chapter 34. Combine the paste with water to cover and boil all day until the liquid turns yellow. It must be yellowish, as pure white *tesguino* is not acceptable. Cool and strain the liquid through a fine-mesh strainer, retaining the sweet-tasting liquid.

• Moisten the brome grass seeds and stalks and pound them into a thick paste. Combine with enough water to cover and sit overnight in a warm spot. Combine the corn and brome grass liquids in a clay pot. Add a handful of any of the optional seasonings at this time. Cover the pot and set aside to ferment for three to four days. When the fermentation stops, the *tesguino* is ready to drink. It is usually poured into bottles and the paste residue discarded.

corn stalks
6 lbs. corn kernels
1 handful *gotoko* root (*Phaseolus metcalfei*) or (*Plumbago scandens*)

• Moisten, sprout, and grind the corn kernels as described in the *tesguino* recipe. Peel the leaves from the corn stalks and pound the stalks between large stones. Squeeze the juice from the stalks. The Tarahumara use an ingenious squeezing net called a *mabihimala* to ring the juice from the stalks into a pot. You can squeeze the juice by hand by ringing the stalks over a large pot. Retain the juice and discard the pulp. Combine the juice with an equal amount of water and strain. Add a handful of the ground root of the *gotoko* to the liquid and boil for two hours.

• Allow the liquid to cool and add the 6 pounds of sprouted corn paste. Cover and set aside to ferment for five days. Bottle when the fermentation stops.

Rice Beer

Rice beer is as common in areas of the world where rice is the main cereal crop as corn beer is in Mexico, proving again that tribal peoples will make maximum use of the natural materials available to them.

The two recipes given here are for rice beer brewed in India. The first recipe is for *handi*, brewed by the Santal people in West Bengal State in western India. The second is for *landa*, brewed by the Gond people in Bastar State in central India.

Handi. *Handi* (also spelled *handia*) is a slightly acidic, sweet-tasting brown beer. Observers report that the aroma is quite noticeable on the breath of consumers. Like *tesguino*, *handi* drinking is preceded by a toast, in this case to the major spirit Maran Buru and to important ancestors, by pouring a little beer on the floor.

2-3 lbs. rice
1 handful *bakhar*
sal (*Shorea robusta*) leaves or other broad leaves such as grape or palm

• Prepare a large earthenware pot for brewing by burning straw inside it on the morning of the day the brewing is to be done. Cool the pot and clean the ashes out before using it.

• Roast the rice, then boil it, then sun-dry it. Grind the rice into a powder and mix in the *bakhar*, a malt made from various tree roots and powdered rice sold at many Indian groceries. Place the rice powder-*bakhar* mix in the pot and fill with cold water. Cover with *sal* leaves and a lid.

Let the liquid ferment for four to five days in the summer or seven to eight days in the winter. Press the fermented liquid through a sieve to remove the pulp. Bottle and drink.

• A second, though weaker, batch of *handi*, called *doja handi*, can be prepared from the pulp by adding hot water to it.

Landa. The Gond people think of *landa* as both a food and a beverage. It is consumed by both children and adults. For a beer, the alcohol content of *landa* is high, averaging 8.6 percent by volume. For the Gond, brewing

In the northern Philippines, wild pigs are sometimes caught by setting out a dish of strong rice wine and malt. The animal becomes drunk and is easily dispatched. Unfortunately, the method does not work very well when more than one or two pigs come around. None of the pigs drink enough to become drunk, and the hunter wastes a quantity of good wine that could have been put to better use.

landa is something of a ceremonial act, with the brewing done by a woman who is a daughter-in-law to the head of the household. The woman is expected to fast on the brewing day.

rice
mandia (*Eleusine coracana*)
siari (elephant creeper, *Bauhinia rahlii*)

• Take a quantity of *mandia* grain equal to the amount of rice to be used, pound it, soak it in water, and store it for two to three days in a covered basket. When the grain sprouts, remove it from the basket and sun-dry for three or four days. Moisten the dry sprouts and grind into a paste.

• Husk, clean, soak, strain, and grind the rice into a flour. Mix the flour with hot water to form a thick paste, then steam the rice paste for 15 minutes.

• Line the bottom of a pot with the *mandia* paste, cover with the rice paste, and add another layer of the *mandia* paste. Fill the pot with cold water, cover with *siari* leaves, and set aside to ferment for five to six days. Bottle and drink.

44
Native American Sports

When we began writing this chapter we thought our problem would be selecting a few Native American outdoor sports from a long list of outdoor sports and games played by Native Americans over the centuries. As it turned out, our problem was just the opposite—finding a few sports suitable for play by contemporary people from a surprisingly short list of Native American outdoor games. The list is short for two reasons. First, Native Americans in both North and South America play only about a dozen basic games that we would consider sports. Although the rules for a particular game might vary from one tribe to another, the basic game is the same. Second, some Native American games differ so much in strategy, technique, and rules from the outdoor games we traditionally play that they would not be much fun. As a rule, Native American outdoor games require large playing areas with loose boundaries; have few rules; call for considerable strength, speed, and endurance on the part of the participants; and require the participants to bet on the outcome. In the past, betting was especially important, with the participants expected to be the heaviest bettors, ensuring that they would then try their hardest. If they did not bet, the spectators would become suspicious and quickly lose interest in the game.

Most Native American games began centuries ago as significant parts of religious ceremonies. Although the ceremony itself disappeared, the game often survived as a popular amusement, with the traditions and customs that connect it with its original purpose still intact. In the widely played hoop and pole game, for example, in which a spear is thrown at a moving ring or netted wheel target, the spear symbolizes the male principle while the hoop symbolizes the female principle. Since the joining of the spear and hoop represent reproduction or fertility, the game was often played as part of fertility rites. The Sioux called it the "elk game," while the Pawnee of the Great Plains called it the "buffalo game" and played it to increase the buffalo herds. The Wasco of the Columbia River in Oregon play it to insure a good salmon run, while the Hopi of the Southwest play it to insure that their soil will be fertile and will yield a rich harvest of corn. In some societies, games occupy a middle ground and are played as both rites and amusements. Many South American tribespeople play games at wakes and funerals, both to send the deceased on his way to the spirit world and to temporarily ease their grief at his passing.

Despite the differences in style and approach, some Native American games still have appeal, especially for large groups congregating in an outdoor area—scouts, Indian guides, school groups, and people attending large social gatherings such as family reunions or corporate barbeques. In reading the instructions that follow keep in mind that few of the games have hard and fast rules. If rules are important to you, make them up as you go along.

Topinagugim Football

The Topinagugim Indians of California played a game that seems a combination of modern rugby, football, and soccer. The game is especially interesting since the rules make for equal competition between teams composed of players of clearly unequal physical strength and speed. The Topinagugim played with teams of men versus women, although teams of older versus younger children work equally well. There are 10 players on each team.

The field is about 600 yards long and up to 600 yards wide and may include obstacles such as trees, ponds, streams, hills, gulleys, etc. to make play more difficult. Goals are two sets of posts set 3 feet apart and 8 feet high at each end of the field. The goal of the game is to drive the ball through the other team's goal. Five goals win the game.

The Topinagugim used a buckskin-covered ball filled with moss or deer hair. You can use any durable, inflatable ball such as a playground ball or soccer ball, although don't expect much to be left of it when the game is over.

The stronger team can advance the ball or take it from the other team only by kicking it with their feet. They cannot touch the ball with their hands. The weaker team can advance the ball or take it from the other team only by using their hands. They can throw the ball or run with it, but cannot kick it.

Play begins with the teams in the alignment shown in Figure 44.1. Five players from each team line up alternately in a line at midfield. The other five players on each team then line up at right angles to the line, with players from one team to the right and players from the other team to the left. A referee starts play by dropping the ball down between the two players in the center of the opening alignment.

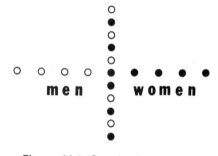

Figure 44.1 *Opening formation for Topinagugim football*

Timbira Log Race

Of the many stories told of the near-superhuman strength and endurance of tribal peoples, none is more amazing than that of the log race, the tribal sport of the Timbira people of the Brazilian Amazon. A race course three or four miles long leading from a clearing in the jungle to the center of a Timbira village is cut out through the jungle. Two huge logs are cut to about 3 feet long and 2 feet in diameter, with each weighing about 150 pounds.

The race is run by two teams of four men each, ranging in age from fifteen to fifty years. The two teams assemble in the clearing in the jungle and three teammates hoist the log on the shoulder of the fourth who is usually their fastest runner. The race starts and the log carrier runs along the course with the log on his shoulder and his teammates running behind him. When he is about to drop from exhaustion, which is usually after about 200 yards, he passes the log to a teammate by twisting his body around and shifting the weight of the log to the teammate's shoulder. He then runs along behind awaiting his next turn as carrier. This running and passing continue as the race goes on until near the end of the race no man is able to run for more than a few yards with the log on his shoulder. The team that reaches the center of the village first wins. There is no prize for the winners, but it is important for every Timbira man to run a log race at least once, since only men who have raced are eligible to marry.

Sometimes after the race is over, the Timbira add to the fun by playing a game of archery with a moving target. An experienced warrior stands about 20 yards from a group of friends and challenges them to shoot at him with their bows and arrows. The warrior gets to keep all arrows that miss him, but must return those that don't!

Seneca Snow Snake

In the game of snow snake, javelins are hurled along ice or snow in a competition to see whose will go the farthest. The game is suitable for play anywhere where there is a snow-covered field. A snow snake is a long, polished rod of wood or bone. It is usually 5 to 10 feet long with a bulging nose which is rounded off to help the snake slide over obstacles (see Figure 44.2).

The snakes are thrown along snow with a frozen crust or in a rut in the snow formed by dragging a log along a straight course for about 500 yards. The Seneca throw the snake with one hand, placing the forefinger at the butt end and steadying the snake with the thumb and other fingers. The throwing technique is something that you just have to learn by trying different motions until you find one that is comfortable and works.

The game begins with the two teams of three players each gathered at the starting line at the base of the rut. They throw their snakes in alternating turns. After their snake stops, they walk down the course and remove it, marking the farthest point it reached. (To speed play along a nonplayer can be stationed down the course as the marker). The team with the longest throw gets one point. An extra point is earned if the two longest throws are by players on the same team. Ten points win the game. Experienced players can throw snakes up to 1,500 feet along a rut.

The Cree Indians of Canada play a somewhat different version of snow snake. They use a shorter, slicker track with barriers along the path. They also use a much shorter (about a foot long) and thicker snake (see Figure 44.3). The goal is to throw the snake so that it passes through the barriers without leaving the track. To win, the snake has to pass through four barriers four times when thrown by the same person or members of the same team. Obviously, it takes much practice and experience to learn just how hard to throw the snake. Losers often lose their snakes to the winners.

The track is formed down the side of a hill by sliding a log for 60 feet or more and then pouring water in the rut to form a slick, icy surface. Snow barriers are then built across the track at 10-foot intervals. Given these shorter dimensions, the Cree version is more suitable for play in urban or suburban areas than is the Seneca version.

Taulipang Jaguar Game

This is a good game for children. In fact, it is the favorite game of Taulipang Indian children in Venezuela. One child plays the jaguar and can move about only by hopping on his hands and one foot—he must hold his other leg up in the air to represent the jaguar's tail (see Figure 44.4). The other children must stay joined together in a line by placing their arms around one another's chest. The jaguar tries to tag the last child in the line. If the last child is tagged, he becomes the jaguar and the old jaguar moves to the head of the line.

Hoop and Pole Games

Hoop and pole games were played in one form or another by every Native American group in North America. The basic game involves

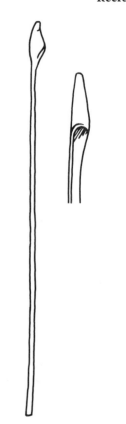

Figure 44.2 *Seneca snow snake*

Figure 44.3 *Cree snow snake*

Figure 44.4 *Jaguar game*

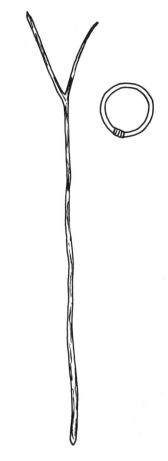

Figure 44.5 *Pomo hoop and pole*

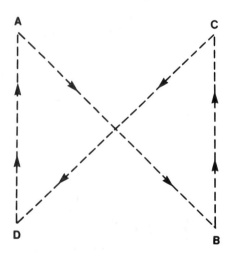

Figure 44.6 *Pomo hoop and pole field*

throwing a spear or dart at a moving hoop or ring, with points counted for the way the spear or dart lies in relation to the hoop target. We describe three versions of the game, all of which can be played with a minimum of equipment.

The *da-ka* game of the Pomo of California is played with a 16-inch green sapling with the ends tied together to form a hoop (a hula hoop or garbage can lid will work) and poles about 9 feet long with forked ends (see Figure 44.5).

Four men each put up a stake, usually money, and take their positions on the playing grid shown in Figure 44.6. The grid is usually laid out on smooth, level ground. Player A rolls the hoop to Player B, who tries to pin it to the ground with the forked end of his pole as the hoop rolls past him. The pole may not leave his hands. Player B then rolls to C, C to D, and D back to A. When a player misses the hoop he is out of the game and loses his stake. The last player left wins all the money. The game is actually far more difficult than it sounds, since the hoop is small and can be rolled rapidly around the course.

The Walapai of Arizona play a more strenuous version of the hoop and pole game called *tu-ta-va*. It is played with two poles, each about 6 feet long, and a hoop 6 inches in diameter. Two contestants compete at a time. Play takes place on a level stretch of ground about 100 feet long by 20 feet wide. A lightly trafficked street is a good course.

The two players stand facing one another at one end of the course. One player holds the hoop and a pole, the other holds just a pole. Both players start to run down the course, and the player with the hoop rolls it down the course ahead of them. The players then hurl or slide their poles down the course with the goal of hitting the hoop and making it fall so that one edge rests on the pole and the other edge rests on the ground, giving the player one point. Ten points win the game. If the pole passes through the hoop, no points are scored. If the hoop falls so that it covers the point of a pole, that player receives four points.

The Eskimo of Hudson Bay play an indoor version of the hoop and pole game called *nugluktug*. A diamond-shaped piece of ivory or wood with a 1-inch hole through the center is suspended from the ceiling of the igloo as a hoop. A heavy weight should be added to the lower end to steady the target (see Figure 44.7). Foot-long wooden darts with sharp points serve as the poles.

The game can be played by up to six people, each of whom has one wooden dart. The object is for a player to jab his dart into the hole in the hoop before any other player does so. This is no easy feat, since the jabs of the other players make the target spin around wildly. Any player can take hold of the target with his free hand, but runs the risk of being stabbed by the darts of the others. If two players hit the hole at the same time, it does not count.

Tarahumara Kickball Race

The favorite sport of the Tarahumara Indians of northern Mexico is a sort of cross-country soccer race. In fact, running is so much a part of Tarahumara life that the name Tarahumara means "foot runners." The course for the race can be from 2 to 12 miles long and is best laid out over flat terrain, although this is rarely possible. If nothing else, having the course cross hills, inclines, rocky areas, rivers, fields, and fences makes it more interesting. The course is marked by hanging bright pieces of cloth from trees and bushes. If the racers are to make more than one lap around the course, a row of stones is set up at the starting line, indicating the number of laps to be run. At the end of each lap, one stone is removed. The Tarahumara use round balls, 3 inches in diameter, carved with a machete from soft pine. If you want to follow tradition, we suggest croquet balls. If you want to protect your feet, we suggest soccer balls.

The race is run between two teams, each with two to twelve members. Each team has one ball which they must kick around the course. The runners on each team pass it ahead to one another by kicking it in the air, which they must do to cross rivers, fences, rock outcroppings, etc. The goal is to bring the ball across the finish line before the other team. The team which can keep the most players in the game (injuries and weariness take their toll) can keep the ball moving along faster and has the best chance of winning.

The race starts with one player from each team at the starting line with a ball between his feet. The other players are staggered in a line down the course, ready to receive the ball and kick it ahead. A runner cannot kick the ball unless he has run the same number of laps as the ball has been kicked around the course. If a runner kicks the other team's ball, he is out of the race. If the ball lodges itself in some difficult place, it can be removed by the runners by means of a stick but it can be moved forward on the course no more than one foot. The strategy is to keep the players spread far enough apart along the course so that the ball can be advanced by passing rather than by individual players dribbling it along the rough course. This strategy takes its toll on the players, as after passing the player must dash ahead to be in position for a pass from a teammate.

The Ring and Pin Game

This is another game played by most Native Americans in North America. The equipment is a series of rings or some other kind of target attached to one end of a leather thong with a pin or needle attached to the other end. The player holds the pin in his hand, and by jerking it quickly, throws the rings up in the air, trying to catch them on the pin as they come down. One person plays against another, with a player keeping control of the ring and pin until he or she misses a point.

The Zuni ring and pin game shown in Figure 44.8 is the basic version. The pin is a 2-foot length of stick, and the ring is green twig bent into a circle and wrapped with blue yarn. Catching the ring on the stick counts one point. Ten points win the game.

The Chippewa ring and pin game is a bit more complicated. The ring and pin consists of seven pieces of bone, each about ½ inch long with holes through their centers, strung on a leather thong about 1 foot long (see Figure 44.9). A piece of fur is attached at one end of the thong to keep the bones from sliding off and a wooden pin is added at the other end. The object is to swing the bones upward and to insert the pin in one of them before they drop. Catching the bone nearest the pin counts seven points, the next pin six points, and so on down to the last pin, which counts one point. The first player to reach fifty points wins.

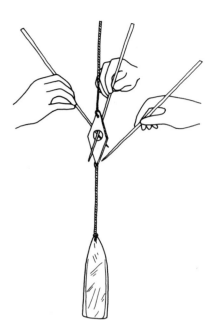

Figure 44.7 *Eskimo hoop and pole game*

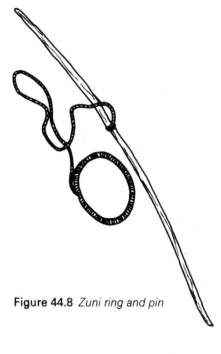

Figure 44.8 *Zuni ring and pin*

Figure 44.9 *Chippewa ring and pin*

The version of the ring and pin game played by the Cree Indians of Saskatchewan is the most complicated of all. The game equipment, shown in Figure 44.10, consists of eight pieces of bone strung on a leather thong with a wooden pin at one end and a diamond-shaped piece of leather with twenty to thirty holes in it at the other end. The game is played to fifty points, with catching one of the bones on the pin counting two points, and sticking the pin through one of the holes in the leather counting ten points. You can make a ring and pin game using the materials listed above, or you can improvise and use a string, a knitting needle for the pin, and any small, circular object with a hole through its center for the ring.

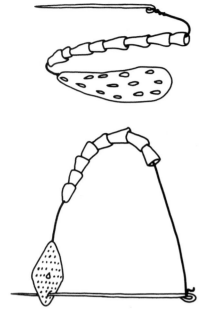

Figure 44.10 *Cree rings and pins*

Figure 44.11 *Tarascan hockey sticks*

Tarascan Hockey

The Tarascan people of the mountains of Mexico play a game of field hockey which dates back to the time of the Aztecs. The game is played by two teams of equal numbers of players of roughly equal ability. Any number of people—men, women, boys, girls—can play. Each player has a wooden stick with a crook in the end like those shown in Figure 44.11. The stick is used to hit a ball about 2 inches in diameter. The Tarascans use a ball made from rags or from a silk-like white substance secreted by a species of green worm found in their region. When playing at night, they sometimes use a piece of burning maguey root, which burns slowly and steadily. When a player strikes the maguey ball, it gives off a shower of sparks. Good substitutes for the traditional equipment are an ice hockey stick and a tennis ball.

The game is played around a street block, making it especially suitable for play at block parties, although you should check with the fire department before using burning maguey root as a ball. The ball can be advanced only by hitting it with the stick. The starting point is always a street intersection. Play starts with one player from each team throwing his ball in the air and knocking it forward to his teammates with his stick. To win the game, one team must take the ball around the block back to the starting point before the other team, as shown in Figure 44.12.

Omaha Shinny

The Omaha game of shinny is quite similar to Tarascan hockey, except that only women are allowed to participate and the game is played on an open field rather than around a city block. The equipment is the same—a crooked stick and a small ball—but the ball can be advanced either by striking it with the stick or kicking it with the feet.

The object of the game is to knock the ball through the other team's goal. The first goal wins the game. Any number of people can play, with some Omaha games having as many as fifty or sixty women on each side. The playing field needs to be large—about 400 yards long without sideline boundaries. Goals of sets of 5-foot poles set in the ground 10 feet apart are set up at each end of the field.

Each player has her own special stick, painted in a unique way to identify its owner. To choose up sides, all of the sticks are thrown in a pile and one woman is blindfolded. She then picks two sticks at a time from the pile and puts them into separate piles, until all the sticks are divided up. The owners of the sticks in the two piles then form the two teams.

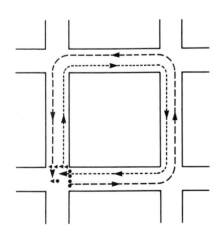

Figure 44.12 *Tarascan hockey course*

45
Head Shrinking

This is not a how-to chapter, nor is it a chapter about psychiatry. It is about how the Jivaro Indians of Ecuador shrink the heads of enemy warriors down to one-quarter of their original size. Since shrunken heads are a tourist item in South and Central America and are on display in many natural history museums, we think it worthwhile to provide the real story of how and why they are made. The Jivaro are the same people who make the blowgun described in Chapter 27. As you may recall, they do not use the blowgun to shoot other human beings. Rather, they use spears and knives to dispatch the enemy warriors whose heads they shrink.

For the Jivaro, head shrinking is more a religious act than an act of military glory. They take and shrink the heads of their enemies to protect themselves from the avenging spirit—the *musiak*—of the enemy. The Jivaro fear that the *musiak* will attempt to avenge a death by killing the murderer or the murderer's son or wife. The *musiak* exists in the corpse, in the immediate vicinity of the corpse, or in the shrunken head—the *tsantsa*—of the victim. If the head shrinking is performed with the correct rituals and ceremonies the *musiak* will enter the head and stay there until it can be safely sent back to its village. If the head is not shrunk, the *musiak* is free to wander about and will eventually take the form of one of three demons: a poisonous snake whose venom will kill the murderous warrior, an anaconda which will tip over the warrior's boat and drown him, or a large tree which will fall on the warrior and crush him. Given these beliefs, it is understandable why the Jivaro take head shrinking so seriously.

After the *tsantsa* is prepared, a series of feasts are conducted to control its power. If the rituals and ceremonies are conducted properly, the *musiak* will remain inside the *tsantsa* and cause no harm. At the conclusion of the final feast the *musiak* is expelled from the *tsantsa* and sent back to its village. As part of the ritual, the Jivaro women chant:

> Now, now, go back to your house where you lived.
> Your wife is there calling you from your house.
> You have come here to make us happy.
> Finally we have finished.
> So return.

The *tsantsa* itself is usually traded or sold by the warrior who took and prepared it to a local trader. One head is worth one rifle in the trade market.

Shrinking the Head

The Jivaro shrink only human heads (usually those of male enemy warriors) and the heads of the tree sloths that inhabit their region. They believe that sloths and humans are the only creatures capable of possessing a *musiak* spirit. Archeological evidence in the form of pottery motifs and stone carvings indicates that head shrinking dates back in Peru prior to the arrival of the Spanish in the 1500s. The Jivaro shrink heads only from people belonging to another tribe. Heads of other Jivaro or heads of blood relatives, even if they belong to another tribe, are not shrunk. Decision making about which warrior's head is to be shrunk is often preceded by an extended discussion of whose relative that warrior is. The warrior who takes the head is considered to be the "lord of the head" and is responsible for its care and shrinking and for hosting the appropriate feasts. In order to avoid any calamities caused by the *musiak*, the warrior usually keeps a low profile until the *musiak* is sent back to its village.

The actual shrinking process takes about twenty hours, although the various steps in the process may be spread out over a period of several days. Since the shrinking is done while that war party returns to its village, when and where the shrinking is actually done depends on the proximity of enemy warriors. Word is sent ahead to the village that a warrior or warriors are returning with *tsantsa* so that preparations for the first feast can be made.

In the past the head was removed from the body with a stone axe and *chonta* palm wood knife, while the flesh was stripped away with a sharpened snail shell and a bamboo knife. Today metal knives are used instead. The head is cut from the corpse as soon after death as possible. A long, lateral incision is made across the back, over the shoulders, and down the chest, forming a V between the nipples. The skin is then peeled up and the neck severed between two neck vertebrae. As much of the neck is left attached to the head as possible.

A long vertical incision is made from the edge of the base of the neck up to the top of the cranium. The scalp and facial skin are then pulled and pried away from the skull and facial bones as in the skinning of any animal. Care is taken to make sure that the facial skin, which is more difficult to remove than the scalp, does not tear or rip. The skull and any flesh adhering to it are discarded. The secret to shrinking the head is removing the bones, leaving only the skin to work with. The eye slits are sewn shut with *chambra* (*Astrocaryum tucuima*) fiber and the lips pegged shut with three or four vertically placed bamboo or *chonta*-palm splinters.

The skin is then boiled in water for no more than thirty minutes to kill any bacteria present and to contract and thicken the skin. After boiling the skin is thick, rubbery, and pale in color. Boiling for more than thirty minutes may cause the hair to fall out. Some observers claim that plant matter with special astringent qualities was added to the boiling water to further shrink the head. This step was evidently optional. The skin is then suspended from a pole to cool.

A ring made from the *kapi* vine is sewn loosely around the neck opening. The long, vertical scalp incision is sewn shut with a bamboo needle and *chambra* fiber thread. With the lips pegged shut, the eyes and scalp incision sewn shut, and the neck opening held open by the vine ring, the head resembles an empty sack.

Three small, round stones are heated in a fire and used to burn out the flesh from inside the head. Using one stone at a time, the hot stone is dropped inside the head and rolled around to singe the flesh. When the stone cools it is replaced by another hot one. The process continues for two to three hours.

Sand is heated in a clay pot and poured into the neck opening to fill the head about two-thirds full. The head is then rolled and shaken so that the hot sand touches all the interior surfaces. When the sand cools it is removed and reheated. While it reheats, flesh is scraped out with the knife. This process continues until the head is shrunk to about one-quarter of its original size, or about the size of a large fist or orange. As it shrinks, the head is continually molded with the fingers and smooth stones to maintain a basically human shape.

Three new *chonta* palm pins, painted red, are skewered through the lips to replace the ones placed there earlier. The pegs are decorated with long strands of cotton fibers which hang down from them. The scalp hair is left as is, which means it will be very long (sometimes two feet or more) in comparison to the head. The facial hair is singed to shorten it. A large, red seed is inserted under each eyelid. Two holes are punched through the skin at the top of the head and a suspension cord strung through them.

The *tsantsa* is blackened either by rubbing it with powdered balsa wood charcoal or by smoking it over a smudge fire for eight hours. It is blackened to prevent the *musiak* from seeing out and causing accidents to the war party on the trip back to the village before the actual ceremonies start. The *tsantsa* is polished to a luster with a soft cloth.

Figure 45.1 *Jivaro shrunken heads (Courtesy American Museum of Natural History)*

Telling a Real from a Fake Tsantsa

Some experts believe that three out of every four shrunken heads traded out of South America are fakes. There are two types of fake heads. First, there are shrunken human heads which, while they really are heads, are prepared neither by the Jivaro nor in the traditional manner with all the required ritual and ceremony. In the past and perhaps even today, these heads are prepared in workshops using a mix of modern and traditional techniques on heads taken from unclaimed bodies. Second, there are so-called shrunken heads that are not heads at all but are pieces of dog or goat skin molded to shape on clay molds. Fake heads of both types have been sold to gullible tourists in South America for over 100 years. Today the selling of *tsantsas* and the transport of them out of Ecuador is illegal.

If you come across a head in a museum or in your travels in South America, the features listed in the following chart will help you distinguish between real and fake *tsantsas*. Keep in mind that you should base your judgement on a number of features, not just one or two. Different preparation techniques and the age of the head, along with its authenticity, influence its appearance.

Feature	Real	Fake
general appearance	distorted human form	human form
size	fist, baseball, orange	larger
nose	distorted, projects forward and upward like a snout with broad, flat nostrils	life-like with little projection
chin	recessed	prominent
forehead	flattened, with indentations on each side	lifelike
facial hair	shortened or removed	present in full length
color	dark or black, polished	yellow, dull
ears	pierced, usually without decoration	decorated with bone or ornaments
skin texture	leathery	brittle
rear incision	from neck to mid-cranium, sewn shut crudely with thick plant fibers	from neck to forward of mid-cranium, sewn shut neatly with thin thread
suspension cord	cord run through one or two holes punched in the scalp	cord stitched through scalp without pre-punched holes
decoration	pendants from lips and long, cotton lip cords	ornaments, feathers, feather headdresses

PART VI
Societies and Customs

46
Ideas of Beauty

Physical appeal is an important part of the formation of sexual and marital relationships in nearly every society around the world. Therefore, it should come as no great surprise that there is general agreement among the people in any given society as to which physical features are attractive and which are unattractive. At the same time, there is no general agreement between people from different societies about which features are attractive and which are unattractive. In fact, there is simply no worldwide ideal of the perfect man or woman. There is so little agreement from one society to another about physical attractiveness that only three general statements can be made with any degree of certainty about ideas of beauty around the world. First, physical beauty and appeal is almost always considered more important for women than for men. In most societies both men and women have a clear picture of what physical features make a woman desirable to men. Men look for women with these features and women often go to great lengths to make sure they have or appear to have the desired features. In men, aside from hair style, physical features are given less consideration. Their ability as providers and fathers, their past achievements, and their wealth, ambition, and trustworthiness are given more attention by potential wives.

The second general statement we can make is that ideas of beauty change over time. Features that were once desirable go out of fashion while others that were thought unappealing become fashionable. We can see this pattern in our own society if we compare the young women featured in *Playboy* magazine two decades ago with those displayed there today. Twenty or so years ago, the ideal woman (the ideal, we presume, for white, upper-middle-class men) in *Playboy* was relatively short, plump, and soft, with short hair and large breasts. The women featured in recent years are relatively tall with medium, athletic builds, long hair, and smaller breasts. This same pattern of change over time exists in all societies and is especially marked in tribal societies in contact with Western civilization. In these societies the Western image of female beauty transmitted through television, film, and magazines often replaces the traditional idea of beauty.

The third and final statement we can make about worldwide ideas of beauty is that in all societies both men and women seek to enhance their appearance and increase their appeal by using a wide range of decorative techniques. Many of these techniques are designed to permanently change, not merely augment, their appearance. The techniques used are far too many to list here, although the following sampling will give you some idea of their variety: tattooing and scarring designs in the skin; coloring the skin with dyes, paints, and powders; smoothing the skin with lotions, creams, oils, butter, and animal fat; decorating the face with paint and clay designs; bleaching the skin; sunbathing to darken the skin; trimming, removing, and styling the scalp hair; powdering, dyeing, oiling, and

greasing the facial and scalp hair; realigning, pulling, and sharpening the
teeth; cutting, shaping, and coloring finger and toe nails; wearing ear, nose,
cheek, and lip rings or plugs; manually stretching the labia majora;
circumcision and clitoridectomy and on and on.

Despite a general lack of agreement around the world as to what
features make for a beautiful person, there are some female features that
have broader appeal than others. A few of these are suggested by the
information listed by Clelland Ford and Frank Beach for a number of tribal
societies featured in their classic *Patterns of Sexual Behavior*:

Female Feature	**Number of Societies**
Body	
plump	13
medium	5
slim	5
Hips	
broad	6
slim	1
Legs	
thin ankles	3
shapely/fleshy calves	5
Breasts	
large	9
long and pendulous	2
upright/hemispherical	2
Genitalia	
elongated labia majora	8
large clitoris	1

As this list suggests, a woman with a plump build, large breasts, broad
hips, fleshy calves, and elongated labia majora would be considered
attractive in the largest number of societies around the world. There are
some societies, however, in which she would be thought unattractive and
not be especially desirable as a wife.

Beyond body build, a woman's eyes and the size and shape of her
breasts capture more attention in more societies around the world than do
any other physical features. The eyes of a woman are thought to be
especially important in many societies, including all seven whose ideals of
beauty are illustrated later in this chapter. Often a woman's eyes are
compared favorably to those of a prized animal. The Zulu of South Africa
speak of a woman having large, soft eyes like those of the gazelle. The
Tarahumara of Mexico prize women's eyes "like those of the mouse." The
Santal of India admire "two eyes like those of the deer." The Balinese of
the South Pacific clearly distinguish among women's eyes, men's eyes, and
the devil's eyes, as shown in Figure 46.1.

w o m e n

m e n

d e v i l

Figure 46.1 *Bali eyes*

Breast shape and size probably draw the most attention around the
world. In many societies distinctions are made between large breasts and
small ones, elongated and hemispherical ones, and upright and sagging
ones. Large, hemispherical, upright breasts are considered a mark of beauty
in most cultures. The Santal of India note the lure of the female breasts in
a number of folksongs, one of which follows:

185

Boy: Your body is radiant like the ripe mango
Your breasts are like two bel-fruits.
For whom is meant your body (for enjoyment), for
whom the breasts?
Girl: Don't, O boy, don't speak about this.
Don't weep, O boy, for this.
This my body, these my breasts,
These are only for you meant.
This loin-cloth and this sheet,
Who will round and use?
Boy: Don't, O girl, don't say like this,
Don't you weep, don't you weep, O my girl,
This loin-cloth and the sheet,
Both of us shall use.

However, in some cultures involvement with a beautiful woman is not without its anxieties, as suggested by the Thonga (Mozambique) proverb: "Do not covet a woman with large breasts if you have no money."

Not all societies emphasize body build, breast size, or the eyes. In some societies other physical features are considered the most important signs of beauty. The Tarahumara of Mexico favor women with large, fat thighs and go so far as to refer to an attractive person as a "beautiful thigh." Zulu men prefer women with large, protruding buttocks, which are so desirable that sometimes a man's sister will help him find a woman with the requisite measurements by enticing other women to raise their skirts and expose their buttocks. The sister will then return home and report to her brother that "so-and-so has an attractive daughter." The Trobriand Islanders in the Pacific prefer that both men and women shave off all body hair. They regularly shave their bodies and faces (including eyebrows) and often bite off each other's eyelashes during lovemaking. This list of examples should give you some idea of the wide variation in preference for physical features found around the world.

The remainder of this chapter is devoted to a series of illustrations of the ideals of physical beauty in seven different tribal societies: the Trobriand Islanders of the Pacific, the Balinese of the South Pacific, the Tarahumara of Mexico, the Siriono of Bolivia, the Zulu of South Africa, the Santal of India, and the people of central Luzon Island in the Philippines. Our original intention was to include illustrations of the ideal for both men and women in each of these seven societies, but we found that the descriptions and photographs available pertain mostly to women. For only three of the societies were we able to include illustrations of men. These illustrations give some idea of both variations and similarities in ideas of physical beauty around the world. The Zulu woman shown in Figure 46.2 is a good example of the widely prized plump build, broad hips, and fleshy calves mentioned above. The Santal and Tarahumara women shown in Figures 46.3 and 46.4 show the elongated and hemispherical breast shapes considered desirable traits in about equal numbers of

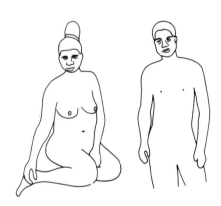

Figure 46.2 *Zulu woman and man*

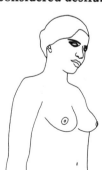

Figure 46.3 *Santal woman*

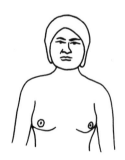

Figure 46.4 *Tarahumara woman*

societies around the world. The Trobriand man shown in Figure 46.5 displays the slim, muscled build found desirable in many societies, while the illustration of the Siriono man in Figure 46.6 suggests that the Siriono prefer somewhat taller, slimmer men. As for Siriono women, the plump build is again favored, along with a large, well-padded vulva.

Figures 46.7 and 46.8 focus on the facial features of women on the island of Bali and women on the Philippine island of Luzon. As mentioned above, and as the illustration shows, Bali men and women put much emphasis on the eyes. Luzon Island Philippinos also value eyes, especially bright, tantalizing ones, the type some Americans would call "bedroom eyes." In fact, Philippino men are intrigued by the tantalizing effects of female beauty and consider a woman to be especially attractive and desirable if she "walks in such a way as to keep the imagination of the man."

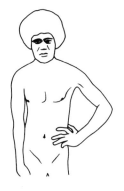

Figure 46.5 *Trobriand man*

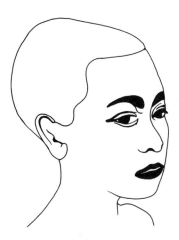

Figure 46.7 *Bali woman*

Figure 46.8 *Philippino woman*

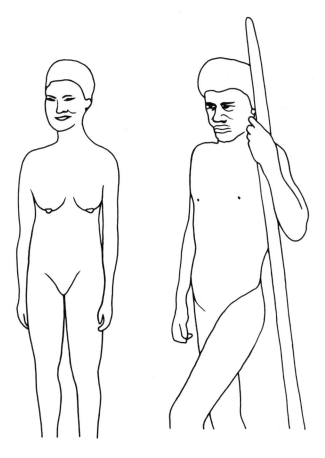

Figure 46.6 *Siriono woman and man*

47
Sign Language

When most people hear "Indian sign language" they think of an Indian chief and a cavalry officer standing face to face in the hot desert sun negotiating a peace treaty by communicating with their hands. While sign languages can serve as a bridge between people speaking different languages, and even between humans and some animals like chimps, they also have many other uses. Sign languages probably developed among tribal peoples as a means for communicating in hunting and war, when silence or secrecy had to be maintained. Many tribes also use sign language when communicating about forbidden or embarrassing subjects such as the dead, ceremonial secrets, or sex. And, just like in our own culture, deaf and mute people use sign language as their regular means of communication. Some tribal people even use signs to get a word in edgewise when they are assaulted by big talkers.

Contrary to popular belief, not all Native American tribes used sign language. Although the tribes of the Great Plains—the Cree, Cheyenne, Sioux, Apache, Comanche, and others—used a single type of sign language, sign language was not used by any other tribes in North America. In fact, there are good descriptions of tribal sign languages from only three places in the world: the North American Plains, Australia, and the State of Maranhao, Brazil, where a unique type of language is used by the Urubu, a jungle tribe of horticulturalists.

The capacity for sign language is unique to humans, and although some of the great apes can be taught to sign, no animal species has ever developed signing in the wild. Like regular languages, sign languages are "open systems"; an unlimited number of new sentences can be produced, and the vocabulary can increase as well.

The largest collection of signs for a single sign language was published in 1880 by U.S. Army Colonel Garrick Mallery, who lists over 3,000 gestures used by the Plains Indians. Don't be put off by this large number; to be able to communicate in normal conversation, you would only have to know 650 to 800 basic signs of any given sign language.

What exactly are the signs that make up a sign language? They are standardized gestures carrying certain conventional meanings. In all known sign languages, these gestures are made mostly with the arms and hands, rather than with the entire body. The Walbiri of Australia recognize this fact in their name for sign language, *raga raga*, meaning "hands." The hands may be formed into several basic shapes: open, clenched, with one or more fingers extended while the others are closed, with one or more fingers curved, etc. Even signs for the action of the feet, such as walking, running, or dancing, are made with the hands. The hands may also be held still or moved in specific ways.

Tribal sign languages are idiographic—signs or gestures represent things or ideas, not individual letters in an alphabet. The idiographic system works well between people who speak different languages, since you don't need to know the language of the person making the signs to understand the signing.

In all three of the known tribal sign languages, the same general principles are applied in making signs represent objects, ideas, and actions. Signs imitate the most conspicuous outlines or properties of an object, or the most striking features of an action. If a sign language user knows a few basic concepts by means of which signs are connected to the things they represent, he or she can often figure out the meaning of any sign even if seeing it for the first time. Some of these concepts are listed below, with examples from the Plains Indian sign language:

Concept	Example
An object or place is designated by pointing at it.	The sign for *ear* is made by pointing at your ear.
An object is designated by making its outline in the air.	The sign for *house* is made by touching the tips of your index fingers together to form a triangle; to make the sign for *tipi*, cross the tips.
An action is designated by mimicking it.	The sign for *go away* is made by moving your extended hand forward, with your palm turned to the left.
An instrument is designated by mimicking its action.	The sign for *saw* is made by holding your clenched fist at your side, and moving it back and forth.
An object is designated by mimicking its preparation.	The sign for *bread* is made by slapping one palm and then the other, as if patting a piece of dough into a cake.
A repeated action is designated by repeating the sign.	The sign for *march* is made by holding your index finger straight up in the air, and moving it forward by steps.
Part of an object is made to stand for the whole object.	The sign for *buffalo* is made by holding your hands on your head with your index fingers extended and the tips curved inward, like a buffalo's horns.

Of course, not all the ideas a sign language user might want to express can be mimicked or drawn in outline. To express grammatical notions such as negation or interrogation certain arbitrary signs are used. The sign for *no*, for example, is made by making a backhanded wave to the right with the open hand, following whatever sign it negates. *Water-no* would mean "there is no water." The sign for asking a question is made by holding the right hand with the palm outward in front of the body, fingers and thumb extended, and turning the hand to the right and left by rotating the wrist. This sign precedes whatever is being asked. Other examples of grammatical signs can be found in the Plains sign language version of the Lord's Prayer in Figure 47.10 at the end of the chapter.

When a sign language user wanted to express an object or thing for which there was no single sign, he often used two or three signs together. Gradually, these compound signs were accepted and widely used. These signs are interesting because they shed light on how tribal peoples think

189

about things. In Plains sign language, "angry" is *brain-twisted*, "annoyed" is *heart-flutter*, "bald" is *hair-wiped out*, "cavalry" is *white-soldier-riding*, "cigarette" is *tobacco-rolled-small*, "coal" is *stone-burn-good*, "divorce" is *woman-throw-away*, "grandfather" is *father-hard-of-hearing*, "vigilant" is *look-much-sleep-not*, and "Navaho" is *Indian-make-blanket-striped*.

A Few Signs

The three best-known tribal sign languages are those used by the Plains Indians in North America, the aborigines in Central Australia, and the Urubu in South America. Although all three languages developed independently and are not mutually intelligible, they are remarkably similar. We give the signs below for ten words and phrases in each of the languages.

Eat
Plains: Bring the tips of the fingers of the right hand up to the mouth and, using the wrist, move the hand downwards.

Urubu: Wave the right hand in front of the mouth with the fingers pointing toward it.

Australia: Bring the closed hand up to the mouth and then drop it quickly in a downward and forward motion, with the fingers extended.

Agent
Plains: Raise the index finger, with the rest of the fingers closed, slowly upward, and then reverse direction and move it downward (same as the sign for *chief*)

Urubu: Rub the chest with a circular motion (the Indian Agent is the only man in the village who has hair on his chest).

Australia: Bring right hand up to forehead, as if saluting.

Woman
Plains: Move the hands from the top of the head down each side, indicating long flowing hair parted in the middle of the head.

Urubu: Cup the right hand under the breast.

Australia: Place fingers of right hand on upturned left palm and move right wrist slightly as if to "shake" the fingers.

Far away
Plains: Place the open palms of the hands together and move them very slowly apart.

Urubu: Extend the index finger of the right hand with the other fingers closed, bring it up to the left shoulder, and fling the hand out, opening the fingers.

Australia: Point to the horizon with the index finger of the left hand.

Wait here
Plains: Hold the closed right hand in front of and a little lower than the right shoulder, and move the hand downward several inches; repeat.

Urubu: Make a pumping gesture with the closed right fist.

Australia: Hold the open right hand out toward the person you are signing to and let it gently fall to your side.

See, look at

Plains: Extend the index and middle fingers of the right hand, with the other fingers closed; bring them up near the eyes and point them outward, with the back of the hand up.

Urubu: Hold the open right hand, with the back of the hand upward, near the eyes.

Australia: Touch the eye with the right index finger.

Water

Plains: Bring cupped right hand up to the mouth, as if drinking from it.

Urubu: Bring the base of the palm of the right hand up to the mouth and make a sucking noise.

Australia: Close the right fist, with the thumb on top and slightly bent, and jerk it two or three times in toward the body.

Sad

Plains: Close the right hand, bring it up to the left breast, and make a small circle with it.

Urubu: Bend the head forward, and bring the open right hand up to the eyes with the fingers falling downward, as if they were tears.

Australia: Extend the thumb, index, and middle fingers of the right hand and make downward movements alternating between the left and the right eye, to suggest tears.

Salt

Plains: Touch the tip of the tongue with the extended right index finger, then hold right hand with fingers closed in front of the body, palm up, open it quickly and move it down and away (= taste bad).

Urubu: Touch the tip of the tongue with the extended right index finger.

Australia: Point to the mouth, then touch the tongue with the extended right index finger.

Pretty, good

Plains: Place the right hand, palm downward, in front of the chest and move it outward.

Urubu: Run the finger tips of the right hand over the back of the left forearm and hand.

Australia: Hold the index and middle fingers of the right hand slightly open with the other fingers closed and make a circle around them with the thumb.

Plains Sign Language Dictionary

Despite the natural connection between signs and the things they represent, all sign languages must be learned; they are unintelligible unless you know the system. We provide here instructions for making 100 signs in the well-described Plains Indian sign language. The 100 signs represent

Sign Language and the Boy Scouts
The Plains Indian sign language is well known by Boy Scouts. The Scout salute—right arm raised, the hand erect, the three middle fingers extended and slightly apart—is an adaptation of the Plains sign for wolf or scout, which differs only in three fingers being raised rather than two. The third finger was added to the salute so that the three points of the Scout oath are represented: honor, God, and country; help others; and obey the Scout law.
The founders of the scouting movement hoped that the use of sign language by Scouts would increase understanding and friendship among Scouts of different nations. Learning sign language is an optional requirement for the Indian lore merit badge.

191

the basic objects, actions, and concepts in the everyday life of people all over the world. Linguists tell us that they are the most frequently used words in any language. If you learn these 100 signs, you will be well on the way to mastering the Plains sign language. Expert Plains Indian "signers" can carry on "conversations" for two or three hours, but that takes years of practice, so it is best to stick to simple sentences and short subjects in the beginning.

I. Point right index finger at chest.

You. Point right index finger at the person you are signing to.

He. With right thumb extend and the rest of the fingers of the right hand closed, gesture in backhanded manner toward the rear.

One through **Ten.** In counting from one to ten, hold closed right hand in front of your right shoulder, palm facing out; for one, extend the little finger; for two, extend the ring finger; for three, extend the middle finger; for four, extend the index finger; for five, extend the thumb. For six, keep the fingers of the right hand extended and separated, bring the closed left hand up in front of the left shoulder, and extend the thumb; for seven, extend the left index finger; for eight, extend the left middle finger; for nine, extend the left ring finger; and for ten, extend the left little finger.

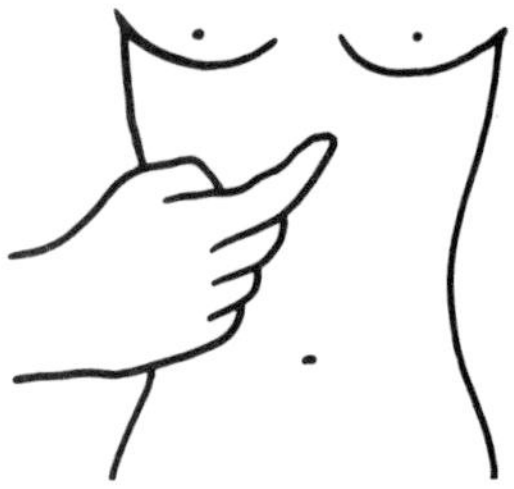

Twenty through **Ninety.** For twenty, bring the closed right hand in front of the right shoulder and the closed left hand in front of the left shoulder, palms facing out, and extend the fingers and close them twice in succession. For thirty, extend them three times, for forty, four times, and so on up to ninety.

One hundred. Bring the hands, palms out, in front of the right shoulder, with the fingers extended and the tips of the thumbs touching, and move the hands to the left and downward.

All. Move the right hand, palm down and fingers extended, in a horizontal circle from right to left, beginning at a point about a foot away from the right shoulder.

Ashes. Bring right hand in front of body, palm down, fingers partially closed, and rub the tips of the fingers with the tip of the thumb a few times.

Bad. Hold right hand with fingers closed in front of body, palm up, open it quickly and move it down and away.

Belly. Indicate the curved surface of a large belly with the hands extended, palms inward.

Big. Bring the hands up in front of the body wth the palms facing each other, a little lower than the shoulders, fingers extended and touching, and slowly separate them.

Black. Hold the extended left hand, palm down, in front of the body; bring the extended right hand, palm down, over on top of it and rub with the inside of the fingers of the right hand the back of the fingers of the left hand. The same sign is used for **color**.

Blood. Bring the right hand, palm inward, the index and middle fingers extended and the other fingers and thumb closed, in front of the mouth; press the tips of the index and middle fingers against the nostrils and move the hand to the right and downward. This mimics the flow of blood from the mouth and nose of a wounded buffalo.

Brother. Place the tips of the right index and middle fingers in the mouth (brothers are fed from the same breast).

Figure 47.1 "I"

Figure Figure 47.2 "One"

Figure 47.3 "Bad"

Figure 47.4 "Big"

Child. Pass the right hand down from the belly and between the legs, indicating how children are born.

Cloud. Bring the extended hands, palms down, in front of and a little higher than the head, and slowly separate them and bring them downward, forming a large semicircle.

Cold. Bring closed hands in front of and close to the body, at the height of the shoulder and a few inches apart, and shake them slightly (as if shivering) while hunching the shoulders.

Come. Hold the right hand, palm inward, index finger extended and pointing upward and other fingers and thumb closed, in front of the body, and bring the hand in quickly toward the body, lowering it slightly.

Day. Hold the extended hands in front of the body, palms down and thumbs touching, at the height of the chest; separate the hands by sweeping them upward, and then bring both down and around, so that the palms end up face up at the height of the shoulders. This indicates the unfolding of darkness.

Dog. Indicate approximate height of dog with right hand, palm downward, and make barking sound.

Ear. Point at ear with right index finger.

Earth. Point with right index finger at the ground.

Egg. Hold the index finger and thumb of the right hand with the tips touching, to suggest the outline of an egg.

Eye. Touch the eye with the right index finger.

Father. Bring the right hand, palm inward, fingers extended and together, up to the right breast, and tap the breast with the fingertips two or three times.

Fire. Hold the right hand, palm up, in front of the body at knee height, fingers partially closed with the thumb resting on the nails of the first three fingers, and raise the hand a little while snapping the fingers a few times.

Grass. Point to ground with right index finger, then turn fingers upward with palms out, to indicate growth.

Green. Point to something green, or make sign for **grass**.

Hair. Touch the hair of the head with the right index finger.

Heart. Bring the right hand, with the fingers together and slightly curved, over the left breast, and touch the tip of the thumb to the tip of the index finger.

Hit. Hold the left hand in front of the body, palm up, fingers extended and pointing out; form the right hand into a fist, and strike the left palm sharply.

Hunt. Hold the right hand in front of the eye, index finger extended outward and other fingers and thumb closed, and move the hand forward in a zigzag motion.

Husband (or **wife**). Hold the right hand in front of the body, palm down, and extend the index and middle fingers outward, with the other fingers and the thumb closed.

Ice. Make the signs for **water**, then **cold**.

Lake. Make the sign for **water**, and then make a large circle in front of the

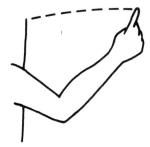

Figure 47.5 *"Come"*

Smoke Signals
Smoke signals are probably the best-known Indian signaling device, thanks to Hollywood westerns. In reality, though, the Indians rarely used smoke signals because the rising smoke pinpointed the signaler's position for both enemies and allies. Thus, another Indian myth goes up in smoke.
Besides sign language, the favorite Indian signaling devices were blankets (they used a code like semaphore), mirrors, flaming arrows, and sparks made at night with flint and steel. Indians also relayed information over long distances by riding their horses in certain distinctive patterns that had previously agreed-upon meanings.

body on the horizontal plane, using the index fingers of the left and right hands.

Laugh. Bring the hands, palms up and fingers extended outward, up to the face, and move them up and down rapidly while smiling.

Left (-hand). Make the left hand into a fist and bring it up in front of the neck, palm to the right; then bring the left elbow into the side, at the same time turning the fist so that the palm faces inward.

Liver. Place the hands, with the fingers extended, on the stomach over the location of the liver, and shake them slightly.

Long. Bring the right hand, fingers extended and plam to the left, from the lower part of the chest upward to about a foot above the head.

Louse. Scratch the head with the fingernails of the right hand, and then closing the nails of the right index finger and thumb as if holding a louse, bring it to the mouth as though eating it (Plains Indians ate lice).

Man. Hold the right hand in front of the body, with the palm down, the index finger extended, and the other fingers closed.

Mother. Make the sign for **father**, but tap the left breast instead of the right.

Mountain. Outline the shape of a mountain against the sky with the right hand.

Name or call. Touch the tip of the right thumb with the right index finger, bring the hand up so that the index finger lays across the mouth, and raise the hand upward and outward. (For **my name**, add the sign for **I**.)

Night. Bring the extended hands, palms down, in front of the body at chest height, and separate and move them downward, forming a semicircle (the fall of darkness).

Nose. With the right index finger partially extended and the other fingers and thumb of the right hand closed, touch the nose from the top to the nostrils.

People. With the index finger of the right hand extended and the other fingers and the thumb closed, bring the right hand, palm to the left, in front of the body and move it around as if indicating different heights.

Rain. Hold the hands at about the height of the head, palms down, and open and close the fingers a few times.

Red. Rub the right cheek in a circular motion with the fingers of the right hand, as if applying warpaint.

Road or trail. Hold the extended hands out in front of the body, palms up, on the same horizontal plane, and move the left hand forward and the right hand back, the right hand forward and the left back, etc., a few times.

Rope. Bring the left hand, palm down, in front of the body at chest height, with the index finger extended and pointing out and the other fingers and thumb closed; bring the right hand up next to it, with the palm down and the index finger extended and parallel to the left index finger; move the right hand to the rear, moving the index finger in a spiral by wrist action.

Sand or dirt. Point to the ground with the right index finger, and make the sign for **ashes**.

Short. Hold the slightly closed right hand, fingers pointing up, to the right and front of the body, and bring it slowly down until it reaches the waist or below.

Figure 47.6 *"Throat"*

Sing. Hold the right hand, palm to the left, in front of the face, index and middle finger extended and separated, other fingers and thumb closed, and make a small circle on the horizontal plane in front of the mouth.

Sister. Make the sign for **brother**, and then make the sign for **woman**.

Sit. Make a fist with the right hand and hold it in front of and a little lower than the right shoulder, palm to the left, and move the hand downward several inches.

Small or **few.** Hold the partially closed hands, palms toward each other and fingers up, in front of the body, and slowly close them until they almost touch.

Smoke. Make the sign for **fire**, but continue raising the right hand until it is above the head.

Snake. Hold the right hand, palm to the left, index finger extended and pointing out and other fingers and thumb closed, in front of the body at waist height; move the hand several inches ahead with a wavy motion.

Snow. Make the sign for **rain**, and from this position lower the hands about a foot, palms down and fingers extended and touching (falls like rain, but lies on the ground).

Speak or **talk.** Bring the right hand, palm down, in front of the mouth, and move it forward a few inches while snapping the thumb and index finger.

Spear. Hold the closed right hand at shoulder height, palm to the left, as if holding a spear and about to throw it.

Star. Make the sign for **night**, and then form a partial circle with the right index finger and thumb, and raise the right hand up toward the sky.

Stone. Make a fist with the right hand, and strike the left palm two or three times with it.

Sun. Form a partial circle with the right index finger and thumb; hold the hand to the east, and move it to the west by making a semicircle on the vertical plane.

Swim. Make the sign for **water**, and then move the hands out in front of the body as if doing the dog paddle (the favorite swimming stroke of the Indians).

Think. Hold the right hand, palm down, against the left breast, index finger extended and pointing to the left, other fingers and thumb closed, and move the hand horizontally outwards and to the right eight or ten inches (this sign means "drawn from the heart").

This, here, that, there. Point the right index finger at the place or object you wish to indicate.

Throat. Point at the throat with the right index finger.

Track. Make the sign for **walk** and point to the ground.

Tree. Point at the ground in front with the right index finger, arm fully extended; raise the arm two or three feet, open the hand and give it a few shakes to indicate the branches.

Warm. Draw the back of the right hand across the forehead, as if wiping off sweat.

Water. Cup the right hand, bring it up to the mouth, palm up, and turn the palm toward the mouth, as if drinking from the hand.

Figure 47.7 *"Sing"*

Wheel. Draw the outline of a wheel on the vertical plane with the right index finger (may also be used for **wagon** or **car**).

Where, what, when, and other questions. Hold the right hand, fingers pointing upward and palm out, at shoulder height, and move it slightly from side to side.

Whiskey. Make signs for **water** and **fire**.

White. With right index finger, point to the sun or to something white.

Wife. Same as sign for **husband**. Some Indians make the sign for **husband** and add the sign for **woman**.

Wind. Indicate with the right hand its direction, and make a whistling sound.

Woman. Move the hands from the top of the head down each side, indicating long hair parted in the middle, or hold the hands cup-shaped over each breast.

Year. Make the sign for **cold**, and then the sign for **one**.

Yes. Hold the right hand, palm to the left, in front of the chest, the index finger extended and pointing up, the other fingers and the thumb closed, and move the hand a little to the left and down, at the same time closing the index finger.

Figure 47.8 *"Yes"*

Figure 47.9 *"No"*

Figure 47.10 *The Lord's Prayer*

48
Figuring Your Family

Everyone has relatives. Some people are happy about it, others wish they didn't. But, like it or not, we are all part of a family. Perhaps the biggest difference between us and people in tribal societies is the little importance we place on our kin. In most modern societies, kin outside the immediate circle of close relatives such as mother, father, husband, wife, son and daughter rarely play much of a role in our lives. We see them at family gatherings once or twice a year and let it go at that. In tribal societies, kin are often very important. In fact, it is often the intricate networks of relationships among kin that form the very fabric of tribal societies. Food gathering, political decision making, child rearing, inheritance of wealth, and other considerations are all affected by the kinship relationships among the people involved. As we saw in Chapter 45, for example, whether or not an enemy warrior's head is shrunk as a trophy depends on whether or not he is someone's relative.

In this chapter we provide basic instructions and charts for figuring out who your kin are and how you are related to them. Before we begin, we need to emphasize three basic concepts about kinship. First, we will be talking about two types of kin: blood relatives (consanguines) and relatives by marriage (affines). Second, we will be using two sets of kin terms: universal terms such as father, mother, brother, sister's son, mother's brother's daughter and American kin terms such as aunt, uncle, niece, and cousin. Third, we will be keeping separate your kin on your father's side (paternal kin) from those on your mother's side (maternal kin).

Figuring Your Blood Kin

To figure your blood kin you will need to see the charts in Figures 48.1 and 48.2. Figure 48.1 shows the relationships among and lists both the American and abbreviated universal kin terms for five generations. You'll notice in the center of the chart a space for the name of *ego*. Ego is you. You will be filling in the chart from the perspective of your position in the family. Ego is always the person from whose perspective the chart is filled out. If it is your mother, she is ego, and you fill the slot for son or daughter. If it is your maternal aunt, your mother's sister, she is ego, and you fill the slot for niece or nephew. To save space, we have abbreviated the universal kin terms. The basic terms spelled out in the margin column are combined to form the other kin terms such as MBs (mother's brother's son) or MBss (mother's brother's son's son). The combinations are easy to work out if you remember that all the terms except the last one take the possessive form.

Don't be put off if some of the rules for figuring your kin and the kin terms used differ from the ones you're familiar with. The rules we provide are those used by middle-class Americans in the northeast. There are ethnic and regional differences in these rules and terms. For example, mothers are called mother, mom, ma, mommy, mummy, mama, muth, old woman, old lady, or by their first names or nicknames.

197

Basic Kin Terms
M = mother
F = father
S = sister
B = brother
d = daughter
s = son

Figures 48.1 and 48.2 allow for only blood relatives. Relatives by marriage such as husband or wife or the husbands or wives of aunts or uncles are not included, although children of these marriages are included. Figure 48.3 allows spaces for kin by marriage.

You are now ready to fill in Figure 48.2. If you have more kin than the chart allows, simply add spaces in the appropriate generations. Begin with ego and enter your name there. Then work back, entering the names of your mother and father, aunts and uncles in the parental generation and likewise for the grandparental generation. Return to your generation and enter the names and then work down through the grandchild generation. Figure 48.1 will give you the relationships and kin terms for all blood relatives. It works best if you enter the American kin term and the person's name on the chart; for example, cousin Ethan, aunt Diane, etc. You may also want to put the chart to practical use by adding the birthdates for each of your relatives.

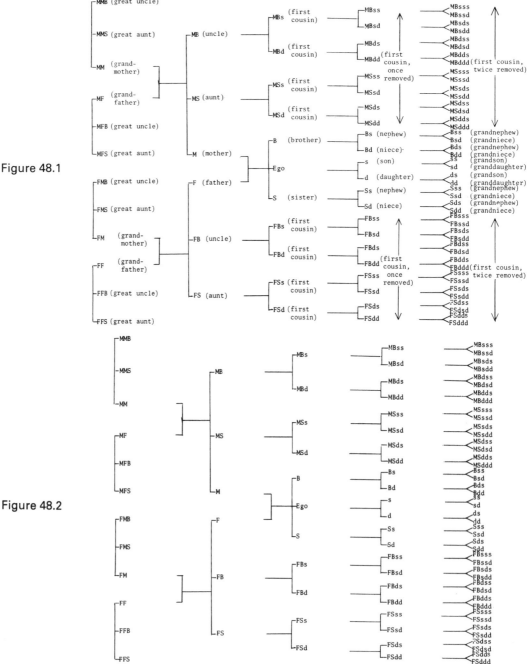

Figure 48.1

Figure 48.2

Figuring Your Affines

Affines are relatives by marriage, people who marry a blood relative, some of whom who are identified as such by the suffix in-law, and the person you marry. Figures 48.3 and 48.4 provide the charts for figuring affines. Figure 48.3 is for the husband's side, Figure 48.4 for the wife's side. Put the two together and you'll have the whole picture. These two charts have a couple of features not included in Figures 48.1 and 48.2. First, they allow for the inclusion of in-laws, designated by the American kin term for the relative followed by "i-l." For example, your sister's husband would be B-i-l (brother-in-law). Second, these charts allow for the inclusion of spouses. A marital sign is indicated by the equal (=) sign. Third, these charts differentiate between blood and affinal kin by linking the blood relatives to ego and to one another with lines. Affines are not so linked. otherwise, the charts are much alike and are filled in the same way. Just enter the names of the relatives, their birth dates, anniversaries or any other useful information.

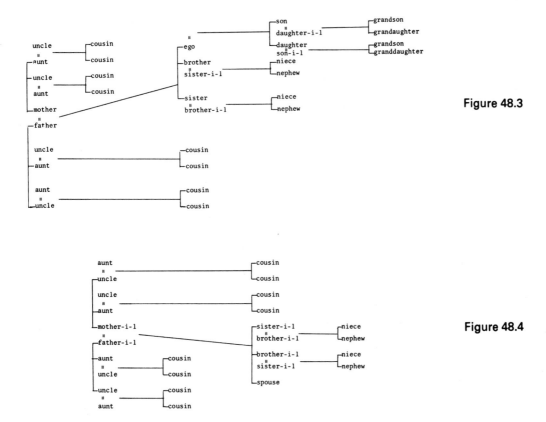

Figure 48.3

Figure 48.4

Cousins

The only American kin term that is confusing is cousin. Different people use the term in different ways or use different terms for the same thing. There are cousins, first cousins, second cousins, third cousins, cousins once removed, cousins twice removed, and country cousins. We have opted to stick with the once and twice removed terms, as they are the easiest to figure. Removed simply means the number of generations away from ego. People sometimes use second cousin to mean what we call once removed and third cousin for twice removed. Others use second cousin to mean children of first cousins. The children are second cousins to each other, the parents are first cousins to each other, and the parents and children are first cousins once removed to each other.

Adoption, Death, Divorce, and Remarriage

The figures are very easy to fill in as long as there are no relatives added or lost due to adoption, death, divorce, or remarriage. Adopted children are treated as blood kin and entered on the chart as son or daughter. If they are doing the chart and know both their blood and legal relatives, they will have to fill out two charts, one for each set of kin.

If you are divorced, you are no longer related to your spouse nor to his or her kin; you no longer have affines related through your marriage. If you have children, however, your ex-spouse and his or her relatives are still your children's relatives and would figure in the children's charts. If you remarry, you add a new set of affines. If you have children with a second or third spouse, your children gain half-siblings. If you had children when you remarried, your children gain a step-parent and your spouse gains step-children. They, of course, are not blood relatives, nor are they really legal relatives. They are social relatives who fill a social role in the family. If a person dies, he or she can be removed from the chart or the date of death listed under the name. Step- and half-relatives can be entered on the charts in the same generation as the full relatives in the appropriate categories.

How We Know What to Call Our Kin

As we grow up we learn who our relatives are, how they are related to us, and what to call them. Aunt Tillie is our aunt because she is mother's sister. Cousin Sid is our cousin because he is father's brother's son.

Underlying our knowledge of where we and our kin fit in the family is a set of criteria we use almost unconsciously to place our kin in the correct categories. (Correct for us, as in other societies different rules and kin terms are used, many of which are far more complicated than the ones we use). In our system, we use five criteria. First, we distinguish between relatives in different generations. Great-grands, grands, parents, brothers and sisters are all kin in different generations. The kin terms tell us what generation they are in. Second, we distinguish between direct and indirect blood relatives. Father, mother, grandfather, grandmother, son, daughter are all direct blood relatives; brother, sister, aunt and uncle are not. Third, we distinguish between male and female kin, except for cousins. Mother versus father, sister versus brother, aunt versus uncle, niece versus nephew all indicate who is male and who is female. Fourth, for some relatives we use the suffix in-law to distinguish blood relatives from relatives by marriage. We distinguish only for close kin, however, not for distant ones like aunt, uncle, cousin, niece, or nephew. Fifth, we distinguish among different categories of kin by calling each other by different kin terms. Fathers call their son, son; mothers call their daughter, daughter; uncles call their nephews, nephew; and so on and vice versa for most categories of kin. The exception is cousins, who use the same term in reference to another cousin.

49
Will Your Marriage Last?

In this time of frequent divorce it would be comforting to be able to predict the chances of a marriage lasting. The Malays of Malaysia have long believed that they have such a system. Based loosely on the zodiac, their system relies on the numerical value of the letters in the first names of the betrothed couple. The system is quite simple, with each letter of the alphabet assigned a numerical value as shown in the following table.

A	B	C	D	E	F	G	H	I
1	2	3	4	5	6	7	8	9
J	K	L	M	N	O	P	Q	R
10	20	30	40	50	60	70	80	90
S	T	U	V	W	X	Y	Z	
100	200	300	400	500	600	700	800	

To determine your marital future, first sum the numerical value of your first names. Then divide the value of each name by nine. For example, if your names are Thomas and Mary, the values of the names are 409 and 831, and the products of the division are 45 and 92, with remainders of 4 and 5. Using the lower remainder first, look up your future in the verse on the following pages. For Thomas and Mary, the future is not bright, as separation is predicted. The only problem with this system is that it fails to account for situations where there are no remainders.

Now listen, youths of noble birth!
If **one** and **one** come together,
It is exceedingly well, of noble youths,
By day and by night you will have peace.
Daily bread will be uncommonly cheap;
Day and by night you will have no idle time,
(As) friends and relations will always be visiting you.
God will preserve you from all misfortune.
You will love each other without cessation,
You will be protected from danger and peril;
There will be love between you and your many relations,
And the Lord will protect you from hurt.

If **one** and **two** come together,
It is an exceedingly good raksi for both,
Which cannot be surpassed by any other,
As it is like that of Adam and Eve.

They will consult each other in all matters.
And will follow one another's advice;
Work easy and difficult will proceed speedily,
And in every occupation they will not counteract one another.
They will be a couple equally faithful,
Who will have pity and compassion on their fellow creatures;
People looking at them will rejoice greatly;
They will not work oppression.

If **one** and **three** come together,
They will live together fairly well,
But there will be suspicion and doubt,
And they will leave each other before long.

If **one** and **four** come together,
They will not agree well;
Work for both will be troublesome,
They will separate and their marriage will not be blessed.

If **one** and **five** come together,
It is not good; they will oppose one another;
They will not take care not to ruin their reputation,
And it will not be long ere they separate.

If **one** and **six** come together,
They will do well in agriculture,
They will be comfortable and not go under,
Nor will their possessions be lost.

If **one** and **seven** come together,
They will not be a good match,
Their hearts will remain far apart,
And it will be like having an enemy in the house.

If **one** and **eight** come together,
It will be good for the seeking of a livelihood.
But there will be knotty problems,
And some people say there will be sorrow.

If **one** and **nine** come together,
They will live well together forever.
But their roads may go apart,
And their daily bread is not sure.

If **two** and **two** come together,
There is some good in the raksi for both,
But according to tradition there will be something amiss,
And at last they will separate.

If **two** and **three** come together,
It will be very bad for both;
They will think badly of each other,
And thus they will separate.

If **two** and **four** come together,
Though the marriage will be lasting, there will be little harmony,
As each of them will have to earn it,
Their livelihood will be less blessed.

If **two** and **five** come together,
The two may live together,
But they will be very proud,
And will be poor ere long.

If **two** and **six** come together,
It is not good, as they will sow anger,
They will be poor and their possessions be lost;
They will live together like fire and a slow match.

If **two** and **seven** come together,
The raksi is good for a match;
They will be of good character and of constant faithfulness,
And in everything will work heartily together.

If **two** and **eight** come together,
It will be a very bad match;
The woman will always have the last word,
And, besides, will be very talkative.
On no account do you come near her,
As this is the raksi which absolutely forbids marriage,
She will not care much for work,
And you should keep away from her as from a loathsome snake.
Do not gaze or look upon her,
Much less make her your legal property;
She will find work in the byways,
And will not abide in her home.
If you cast your eyes on her,
In your heart do not long for her,
Though she be beautiful to look at,
In the end she will bring you sorrow.

If **two** and **nine** come together,
The raksi is good and well matched;
Your friends and acquaintances will be glad of the marriage,
Which afterwards will not lead to regret.
It will be very well for you to make her your wife,
For you will never tire of watching her face;
Pleasure will teach you wisdom,
In her heart she will be glad to entertain you.

As regards **three** and **three**,
It is not good for either party,
Their work will never be calculated,
And in the end they will separate.

If **three** and **four** come together,
The two will not harmonize well;
Their work will be troublesome,
They will separate and not stick together.

If **three** and **five** come together,
It is not good that the two should be united;
Within four months, or in the fifth,
The divorce offered will be quickly accepted.
She will be a discreditable wife,
Who moreover will break faith,
And will refuse to learn;
Many people do not praise her.

If **three** and **six** come together,
It is well for rice growing and planting,
But the heart will be overwhelmed with its thought,
and a multitude of lies will bring destruction.

If **three** and **seven** come together,
The raksi is auspicious for a good match;
You will not have many altercations,
Nor many disturbances of your peace.

If **three** and **eight** come together,
It is good for the earning of the livelihood;
You will find your daily bread everywhere around you,
But there will be suspicion and the marriage will not be permanent.

If **three** and **nine** come together,
It is not an appropriate omen;
The one or the other will seek his own way,
And in the end it will lead to regret.
Therefore do not marry in haste,
But look out for a woman with a good name;
So that you marry not in vain,
But with luck love for long.

As regards **four** and **four**,
The two will not agree well;
They will only injure one another's good name,
And will separate and not stick together.

If **four** and **five** come together,
Their love will not last long;
They will not heed the ruin of their good names,
And their union will not be lasting.

If **four** and **six** come together,
They will not be lucky in trade or agriculture;
Their thoughts will faint with the planting of anger,
And thus in the end they will come to destruction.

If **four** and **seven** come together,
Hearts will be divided in disputation day and night;
Like a house that is not firmly built,
That falls down once in seven days.

If **four** and **eight** come together,
There will be no permanent union between the two;
Some people, however, say that it will be advantageous,
Though there is one school that denies this.

If **four** and **nine** come together,
That, too, is not appropriate,
As the only means to get on well together,
Is to abandon much of their work.

As regards **five** and **five**,
They will not get on well together,
Their conduct will not improve their reputation,
And they will separate ere long.

If **five** and **six** come together,
It will be (smooth) like water in a well;
They will live in mutual love day and night,
And will be like a ring and its sapphire.

If **five** and **seven** come together,
It is good the parties match,
But there will be some differences,
And they should not go far from each other.

If **five** and **eight** come together,
The union will not be lasting;
Though it will be well as regards the earning of a livelihood,
There will be trouble in the end.

If **five** and **nine** come together,
The two will keep even with each other;
Force will meet force,
And gentleness will meet gentleness.

As regards **six** and **six**,
Both will be lucky in agriculture,
When they move their seedlings they will not be submerged,
And will escape ruin and loss.

If **six** and **seven** come together,
Though the union will be lasting, there will be quarrels;
The heart within will be angry,
And besides, there will not be secure fidelity.

If **six** and **eight** come together,
There may be hope;
Some people say the union may be permanent,
But others do not confirm it.

If **six** and **nine** come together,
They will be able to earn a good livelihood,
But they will meet with ill-luck,
As in their hearts they will feel regret.

As regards **seven** and **seven**,
It is not good; they will quarrel in their hearts,
And their hearts will not be clean towards one another;
It will be like keeping many enemies (in the house).

If **seven** and **eight** come together,
They will not be lucky in earning their livelihood;
They will make mistakes all around,
And will be put to shame ere long.

If **seven** and **nine** come together,
It is well for them to become comrades.
But there will be some regret,
As she will be lazy and a gadder.

As regards **eight** and **eight**,
It is a raksi which means permanency,
And an easy earning of the livelihood,
Which will provide you with the daily bread and all necessities.

As regards **eight** and **nine**,
It is a very reliable raksi;
You will be sure to have children,
And you will never feel regret.

As regards **nine** and **nine**,
It is a good and appropriate raksi;
Your orders will be followed honestly,
You will be as star and moon.

50
Witchcraft and Sorcery

In many societies around the world, the most sinister threat to life, the most frequent cause of death, is witchcraft. Beliefs in witchcraft and sorcery are not exotic bugaboos, as we sometimes think, but an actual and vital part of the daily lives of a majority of people on earth. And even in our own society, as late as 1692, nineteen people were hanged and one person crushed with rocks until dead for being suspected witches during the Salem witchcraft scare.

Witches and sorcerers are quite different types of people, as most tribespeople will tell you. A sorcerer achieves his evil ends by magical impersonal supernatural forces, which he believes control the succession of events and the destiny of the universe. Witches, on the other hand, achieve their evil ends by mystical power inherent in their own personalities, part of their own personal makeup. Their ability to practice witchcraft is usually believed to be hereditary, something like a birth defect. Sorcery demands no special personal attributes and can be practiced by anyone who acquires the necessary magical substances or spells and incantations.

Information on witches and sorcerers is hard to come by. Hardly anyone will admit to being a witch, as in societies where people believe in witchcraft it is almost always punishable by horrible torture and death. Sorcery is too, and there is an additional problem in collecting formulas and spells from tribal peoples—the demand is so great for them, they cost a fortune! So an anthropologist who wants to learn sorcery not only has to spend great sums of money, he may even be killed for his efforts. In this chapter, we will tell you what witches are like in a number of places, so you will know one if you see one, and we will teach you some magic whose effectiveness has been proven by generations of sorcerers. But first: do witchcraft and sorcery really "work"?

The answer is yes. It is an established fact of modern medicine that severe psychic stress—"shock"—can cause illness and death. Equally true is the belief that witchcraft can cause the death of a person who truly believes himself to be bewitched. A person who believes he has been bewitched is thoroughly convinced that he is doomed, in accordance with all the religious beliefs of his culture, and goes into shock. Fear, like rage, causes intense and disorganized activity of the sympathetic nervous system, which controls involuntary responses to alarm, such as the speeding up of the heart rate, raising of the blood pressure, and dilating of the pupils of the eyes. The witchcraft victim, in the throes of intense anxiety, will not eat or drink, which causes dehydration and increased permeability of the capillary vessels. This, in combination with the

Psychedelic Witchcraft
One widely held belief about witches is that they do their evil work in spirit form while they lay in bed asleep. Strangely enough, this belief may have a factual basis, if we consider the widespread use of hallucinogenic drugs by aspiring witches. Witches in the late medieval and Renaissance periods in Europe, for example, commonly rubbed their bodies with salves and ointments of deadly nightshade, henbane, mandrake, and thorn apples (see Figures 50.1 through 50.4). All of these plants contain tropane alkaloids, which are absorbed into the skin and produce vivid hallucinations including feelings of disembodiment, sensations of flying and sexual excitement, and delusions of being an animal. The traditional witch's broomstick served as an internal applicator for these ointments to the sensitive vaginal membranes and also was suggestive of riding on a steed, a typical mode of travel to the witches' sabbat. Modern psychiatric tests have shown the incredible strength of these ointments. One subject, after taking a dose of harmaline, first believed that he was a bird flying through the air, complete with feathers, and then thought he had changed into a wolf. Snarling and howling, he mistook one of the nurses for a deer, and had to be restrained from biting her on the neck. Given the power of these drugs, it is easy to understand how people truly believed that they were witches or werewolves.

207

speeding up of the heart rate, causes a decrease in the volume of blood (it literally seeps out of the veins), a drop in blood pressure, and then usually fatal damage to the circulatory organs such as the heart and lungs. Similar traumas in our own society may be caused by bombings, car accidents, and surgical operations. As far as witchcraft goes, if you think you will die, you really will die. The best defense against witchcraft and sorcery is complete disbelief.

Witches and Witchcraft

One of the strangest things about witchcraft is that in tribe after tribe witches are said to have the same group of traits that distinguish them from ordinary people and allow them to be singled out and punished. First, witches are almost always adults and usually women. They have some physical mark which gives them away—a red eye, a snake in the belly, a wart on the nose, or a special witchcraft substance that flows in the veins instead of blood.

Second, witches cause everyday accidents and calamities that have no explanation but "bad luck"—a fall from a ladder, a drought, an epidemic of the plague. Third, witches turn against their own relatives and neighbors; they never attack strangers. Fourth, witches work from envy, malice, or greed, not for any specific material gain. Fifth, witches work in secret, usually at night, and almost always are able to fly, using a broomstick, a dead goat, or simply their own mysterious powers.

Sixth, witches are not ordinary people. If a witch wishes you harm, the harm is as good as done. They may be possessed by spirits, the devil, or evil gods; they may have human form or turn into animals. Seventh, witches are always immoral. Witchcraft, unlike homicide, is never thought to be justifiable. Eighth, witches reverse all normal standards. They practice incest and bestiality, they eat their own children, they dig up corpses and eat them or have sex with them, they go naked instead of clothed.

Sound like anyone you know? The question is not as far-fetched as it sounds for people in the six societies listed below, who live in constant dread of witchcraft. The Dobu Islanders of the South Pacific say that all witches are women; they fly around at night, with fire streaking from their pubes, and steal the souls of men and children.

The Tswana tribe of Botswana, Africa, claims that witches are old women not content to use their evil magic to destroy some specific target; they must destroy people in general. They meet at night in small groups, run about naked, and smear their bodies with white ashes or the blood of the dead. To join such a group, a woman must first show her enthusiasm by murdering a close relative, preferably her firstborn child. The witches perform various rites. They remove fresh corpses from their graves to feast on and fornicate with by using a special magic which causes the grave to open and the corpse to float upward. They have a special medicine which enables them to put the occupants of a homestead into a deep sleep so the witches can enter and do as they wish. They cut open the bodies of their victims and insert small stones, pieces of flesh, or excrement, which cause the victim to take sick and die. Tswana witches ride hyenas when they travel. They keep one leg on the ground while putting the other on the hyena's back.

In Medieval Europe, witches were old women who made secret pacts with the devil, the Prince of Darkness. At night they annointed themselves with "devil's grease" made from the fat of murdered children, slipped out of cracks, keyholes, and chimneys, mounted brooms, spindles, or flying goats and went on a long journey to the witches' sabbat. Sabbats were held once a week, every Thursday. Once there, the witches were surprised to see all their friends, relatives and neighbors, whom they never suspected of being witches. At the sabbat they made love with scores of demons and with the god of their worship, the devil himself, who appeared as a big, black, bearded man or as a stinking goat or huge toad. They kissed him on the lips if he was a toad or under the tail if he was a goat. They had sexual orgies and feasted on roasted or boiled children, exhumed bodies, fricassees of bats, or roast beef and beer.

The Nyakyusa people of Tanganyika believe that witches exist as pythons in the bellies of certain people, both men and women. These snakes are inherited, although their presence can be detected through an autopsy. The main incentive to witchcraft is good food. Witches lust for meat and milk and they delight in eating human flesh, gnawing at people on the inside and eventually causing death. They also steal milk, sucking at the udders of cows so that the cows dry up and later abort. Witches fly about at night, either as pythons or "on the wind." They are proud and boastful, morose and aloof, and unsympathetic to neighbors in trouble.

Witches in the Lugbara tribe of Zaire walk about at night, entering their victims' huts silently "like a rat creeping on a wall." They may take the form of animals, especially a leopard, snake, owl, or screech monkey. They vomit blood on their victims' doorsteps; in the morning the victims touch it and become ill. Witches may be seen as a light on the top of a hut or as a light moving rapidly across the fields. All witches have glowing lights at their wrists and anus. Day witches walk about during the day killing children by spitting on their heads. A witch is a witch because his heart is bad, and witchcraft can be inherited. The face of the witch is grey and drawn, like a corpse, he has red eyes and squints, he vomits blood, and he fornicates with nocturnal animals.

Among the Fipa, a Bantu tribe of southwest Tanzania, witches are old men who go around the village naked at night, entering the huts and removing head and pubic hair from the magically stupified occupants. The hair is later used in potions. The old man might be accompanied by his wife, also naked, who carries her husband upside down from her shoulders while she clasps his lower legs to her breasts. They turn their victims into zombies, forcing them to work in their gardens at night, while the witches sleep atop the victim's hut during the day.

Sorcery and Magic

Sorcerers and their magic come in all different shapes and sizes. Some sorcerers specialize in black magic and use it to kill their enemies; others use rain and crop magic to ensure bountiful harvests; others use love magic, fertility magic, and sex magic to satisfy their lust. Since our emphasis is on how-to, we'll stick to love, sex, and fertility and provide a few spells and potions you can try without causing anyone harm or taking the risk of being burned at the stake. Before you try this magic on a member of the opposite sex, however, remember that the people you work the magic on will be affected for the rest of their lives. Many is the story of tribal sorcerers who overdid it and literally got "loved to death"!

The standard aphrodisiac used by the Moche and peasants in coastal villages in Peru is *huanarpo* (*Jatropha macrantha*). It is as easy to buy in markets as milk, bread, and eggs. *Huanarpo* looks like dried mushroom and comes in two forms, male and female, depending on the buyer's sexual preference. The male type has a shriveled stalk with a penis-like head, and the female type has a short stalk and a large, soft head with a hole in the middle. The plant is crushed into a fine powder and put into the victim's food or drink (the male type for a man, the female type for a woman). The

Figure 50.1 *Deadly nightshade* (Atropa belladonna)

Figure 50.2 *Mandrake (*Mandrogora sp.)

209

Figure 50.3 *Henbane (Hyoscymus sp.)*

Figure 50.4 *Thorn apple (Datura sp.)*

Figure 50.5 *A common insignia of English witch covens. The triangle is an ancient Egyptian phallic symbol. The two figures have eight points and thirteen sides, symbolizing the eight rituals of witchcraft and the thirteen lunar months, as well as reincarnation and eternity.*

buyer can even take it himself to increase his potency and desire. Overdosing can be harmful or fatal, which explains the local Spanish nickname for the plant—*la muerte dulce* ("the sweet death").

Love spells are cast by the Cheremis peasants of the Soviet Union in the following way. In the spring they catch two spawning frogs, wrap them in a white cloth, and bury them in an anthill. A month later, after the ants have consumed the frog flesh, the sorcerer takes two curved bones of the male and female frog from the anthill and touches them against his victim, causing her to fall passionately in love with him. If the sorcerer tires of a lover, he can prevent marriage by entangling the legs of a table with rope. But if the girl's father hears of it, he can break the spell and force them to marry by chopping up both the rope and the table legs. The Cheremis also believe that if a man copulates with a woman lying on her right side she will bear a male child.

The sex and fertility magic of the Australian aborigines of western Arnhem Land is simplicity itself—just draw what you want to happen. Using ochre paints or sometimes blood, male sorcerers draw women with human, reptile, or bird heads, several arms, accentuated breasts, and elongated vulva streaming with semen on the ceilings of rock shelters or on special, stringy bark. They believe that the drawings will cause the women depicted in them to want to have sex with the sorcerer. To retain the affection of the woman, the drawing must be retouched or redrawn from time to time. Often, the drawing isn't necessary. The women are so fearful of being vexed by this sort of magic that a sorcerer need only threaten, "If you don't come into the bush with me, I'll draw you," to gain their affections. Married sorcerers use the same technique to cause their wives to be fertile; they draw them with babies sucking at their breasts, with their stomachs cut away to show fetal growth, or performing the sex act.

Sorcerers who can work love magic among the Black Carib of Belize are known as *gasohaditi* ("stingers") or *gabacahaditi* ("ones who can make it hot"). Women use their own menstrual blood or a special kind of worm for this purpose, slipping it into the food or drink of the man they desire. These potions are very powerful, and the Carib say that "they can turn a boy mad." The love magic of male sorcerers is much less harmful. They use the following recipe. The sorcerer takes a *hua*, a large species of frog or toad, and puts it in a box containing tiny holes. He then buries the box in an anthill. When the ants have finished with the *hua*, the sorcerer sifts through the bones for the one shaped like a fishhook. He hangs the fishhook on the dress of a girl or woman he desires and she cannot resist him. To break the spell, the sorcerer again sifts through the bones, this time looking for one shaped like a saucer. When he finds the victim's attentions exhausting, he passes the saucer-shaped bone over her forehead and she soon forgets him.

If a Carib sorcerer is angry with a woman he loves because she has been made pregnant by another man, he may "tie the months on her" so she will not give birth to the child. He does this by tying knots in a black thread for the number of months he wants her to continue to carry the child. He may also steal her menstrual cloth or drawers from the time of her last menstruation and stick seven black-headed pins in the crotch to form a cross. He then buries the cloth and pins underneath the hearth. Until someone discovers the cloth or drawers with the pins, the woman will be unable to give birth. An eclipse of the moon is also believed to be dangerous for pregnant women. When a lunar eclipse occurs, Carib women take off their clothes, spread sheets on the ground outside their huts, and lie naked on the sheets, face down, "mooning the moon" so it does not harm their unborn children, causing them to be born deformed.

Appendix A. The People

Aleut. The Aleuts are Eskimoan-speaking inhabitants of the Aleutian Islands in Alaska and the Commander Islands in the Soviet Union. Their life, both aboriginally and today, is based on the sea, with fishing and hunting of sea mammals their primary activities.

Ashanti. The Ashantis are a Twi-speaking people of southern Ghana, numbering nearly one million people. They practice tropical forest agriculture, cultivating yams, bananas, and cocoa, the latter as a cash crop (Ghana provides 30 percent of the world's supply). Originally, Ashanti society was stratified into royalty, elders, commoners, and slaves.

Azande. The Azandes are a large tribe of roughly one million people who inhabit large parts of the Sudan, the Central African Republic, and Zaire. Their economy is based largely on agriculture. In aboriginal times, the entire population formed an empire divided into a number of kingdoms, each ruled by a paramount chief.

Black Carib. The Black Caribs are descendants of African negroes brought to the West Indies as slaves. The original ancestors of the Black Caribs escaped from their masters and took refuge among the Carib Islanders of St. Vincent, British Honduras (now Belize). Although they maintain many customs and beliefs of their African homeland, today they work mainly as seamen and sailors and in seasonal jobs in the mahogany logging and grapefruit canning industries.

Blackfoot. Before they were placed on reservations in the latter half of the nineteenth century, the Blackfoot tribe were nomadic tipi dwellers who hunted buffalo and warred with neighboring tribes, both with the aid of guns and horses. In many ways the archetypal "Plains Indians," they once numbered over 20,000 and inhabited a large territory stretching from the North Saskatchewan River in Canada to the Missouri River in Missouri. Today, about 8,000 Blackfoot live on reservations in Montana and Alberta, Canada.

Cheremis. The Cheremis are an ethnic group of about 85,000 people living in the Bashkir Autonomous Soviet Socialist Republic in the Soviet Union. They live as subsistence farmers, and many work as wage laborers in the numerous lumber mills in the region.

Chippewa. See *Ojibwa.*

Cree. The Crees are a large Native American group who inhabit great tracts of land in northern Quebec, Ontario, Manitoba, Saskatchewan, and Alberta, Canada. Although most of the Western Crees adopted a "Plains Indian" life-style of living in tipis and hunting buffalo, those in the north and east lived by hunting caribou and moose and trapping small, fur-bearing animals. Many continue this same style of living today.

Dobu. The natives of the Dobu Islands, rocky, volcanic upcroppings located in the d'Entrecasteaux group off the southern shore of Eastern New Guinea, are small-scale cultivators and fishermen. They have acquired a reputation among neighboring islanders of lawlessness and treachery and are believed to practice an extremely vicious form of sorcery.

Eskimo. The Eskimos (also called the Inuit), including the Netsilik, are the inhabitants of a broad strip of land across the northern coast of North America and the coast of Greenland. In the past, caribou, seal, and fish were their mainstays, providing most of the necessities of life. Today, about 85,000 Eskimos live in small towns or on reservations in the United States and Canada.

Fellahin Arabs. The Fellahin Arabs number well over 20 million people and constitute the largest single ethnic group in Egypt. Islamic in religion, they are mainly peasant agriculturists, although many have begun migrating to Egyptian towns and cities in search of wage labor.

Fipa. The Fipas are a Bantu ethnic group inhabiting the high plateau at the south end of Lake Tanganyika in Southwest Tanzania.

Galela. The Galelas are a group of about 15,000 people who live on the island of Halmahera at the northern end of the Molucca Islands (now called Maluku) in Indonesia. They are hunters, fishermen, and slash-and-burn cultivators of millet.

Gond. The Gonds are one of the largest Dravidian-speaking tribes of India, numbering well over three million people. Living primarily in Madhya Pradesh and other central states, they occupy the hill lands and form occupational castes of farm laborers, ironworkers, minstrels, carpenters, and fortune-tellers.

Guiana Indians. The Guiana Indians, including the Makusi, Wapishana, and Taruma tribes plus many others, are among the most technologically primitive people in the world. Inhabiting the dense jungles of the Amazon, they live by slash-and-burn cultivation of manioc and other crops; collecting wild fruit, honey, insects, and reptiles; and hunting and fishing with blowguns, spears, bows and arrows, and harpoons. No population estimates are available for these tribes, who live in almost complete isolation from the rest of the world.

Iban. The Ibans or Sea Dayaks are a riverine group of rice farmers who inhabit the interior hill country of Malaysia (now Sarawak) and sections of Indonesian Borneo. Famous as head-hunters, this group of 330,000 people still live in longhouses hidden in the jungle and continue their traditional lifeways.

Ifugao. The Ifugaos are a tribe of about 100,000 people, primarily rice farmers, who live in the mountainous regions of northern Luzon in the Philippines. They construct elaborate terraces on the rugged Luzon mountainsides to grow their crops.

Ingalik. The Ingaliks, whose name comes from the Eskimo word meaning "having louse's eggs," are an Athapaskan Indian group who inhabit a large area of the lower Yukon drainage in Alaska.

Iroquois. The Iroquois nation includes members of the Mohawk, Oneida, Onondaga, Cayuga, and Seneca tribes. They lived aboriginally in central and northern New York State and in southern Ontario, as farmers and hunters. Today there are bout 20,000 Iroquois scattered among reservations in New York, Ontario, Quebec, Wisconsin, and Oklahoma.

Jivaro. The Jivaros live in the tropical rainforest on the eastern slopes of the Ecuadoran Andes. Men hunt and fish while women handle the more important slash-and-burn horticultural tasks. This tribe of about 20,000 is best known for its shrunken head trophies displayed in museums around the world.

Kapauku. The Kapaukus, numbering about 45,000, are a Papuan ethnic group of pig herders and slash-and-burn horticulturists living on a small tract of land in the central highlands of western New Guinea. Their lives have been relatively little affected by the encroachment of modern European civilization.

Karen. The Karens are an ethnic group of about 3.5 million people living in southern and eastern Burma and western Thailand. They are Burma's largest ethnic group and were originally a hill people living by means of hunting, fishing, and slash-and-burn horticulture. In the last 100 years many Karens have moved down into the plains and deltas and become wet rice agriculturists.

Klamath. The Klamaths, who call themselves Maklaks, were a riverine people of southeastern Oregon and northern California who lived by fishing and gathering vast quantities of water lily seeds. Numbering about 1,000 people in the 1880s, their population has increased to about 2,200, with most of them residing on the Klamath reservation in Klamath County, Oregon.

Lapp. The Lapps are an ethnic group of about 35,000 people who inhabit a broad belt of territory in northern Scandanavia including parts of Russia, Finland, Norway, and Sweden. Calling themselves *Samek*, they farm, raise cattle, fish, and hunt. Probably the best-known subgroup are the reindeer-herding Mountain Lapps.

Lugbara. The Lugbaras are an African people living along the open, fertile uplands of the Nile-Congo divide between northwest Uganda and northeast Zaire (formerly the Belgian Congo). Numbering about 250,000 people, they are mainly agriculturists.

Makusi. See *Guiana Indians*.

Malay. The coastal Malays are an Islamic ethnic group of between four and five million people who are concentrated mainly on the Malay peninsula and along the neighboring coast of eastern Sumatra. They became involved in the European spice trade soon after colonization of the East Indies and are known today as middlemen and merchants.

Malekula. Malekula is a small island about 60 miles long in the northwest section of the archipelago formed by the islands of New Hebrides in the South Pacific. The native groups of Melanesians who inhabited this island were once wide-ranging canoe fisherman and slash-and-burn agriculturists. Regular contact with Europeans has decimated their population and the traditional culture has almost entirely disappeared.

Maori. The Maoris are a large tribe of over 100,000 people native to the volcanic island of New Zealand. Tall, strong, and well-built, they lived by fishing and agriculture and excelled in athletic sports and warfare.

Moche. Moche is a small, coastal village in northern Peru with a population of about 4,000 people. Formerly a community of Indian farmers and fishermen, it is now in the last stages of losing its unique identity as it is absorbed into the Peruvian national society and economy.

Modoc. The Modocs are a small Native American group of a few hundred persons who lived aboriginally in the area around Modoc Lake in southwestern Oregon. Having ceded all of their land to the United States in 1864, they were sent to live on the Quapaw and Klamath reservations. Under these conditions their culture has gradually disintegrated.

Montagnais. The Montagnais Indians of Quebec and the Labrado Peninsula of Canada were hunters of caribou and moose and trappers of beavers and other small animals. Today, most of the 5,000 Montagnais live as welfare recipients on reservations.

Navajo. The Navajos are the largest American Indian group, numbering about 200,000. The majority of Navajos live on their reservation in the Four Corners region of Arizona, New Mexico, Utah, and Colorado. The ancestors of the modern-day Navajos migrated to the Southwest from what is now Canada about one thousand years ago. At the time of contact with the Spanish, they were primarily hunters. This way of life was eventually replaced by agriculture and sheepherding, and today they rely heavily on wages as well as tourism, lumbering, and mineral production. In addition to sandpainting, the Navajos are renowned for their silver and turquoise jewelry and their weaving.

Netsilik. *See Eskimo.*

Nyakyusa. The Nyakyusas and the closely related Ngondes are a large African ethnic group of one million people. They live in large villages, grouped into kingdoms led by hereditary chiefs, located along the river dividing Tanzania from Malawi. They herd cattle and cultivate bananas, maize, millet, and manioc.

Ojibwa. The Ojibwas are a large Native American group of about 70,000 people centered around the upper Great Lakes in the United States and Canada. The Northern Ojibwa or Salteaux and the Southern Ojibwa or Chippewa tribes lived by fishing, trapping, and gathering plants such as wild rice. The Bungi or Plains Ojibwas lived in the northern plains and hunted buffalo.

Omaha. The Omahas are a Native American group who originally lived in the area adjacent to the upper Missouri River in Iowa and Nebraska. They formed and hunted buffalo, lived in earth lodges and skin tents, and were continually at war with their Sioux neighbors.

Ona. The Onas were a South American Indian group of about 3,500 people who occupied much of the island of Tierra del Fuego at the southern tip of South America. They subsisted mainly by hunting guanaco and marine animals and are now extinct as an ethnic group.

Penang. The Penang Malays are an ethnic subgroup of the Coastal Malays, numbering about 50,000 people. They live on the island of Penang, located in the Strait of Malacca off the northwest coast of the Malay Peninsula. The island's rice, rubber, coconut, and fruit plantations provide work for its inhabitants, most of whom are Chinese.

Penobscot. The Penobscots are a small subgroup of the Eastern Abenaki Indians who once inhabited the area around Penobscot Bay in northern Maine. They were one of the first groups of Native Americans to come into contact with Europeans, after which their numbers were quickly decimated by warfare and epidemics. Today, the 850 Penobscot people live mostly by welfare and wage labor and occupy a small reservation in Old Town, Maine.

Pomo. The Pomos are a sedentary people numbering only a few hundred who formerly lived in small villages along the central California coast. They are well known for their outstanding basketry. Aboriginally, they lived by collecting acorns and buckeye nuts; fishing; and hunting deer, elk, and antelope.

Ponape. Ponape and its satellite islands are located in the eastern Carolines in the South Pacific not far north of New Guinea. Its inhabitants live by fishing and cultivating breadfruit, coconut, taro, and bananas.

Romonum Islanders. See *Trukese*.

Rural Irish. The rural Irish who make up much of the island's population live in Donegal, Mayo, Galway, Clare, and Kerry counties in the poor and mountainous western part of the island. These peasants, who are extremely conservative, practice subsistence agriculture with primitive tools such as the digging stick and spade. They generally live outside the Irish market economy; barter is their primary means of exchange.

Samoans. The Samoans, made famous by Margaret Mead, are a Polynesian ethnic group of about 100,000 people who live on a small chain of volcanic islands in the South Pacific. Samoan villages, half-hidden by coconut groves, with fishing canoes floating in lagoons and black-haired women in grass skirts on the beaches epitomize for many Americans the typical South Sea island.

Santal. The Santals, numbering three million people, are one of the largest ethnic groups in India. They occupy parts of Bihor, West Bengal, and northern Orissa states in north-central India. Formerly hunters and rice farmers, they have migrated widely throughout India and are employed now mainly as agricultural and industrial laborers.

Semang. "Semang" is a term applied by the Malays of Kedah to the negrito aborigines who live on the Malay Peninsula. Extremely primitive, the Semangs grow no crops, dwell in portable huts made from palm branches, and live by gathering fruits and roots and hunting animals that inhabit the jungle-covered land over which they roam. In 1964 the total Semang population was about 2,000.

Seneca. See *Iroquois*.

Shakers. The Shakers (The United Society of Believers in Christ's Second Appearing) are an American communal society that began in the late 1700s. Numbering some 5,000 members in the mid-nineteenth century in at least 19 communities, the group has now dwindled to about a dozen members in two communities in Cantebury, New Hampshire, and Sabbathday Lake, Maine. Shakers are widely known today for their simple, high quality manufactured goods produced in the spirit of "hands to work and hearts to God."

Siriono. The Sirionos are a small band of semi-nomadic hunter-gatherers and slash-and-burn horticulturists living in the high rainforests of eastern Bolivia. Their population was about 2,000 in 1940.

Somali. The Somalis, a large ethnic group of over three million people, were traditionally nomadic pastoralists. Today, they are slowly being assimilated into European culture. They live in the northern part of the Somali Democratic Republic in northeast Africa.

Tarahumara. The Tarahumara Indians live in the Sierra Madre Mountains of the state of Chihuahua in northwest Mexico. The 50,000 or so Tarahumaras live mostly by maize agriculture, animal husbandry, and the tourist trade.

Tarascan. The Tarascans are a group of about 70,000 Indians living in the cool, green mountains of northwestern Michoacán in western Mexico. They are primarily a farming society and live in small towns. Although largely Hispancized, they have preserved their native language.

Taruma. See *Guiana Indians*.

Taulipang. The Taulipangs are subgroup of the Pemon, a South American Indian tribe occupying an area known as the *Gran Sabana* in southeastern Venezuela. They live in villages made up of several round, communal huts with conical thatched roofs. They exist primarily by means of slash-and-burn horticulture supplemented by hunting and fishing. Population estimates for this little-known tribe range from 250 to 2,500.

Timbira. The Timbiras are a relatively primitive and little-known group of hunters and manioc cultivators living in the northeastern part of the central Brazilian steppes. Their population has steadily declined since contact with the White-Brazilian culture was established, and today they number no more than 1,000 individuals.

Tonga. The Tonga tribe includes a number of quite distinct ethnic groups living in Zambia (formerly Northern Rhodesia) and Rhodesia (formerly Southern Rhodesia). The Gwembe Tongas mentioned in this book are a group of around 85,000 people who traditionally lived in large permanent villages and farmed sorghum and finger millet.

Torres Straits Islanders. The Melanesian natives of the Torres Straits occupy the numerous islands in the broad, shallow sea passage that separates the western part of Papua in New Guinea from the Cape Youk Peninsula in northeastern Australia. A seafaring people, they also practice some agriculture and dive in the waters of the strait for pearls and pearl shell.

Trukese. The Trukeses, including the Romonum Islanders, are the inhabitants of the Truk atoll of the Caroline Islands in Micronesia in the tropical South Pacific. In the past, the population of 20,000 survived mainly by farming and fishing. Today, the small island nation is being integrated into the world economy.

Tswana. The Tswanas, numbering in all about 800,000 people, are a large African Bantu Group inhabiting Botswana (formerly called Bechuanaland). Traditionally, the Tswanas were stratified into four classes of aristocracy, commoners, aliens, and hereditary serfs, with the chiefs collecting tribute through a complex and far-reaching administrative organization.

Urubu. The Urubus live in the tropical rainforest of Maranhão, Brazil, as slash-and-burn cultivators of manioc, cotton, urucu, bananas, and oranges. The several hundred people occupy small villages containing a series of long, rectangular huts which serve as communal living quarters.

Walapai. The Walapais or "pine tree folk" are a small group of Native Americans who once roamed over much of Arizona hunting and gathering roots and seeds. Today, they are confined to a small reservation in northwest Arizona and, according to one authority, "are making little progress in civilization." They live primarily as farmers and horse ranchers.

Wapishana. See *Guiana Indians*.

Woleai. The Woleais are a group of nearly 1,500 people living in the Yap district of the Central Caroline Islands in the South Pacific. They live on 53 islands and atolls covering only 3.3 miles of land surface. Coconuts and fish are their principal foods, with dogs, hogs, and chickens their only domesticated animals. In the past they often traveled over 600 miles in their outrigger canoes to trade and war with other tribes.

Yagua. The Yaguas, who call themselves the Nihamwo, are a primitive South American tribe of 1,000 people who inhabit the dense jungle lowlands surrounding the Maranon River in northeastern Peru. Because of their isolated location, they have maintained many of their traditional ways, and many of them still live by hunting peccaries, deer, tapir, and monkeys with blowguns and by cultivating bananas and yucca using slash-and-burn horticulture.

Yao. The Yaos are a Bantu tribe of over 350,000 people living in Malawi, Tanzania, and Mozambique on the east coast of Africa. They are subsistence cultivators who own no cattle and whose largely vegetarian diet is based on sorghum and maize. Most have converted to Islam.

Yokuts. The aboriginal home of the Yokuts Indians was the San Joaquin Valley in central California. At one time numbering as many as 20,000 people, they lived by gathering acorns and hunting deer, elk, and antelope.

Yugoslav Peasants. The Yugoslavs mentioned in this book live in the Bosnia region of central Yugoslavia. The republic of Bosnia-Herzegovina, with a population of about 1.5 million people, about a third of whom are Moslems, is the most mountainous and therefore the least densely populated region of Yugoslavia. Most people live as farmers, growing tobacco, corn, wheat, oats, flax, and hemp and keeping a few cattle, horses, and sheep.

Zuni. The Zunis, who call themselves the Ashiwi, are a Pueblo Indian group of about 2,500 people. They have managed to maintain much of their traditional way of life in their single village or "pueblo" located in west-central New Mexico.

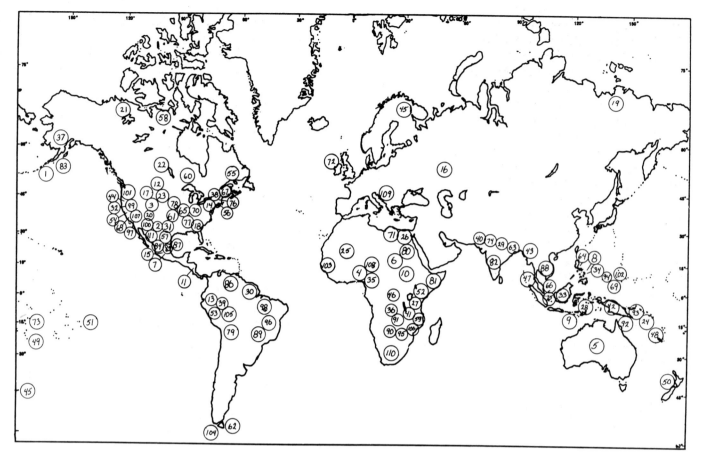

Key To The Tribal Map

1. Aleut (North America)
2. Apache (North America)
3. Arapaho (North America)
4. Ashanti (Africa)
5. Australian Aborigines (Australia)
6. Azande (Africa)
7. Aztecs (Central America)
8. Bagabo (Southeast Asia)
9. Balinese (Southeast Asia)
10. Bantu (Africa)
11. Black Carib (Central America)
12. Blackfoot (North America)
13. Cagaba (South America)
14. Canarsee (North America)
15. Chamula (Central America)
16. Cheremis peasants (Soviet Union)
17. Cheyenne (North America)
18. Choctaw (North America)
19. Chuckchee (Soviet Union)
20. Comanche (North America)
21. Copper Eskimo (North America)
22. Cree (North America)
23. Crow (North America)
24. Dobu (South Pacific)
25. Dogon (Africa)
26. Fellahin Arabs (Middle East)
27. Fipa (Africa)

28. Galela (Southeast Asia)
29. Gond (India)
30. Guiana Indians (South America)
31. Hopi (North America)
32. Hupa (North America)
33. Iban (Southeast Asia)
34. Ifugao (Southeast Asia)
35. Igbo (Africa)
36. Ila (Africa)
37. Ingalik (North America)
38. Iroquois (North America)
39. Jivaro (South America)
40. Kafir (Asia)
41. Kagaru (Africa)
42. Kapauku (South Pacific)
43. Karen (Asia)
44. Klamath (North America)
45. Lapp (Scandinavia)
46. Lugbara (Africa)
47. Malay (Southeast Asia)
48. Malekula (South Pacific)
49. Mangaia (South Pacific)
50. Maori (South Pacific)
51. Marquesans (South Pacific)
52. Masai (Africa)
53. Moche peasants (South America)
54. Modoc (North America)

55. Montagnais (North America)
56. Narraganset (North America)
57. Navaho (North America)
58. Netsilik Eskimo (North America)
59. Nyakyusa (Africa)
60. Ojibwa (North America)
61. Omaha (North America)
62. Ona (South America)
63. Oraon (India)
64. Pangasinan (Southeast Asia)
65. Pawnee (North America)
66. Penang (Southeast Asia)
67. Penobscot (North America)
68. Pomo (North America)
69. Ponape (South Pacific)
70. Potawatomi (North America)
71. Riyadh Arabs (Middle East)
72. Rural Irish (Europe)
73. Samoans (South Pacific)
74. Santal (India)
75. Semang (Southeast Asia)
76. Shakers (North America)
77. Shawnee (North America)
78. Sioux (North America)
79. Siriono (South America)
80. Siwans (Middle East)
81. Somali (Africa)
82. Tamil (India)
83. Tanaina (North America)

84. Tarahumara (Central America)
85. Tarascans (Central America)
86. Taulipang (South America)
87. Tepotzlan peasants (Central America)
88. Thai (Southeast Asia)
89. Timbira (South America)
90. Tlokwa (Africa)
91. Tonga (Africa)
92. Torres Straits Islanders (South Pacific)
93. Trobriand Islanders (South Pacific)
94. Trukese (South Pacific)
95. Tswana (Africa)
96. Tupi (South America)
97. Tupinagugim (North America)
98. Urubu (South America)
99. Ute (North America)
100. Walapai (North America)
101. Wasco (North America)
102. Woleai (South Pacific)
103. Wolof (Africa)
104. Yaghan (South America)
105. Yagua (South America)
106. Yao (Africa)
107. Yokuts (North America)
108. Yoruba (Africa)
109. Yugoslav peasants (Europe)
110. Zulu (Africa)
111. Zuni (North America)

Appendix B. Sources

We gathered the information presented in this book from three main sources. First, we used hundreds of books, articles, and unpublished manuscripts containing descriptions of the ways of life of tribal and folk people around the world. Nearly all of these documents are first-hand accounts written by trained observers (usually anthropologists) who participated in the everyday activities of the tribal and folk people among whom they lived. Second, we interviewed craftspersons (weavers, embroiderers, basketmakers, etc.) who practice their crafts using traditional techniques and/or materials. Third, we relied on our own experiences making many of the projects or doing the activities described in the book, always following the instructions given in the documents or by the craftpersons.

As our goal was to provide accurate and complete descriptions or instructions for tribal arts, crafts, technologies, and lifeways, we went to considerable lengths to find trustworthy first-hand accounts. Of great help on this score was the Human Relations Area Files (HRAF) data archive. The archive is a collection of 6,000 documents describing the ways of life of 325 different tribal and folk societies around the world. Beyond providing a wealth of basic information, the archive was especially useful in two other ways. First, it contains hundreds of first-hand accounts that were translated from two dozen languages into English. These accounts, available only in the archive, are often among the best reports written on a particular tribal society and therefore provided us with much information that would have been unavailable otherwise. Second, the archive contains multiple reports on each of the 325 societies covered therein. We checked the accuracy and completeness of these reports by comparing them to one another.

The reports listed below are the main ones we consulted. Insofar as we could determine, they contain the most accurate and complete descriptions of the projects or activities we have described. Some of them are quite old—early 1900s or even 1800s—and were often so detailed that later authors simply referred the reader to the earlier account while moving on to other matters.

Dwellings

Balikci, Asen. 1970. *The Netsilik Eskimo.* Garden City, N. Y.: Natural History Press.

Densmore, Frances. 1929. *Chippewa Customs.* U.S. Bureau of American Ethnology Bulletin no. 86. Washington, D.C.: Government Printing Office.

Jenness, Diamond. 1922. *The Life of the Copper Eskimos.* Canadian Arctic Expedition, 1913-1918, Report no. 12. Ottawa: F. A. Acland, King's Printer.

Lebar, Frank. 1964. *The Material Culture of Truk.* Yale University Publications in Anthropology, no. 68. New Haven, Conn.: Department of Anthropology, Yale University.

Spier, Leslie. 1930. *Klamath Ethnography.* University of California Publications in American Archaeology and Ethnology, no. 30. Berkeley: University of California Press.

Vorren, Omuly, and Ernst Manker. 1962. *Lapp Life and Customs: A Survey.* London: Oxford University Press.

Basic Skills and Materials

Balfour, Henry. 1907. The fire piston. In *Anthropological Essays Presented to Edward Burnett Tylor in Honor of His 75th Birthday, October 2, 1907,* ed. Henry Balfour, pp. 17-50. Oxford: Clarendon.

Best, Elsdon. 1942. *Forest Lore of the Maori.* Wellington, New Zealand: Polynesian Society & Dominion Museum.

Burrows, Edwin G. 1949. The people of Ifalik: A little-disturbed atoll culture. Unpublished.

Densmore, Frances. 1929. *Chippewa Customs.* U.S. Bureau of American Ethnology Bulletin no. 86. Washington, D.C.: Govemment Printing Office.

Evans, Emyr E. 1942. *Irish Heritage: The Landscape, the People and Their Work.* Dundalk, Ireland: Dundalgan Press.

———. 1957. *Irish Folk Ways.* London: Routledge and Paul.

Flint Institute of Art. 1973. *The Art of the Great Lake Indians.*

Hodges, Henry. 1976. *Artifacts: An Introduction to Early Materials and Technology.* London: John Baker.

Holmberg, Allan R. 1950. *Nomads of the Low Bow: The Siriono of Eastern Bolivia.* Smithsonian Institution Institute of Social Anthropology, Publication no. 10. Washington, D.C.: Govemment Printing Office.

Itkonen, Toivo I. 1948. *The Lapps in Finland up to 1945.* Porvoo, Helsinki: Wemer Soderstrom Osakeyhtio. (Translation of the Human Relations Area Files.)

Jochelson, Vladimir I. 1933. *History, Ethnology and Anthropology of the Aleut.* Washington, D.C.: Camegie Institution of Washington.

Layard, John W. 1942. *Stone Men of Malekula.* London: Chatto and Windus.

Mason, Otis T. 1894. Primitive travel and transportation. In *Annual Report of the Board of Regents of the Smithsonian Institution,* pp. 237-594. Washington, D.C.: Govemment Printing Office.

Morgan, Lewis H. 1954. *League of the Ho-De-No-Sau-Nee or Iroquois.* New Haven, Conn.: HRAF Press.

Oakley, Kenneth P. 1952. *Man the Tool-Maker.* London: Trustees of the British Museum.

Osgood, Comelius. 1970. *Ingalik Material Culture.* Yale University Publications in Anthropology, no. 22. New Haven, Conn.: HRAF Press.

Pennington, Campbell W. 1963. *The Tarahumar of Mexico: Their Environment and Material Culture.* Salt Lake City: University of Utah Press.

Pospisil, Leopold J. 1963. *Kapauku Papuan Economy.* Yale University Publications in Anthropology, no. 67. New Haven, Conn.: HRAF Press.

Stannus, Hugh S. 1922. The Wayao of Nyasaland. *Harvard African Studies* 3:229-372. 213

Thompson, Laura. 1940. *Southern Lau, Fiji: An Ethnography.* Honolulu: Bernice P. Bishop Museum.

Crafts

Adney, Edward T., and Howard I. Chapelle. 1964. *The Bark Canoes and Skin Boats of North America.* United States National Museum, Bulletin no. 230. Washington, D.C.: Smithsonian Institution.

Blackman, Winifred S. 1927. *The Fellahin of Upper Egypt: Their Religious, Social, and Industrial Life Today With Special Reference to survivals from Ancient Times.* London: Harrap.

Disney, Rosemary (1972). *The Splendid Art of Decorating Eggs.* New York: Dover.

Eckstrom, Fannie H. 1932. *The Handicrafts of the Modern Indians of Maine.* Robert Abbe Museum, Bulletin no. 3. Bar Harbor, Maine: Robert Abbe Museum of Stone Age Antiquities.

Farnham, A.B. n.d. *Home Manufacture of Furs and Skins.* Columbus, Ohio: Harding.

Haddon, Alfred C., and James Hornell. 1936–38. *Canoes of Oceania.* Volumes 1-3, Bernice P. Bishop Museum, Special Publications nos. 27-29. Honolulu: Bernice P. Bishop Museum.

Hornell, James. 1970. *Water Transport: Origins and Early Evolution.* Newton Abbot: David and Charles.

Joe, Eugene Baatsoslanii, and Mark Bahti (1978). *Navajo Sandpainting Art.* Tucson: Treasure Chest Publications.

Lowie, Robert H. 1910. Notes concerning new collections. *Anthropological Papers of the American Museum of Natural History* 4:282.

Lyford, Carrie A. 1940. *Quill and Beadwork of the Western Sioux.* Washington, D.C.: Bureau of Indian Affairs, U.S. Department of Interior. Reprint ed., 1974. Boulder: Johnson Books.

———. 1945. *Iroquois Crafts.* Lawrence, Kan.: Haskell Institute.

Orchard, William C. 1971. *The Technique of Porcupine Quill Decoration among the Indians of North America.* New York: Heye Foundation, Museum of the American Indian.

———. 1971. *Beads and Beadwork of the American Indians.* New York: Heye Foundation, Museum of the American Indian.

Osgood, Cornelius. 1970. *Ingalik Material Culture.* Yale University Publications in Anthropology, no. 22. New Haven, Conn.: HRAF Press.

Rye, Owens, and Clifford Evans. 1976. *Traditional Pottery Techniques of Pakistan.* Smithsonian Contributions to Anthropology, no. 21. Washington, D.C.: Smithsonian Institution.

Speck, Frank G. 1976. *Penobscot Man.* New York: Octagon Books.

Start, Laura E. 1939. *The Durham Collection of Garments and Embroideries from Albania and Yugoslavia.* Halifax, England: Bankfield Museum.

Wissler, Clark. 1910. Material culture of the Blackfoot Indians. *Anthropological Papers of the American Museum of Natural History* 5:1-175.

Wyman, Leland C. *Sandpaintings of the Navaho Shootingway and the Walcott Collection.* Washington D.C.: Smithsonian Institution Press.

Food Quest

Anonymous. 1749. *The Complete Family-Piece; and Country Gentlemen, and Farmer's Best Guide.* In three parts. Fifth ed., improved. London: George Faulkner.

Barton, Roy F. 1922. Ifugao Economics. University of California Publications in American Archaeology and Ethnology, no. 15. Berkeley: University of California Press.

Bennett, Wendell C. 1933. New Ethnological specimens. *Natural History* 33:660-661.

Bennett, Wendell C., and Robert M. Zingg. 1935. *The Tarahumara: An Indian Tribe in Northern Mexico.* Chicago: University of Chicago Press.

Bodenheimer, W. 1951. *Insects as Human Food: A Chapter in the Ecology of Man.* The Hague, Netherlands: Dr. W. Junk.

Bollig, Laurentius. 1927. *The Inhabitants of the Truk Islands: Religion, Life, and a Short Grammer of a Micronesian People.* Munster in Westphalia, Germany: Aschendorffsche Verlags buchhandlung. (translation of the Human Relations Area Files)

Bruning, Hans H. 1928. Journeys into the region of the Aguaruna. *Baessler-Archiv* 12:46-85. (Translation of the Human Relations area Files)

Burton, Richard F. (1987). *The Book of the Sword.* New York: Dover.

Cooper, John M. 1946. Traps in *Handbook of South American Indians*, ed. Julian H. Steward. U.S. Bureau of American Ethnology, Bulletin no. 143. Washington, D.C.: Government Printing Office.

Culwick, Geraldine M. 1950. *A Dietary Survey among the Zande of the South-Western Sudan.* Khartoum: Sudan Government.

Densmore, Frances. 1929. *Chippewa Customs.* U.S. Bureau of American Ethnology Bulletin no. 86. Washington, D.C.: Government Printing Office.

Evans, Emyr E. 1957. *Irish Folk Ways.* London: Routledge and Paul.

Fejos, Paul, 1943. *Ethnography of the Yagua.* Viking Fund Publications in Anthropology, no. 1. New York: Wenner-Gren Foundation.

Grinnell, George B. 1962. *Blackfoot Lodge Tales: The Story of a Prairie People.* Lincoln: University of Nebraska Press.

Gusinde, Martin. 1931. The Selk'nam: On the Life and Thought of a Hunting People of the Great Island of Tierra del Fuego. Modling bei Wien: Verlag der Internationalen Zeitschrift Anthropos. (translation of the Human Relations Area Files).

Hilger, M. Inez. 1951. *Chippewa Child Life and Its Cultural Background.* U.S. Bureau of American Ethnology Bulletin no. 146. Washington, D.C.: Government Printing Office.

Hornell, James, 1970. *Water Transport: Origins and Early Evolution.* Newton Abbot: David and Charles.

Innokentii, Metropolitan of Moscow. 1840. *Notes on the Islands of the Unalaska District.* Vol. 3, by Ivan E.P. Veneaminov. Sankpeterburg: Izdano Izdiveniem Rossiisko-Amerikonskoi Kompanii. (Translation of the Human Relations Area Files).

Ishige, Naomichi. 1980. *The Galela of Halmehera.* Senri Ethnological Studies no. 7. Osaka: National Museum of Ethnology.

Kraemer, Augustin. 1932. *Truk.* Hamburg: de Gruyter. (Translation of the Human Relations Area Files)

Latta, Frank F. 1949. *Handbook of the Yokuts Indians.* Bakersfield, Claifor.: Kern County Museum.

Lebar, Frank. 1963. The material culture of Truk. Unpublished.

Marshall, Henry T. 1922. The Karen people of Burma: a study in anthropology and ethnology. Contributions in History and Political Science, no. 8. *Ohio State University Bulletin* 26.

Mason, Bernard S. 1974. *Boomerangs: How to Make and Throw Them.* New York: Dover Publications.

Mason, Otis T. 1884. Throwing-sticks in the national museum. Annual Report of the Board of Regents, Smithsonian Institution, Washington, D.C.

————. 1900. Traps of the Amerinds—a study in psychology and invention. *American Anthropologist* 2:657-675.

Osgood, Cornelius. 1970. Ingalik Material Culture. Yale University Publications in Anthropology, no. 22. New Haven, Conn.: HRAF Press.

Popisil, Leopold. 1972. *Kapauku Papuan Economy.* Yale University Publications in Anthropology, no. 67. New Haven, Conn.: HRAF Press.

Quimby, George I. 1944. *Aleutian Islanders: Eskimos of the North Pacific.* Anthropology Leaflet no. 35. Chicago: Natural History Museum.

Rivet, Paul. 1908. Les Indiens Jibaros: étude géographique, historique et ethnographique. *Anthropologie* 19:235-259.

Savishinsky, Joel S. 1970. *Stress and Mobility in an Arctic Community: The Hare Indians of Colville Lake, Northwest Territories.* University Microfilms International.

Spencer, Walter B., and F. J. Gillen. 1927. *The Arunta: A Study of a Stone Age People.* London: Macmillan.

Speir, Leslie. 1930. *Klamath Ethnography.* University of California Publications in American Archaeology and Ethnology, no. 30. Berkeley: University of California Press.

Stegmiller, P. F. 1925. Arrow-shooting and hunting of the Khasi. *Anthropos* 20:607-623. (Translation of the Human Relations Area Files)

Stirling, Matthew W. 1938. *Historical and Ethnographic Material on the Jivaro Indians.* U.S. Bureau of American Ethnology Bulletin no. 132. Washington, D.C.: Government Printing Office.

Taylor, Robert B., Jr. 1960. *Teotitlan del Valle: A Typical Mesoamerican Community.* University Microfilms. Ann Arbor: University Microfilms International.

Up de Graff, Fritz W. 1923. *Head-Hunters of the Amazon: Seven Years of Exploration and Adventure.* New York: Duffield.

Wissler, Clark. 1910. Material culture of the Blackfoot Indians. *Anthropological Papers of the American Museum of Natural History* 5:1-175.

Recreation

Anonymous. 1749. *The Complete Family-Piece; and Country Gentlemen, and Farmer's Best Guide.* In three parts. Fifth Ed., improved. London: George Faulkner.

Beals, Ralph L., and Pedro Carrasco. 1944. Games of the Mountain Tarascans. *American Anthropologist* 46:516-522.

Bennett, Wendell C., and Robert M. Zingg. 1935. *The Tarahumara: An Indian Tribe of Northern Mexico.* Chicago: University of Chicago Press.

Best, Elsdon. 1925. *Games and Pastimes of the Maori.* Museum Bulletin no. 8. Wellington, New Zealand: Dominion Museum.

Biswas, P. C. 1956. *The Santals of the Santal Parganas.* Delhi: Bharatiya Adimjati Sevk Sangh.

Cooper, John M. 1949. Games and gambling. In *Handbook of South American Indians,* ed. Julian H. Steward. U.S. Bureau of American Ethnology bulletin no. 143. Washington, D.C.: Government Printing Office.

Culin, Stewart. 1907. *Games of the North American Indians.* U.S. Bureau of American Ethnology Report no. 24. Washington, D.C.: Government Printing Office.

Densmore, Frances. 1928. *Use of Plants by the Chippewa Indians.* U.S. Bureau of American Ethnology Report no. 44. Washington, D.C.: Government Printing Office.

Dorsey, J. Owen. 1884. *Omaha Sociology.* U.S. Bureau of American Ethnology Report no. 3. Washington, D.C.: Government Printing Office.

Drake-Brockman, Ralph E. 1912. *British Somaliland.* London: Hurst and Blackett.

Dussek, O. T. 1919. Notes on Malay indoor games. *Journal of the Royal Asiatic Society, Straits Branch* 80:68-71.

Elwin, Verrier. 1943. *Maria Murder and Suicide.* Bombay: Oxford University Press.

Gamble, David P. 1957. *The Wolof of Senegambia, Together with Notes on the Lebu and the Serer.* London: International African Institute.

Graff, Herbert. 1982. An annotated bibliography of riddles. *Behavior Science Research* 17:115-157. (See also sources cited in this article.)

Grigson, Wilfred V. 1949. *The Masai: Their Language and Folklore.* Oxford: Clarendon Press.

Haile, N.S. 1951 A Dyak game. *Sarawak Museum Journal* 5:442-445.

Harner, Michael J. 1973. *The Jivaro: People of the Sacrd Watefalls.* Garden City, N.YU.: Anchor Press/Doubleday.

Hollis, Alfred C. 1905. *The Masai: Their Language and Folklore.* Oxford: Clarendon Press.

Hornell, James. 1927. *String Figures from Fiji and Western Polynesia.* Museum Bulletin no. 39. Honolulu: Bernice P. Bishop Museum.

Jayne, Caroline F. 1962. *String Figures and How to Make Them: A Study of Cat's-Cradle in Many Lands.* New York: Dover Publications.

Karsten, Rafael. 1935. *The Head-Hunters of Western Amazonas: The Life and Culture of the Jibaro Indians of Eastern Ecuador and Peru.* Helsingfors: Central tryckeriet.

Marin, G. 1931. Somali games. *Journal of the Royal Anthropological Institute of Great Britain and Ireland* 61:499-511.

Mukherjea, Charulal. 1962. *The Santals.* Calcutta: A. Mukherjee.

Nimuendja, Curt. 1946. *The Eastern Timbira.* Trans. and ed. Robert H. Lowie. University of California Publications in American Archaeology and Ethnology, no. 41. Berkeley: University of California Press.

Pennington, Cambell W. 1963. *The Tarahumara of Mexico: Their Environment and Material Culture.* Salt Lake City: University of Utah Press.

Raghavaiah, V. 1972. *Tribes of India.* 2 vols. New Delhi.

Rattray, Robert S. 1927. *Religion and Art in Ashanti.* Oxford: Clarendon Press.

Reynolds, Barrie. 1968. *The Material Culture of the People of the Gwembe Valley.* New York: Praeger.

Roth, Walter E. 1924. *An Introductory Study of the Arts, Crafts, and Customs of the Guiana Indians.* U.S. Bureau of American Ethnology, Report no. 38. Washington, D.C.: Government Printing Office.

———. 1929. *Additional Studies of the Arts, Crafts and Customs of the Guiana Indians, with Special Reference to those of Southern British Guiana.* U.S. Bureau of American Ethnology, Bulletin no. 91. Washington, D.C.: government Printing Office.

Schebesta, Paul. 1954. The Negritos of Asia; 2. *Ethnography of the Negritos; Half-Volume 1, Economy and Sociology. Wein-Modling:* St. Gabriel-Verlag. (Translation of the Human Relations Area Files).

Smith, Edwin W., and Andrew M. Dale. 1920. *The Ila-Speaking Peoples of Northern Rhodesia.* London: Macmillan.

Speck, Frank G. 1937. *Montagnais Art in Birch-Bark, a Circumpolar Trait.* New York: Heye Foundation, Museum of the American Indian.

Turner, George. 1884. *Samoa, A Hundred years Ago and Long Before. Together with Notes on the Cults and Customs of Twenty-three Other Islands in the Pacific.* London: Macmillan.

Societies and Customs

Bennett, Wendell C., and Robert M. Zingg. 1935. *The Tarahumara: An Indian Tribe of Northern Mexico.* Chicago: University of Chicago Press.

Berndt. Ronald M., and Catherine H. 1951. *Sexual Behavior in Western Arnhem Land.* Viking Fund Publications in Anthropology, no. 16. New York: Wenner-Gren Foundation.

Bryant, Alfred T. 1949. *The Zulu as They were Before the White Man Came.* Pietermaritzburg. South Africa: Shuter and Shooter.

Clark, W. P. 1982. *The Indian Sign Language.* Lincoln: University of Nebraska Press.

Covarrubias, Miguel. 1938. *Island of Bali.* New York: Knopf.

Fletcher, Alice C., and Francis LaFlesche. 1906. *The Omaha Tribe.* U.S. Bureau of American Ethnology Report no. 27. Washington, D.C.: Government Printing Office.

Ford, Clellan S., and Frank A. Beach. 1951. *Patterns of Sexual Behavior.* New York: Harper and Row.

Gillin, John. 1945. *Moche: A Peruvian Coastal Community.* Smithsonian Institution Institute of Social Anthropology, Publication no. 3. Washington, D.C.: Government Printing Office.

Guisinde, Martin. 1937. *The Yahgan: The Life and Thought of the Water Nomads of Cape Horn.* Modling bei Wein: Antrhopos-Bibliothek. (Translation of the Human Relations area Files)

Harner, Michael J. 1973. *Hallucinogens and Shamanism.* New York: Oxford University Press.

Heibert, Paul G. 1976. *Cultural Anthropology.* Philadelphia: J. B. Lippincott Co.

Holmberg, Allan R. 1950. *Nomads of the Long Bow: The Siriono of Eastern Bolivia.* Smithsonian Institution Institute of Social Anthropology, Publication no. 10. Washington, D.C.: Government Printing Office.

Karsten, Rafael. 1935. *The Head-Hunters of Western Amazonas: The Life and Culture of the Jibaro Indians of Eastern Ecuador and Peru.* Helsingfors: Central tryckeriet.

Mair, Lucy. 1969. *Witchcraft.* New York: McGraw-Hill.

Malinowski, Bronislaw. 1929. *The Sexual Life of Savages in Northwestern Melanesia: An Ethnographic Account of Courtship, Marriage and Family Life among the Natives of the Trobriand Islands, British New Guinea.* New York: Horace Liveright.

Marwick, Max. 1970. *Witchcraft, and Curing.* American Museum Sourcebooks in Anthropology. Garden City, N.Y.: The Natural History Press for the American Museum of Natural History.

Mukherjea, Charulal. 1962. *The Santals.* Calcutta: A. Mukherjee.

Overbeck, H. 1923. Shaer raksi. *Journal of the Royal Asiatic Society, Malayan Branch* 1:282-307.

Schneider, David M. 1968. *American Kinship: A Cultural Account.* Englewood Cliffs, N.J.: Prentice-Hall.

Sebeok, Thomas A., and Frances J. Ingemann. 1956. *Studies in Cheremis: The Supernatural.* Viking Fund Publications in Anthropology, no. 22. New York: Wenner-Gren Foundation.

Stirling, Matthew W. 1938. *Historical and Ethnographical Material on the Jivaro Indians.* U.S. Bureau of American Ethnology Bulletin no. 132. Washington, D.C.: Government Printing Office.

Taylor, Douglas M. 1951. *The Black Carib of British Honduras.* Viking Fund Publications in Antrhopology, no. 17. New York: Wenner-Gren Foundation.

Umiker-Sebeok, D. Jean, and Thomas A. Sebeok. 1978. *Aboriginal Sign Languages of the Americas and Australias.* 2 vols. New York: Plenum Press.

Society/Geographical Index